Role of Paramilitary and Central Armed Police Forces in India's National Security

Role of Paramilitary and Central Armed Police Forces in India's National Security

Rohit Singh

Centre for Land Warfare Studies

Pentagon Press

"The contents of this book are based on the analysis of materials accessed from open sources and are the personal views of the author. The contents, therefore, may not be quoted or cited as representing the views or policy of the Government of India, or Integrated Headquarters of MoD (Army), or the Centre for Land Warfare Studies."

Centre for Land Warfare Studies
RPSO Complex, Parade Road, Delhi Cantt, New Delhi-110010
Phone: 011-25691308 • Fax: 011-25692347
email: landwarfare@gmail.com • website: www.claws.in

First Published in 2013

ISBN 978-81-8274-732-6

Published by

PENTAGON PRESS
206, Peacock Lane, Shahpur Jat, New Delhi-110049
Phones: 011-64706243, 26491568
Telefax: 011-26490600
email: rajan@pentagonpress.in
website: www.pentagon-press.com

Printed at Aegean Offset Printers, Greater Noida, U.P.

Contents

PART 3
Paramilitary Forces of China & Pakistan

PART 4

Foreword

Since independence, India has faced a large number of external and internal security challenges. The Indian Army, the paramilitary forces and the Central Armed Police Forces (CAPFs) have worked hand-in-hand to manage and neutralise these challenges. While the army has been responsible to maintain the integrity of the country's long land boundaries through four wars and the Kargil conflict, the CAPFs have been largely responsible to manage the land borders and lend a helping hand to the army for counter-insurgency operations. Some insurgencies are now being fought primarily by the CAPFs by themselves.

In May 2001, the Cabinet Committee on Security (CCS) had approved the concept of "one border, one force". The Line of Actual Control (LAC) along the border with Tibet is now being managed largely by the Indo-Tibetan Border Police (ITBP). In the west, the entire border with Pakistan is manned by the Border Security Force (BSF) except the Line of Control (LoC) in Jammu and Kashmir (J&K). Maintaining the sanctity of the LoC is the responsibility of the army and some BSF battalions have been placed under its operational control for this purpose. For over 50 years since the Kashmir conflict began in 1947-48, soon after independence, the two armies were engaged in a so-called 'eyeball-to-eyeball' confrontation with daily loss of life and property that could justifiably be called a 'low intensity limited war'. An informal cease-fire has been in place all along the LoC, including at the Actual Ground Position Line (AGPL) along the Saltoro Range west of the Siachen Glacier, since November 25, 2003.

The border with Nepal was virtually un-attended till very recently as Nepalese citizens have free access to live and work in India under a 1950 treaty between the two countries. Since the eruption of a Maoist insurgency in Nepal, efforts have been made to gradually step up vigilance along this border to prevent the southward spread of Maoist ideology. The responsibility for this has been entrusted to the Sashastra Seema Bal (SSB), erstwhile Special Security Bureau that is now a Ministry of Home Affairs force. The Bhutan border is also managed by the SSB. Since the Royal Bhutanese Army drove out the Bodo and ULFA insurgents from its territory some years ago, the border has been relatively quiet. The border with Myanmar also remains operationally active. Several insurgent groups have secured sanctuaries for themselves in Myanmar despite the cooperation extended to India by the Myanmarese army. The cross border movement of Nagas and Mizos for training, purchase of arms and shelter when pursued by Indian security forces, combined with the difficult terrain obtaining in the area, makes this border extremely challenging to manage. This border is manned by the Assam Rifles (AR), India's oldest paramilitary force.

Along the Bangladesh border that has seen some action in recent years, the BSF is in charge. This border remains in the news as there are frequent clashes between the BSF and the Bangladesh Rifles (BDR). Managing this border is a peculiar challenge that is usually referred to as 'Enclaves and Adverse Possessions'. There are 111 Indian enclaves (17,158 acres) within Bangladesh and 51 Bangladeshi enclaves (7,110.02 acres) in India. Thirty-four tracts of Indian land are under the adverse possession of Bangladesh and 40 pieces of Bangladeshi land are in India's adverse possession. Though the Land Border Agreement of 1974 has provisions for the settlement of the issue of adverse possession, it has not been implemented so far as the problem is politically sensitive.

The CCS had also approved the nomination of the Central Reserve Police Force (CRPF) as the country's primary counter-insurgency force. Since then, the BSF has been withdrawn from internal security duties in J&K and has been replaced by CRPF battalions. The CRPF is also the primary strike force for anti-Naxalite or anti Maoist operations in the left wing extremism (LWE) affected states in central India. Though it has suffered many casualties in operations so far, it is gradually gaining experience in counter-insurgency operations and will without doubt acquit itself creditably in future.

Over the last few decades, the CAPFs have seen rapid expansion, some of which appears to have been hastily undertaken. Also, there appears to lack of inter-departmental coordination such that the combat potential of the various forces is not being optimally exploited in the nation's best interests. To examine these issues, a need was felt at CLAWS to undertake a study into the role and the organisational as well as the command and control structure of the CAPFs in detail. The project 'The Role of Para Military and Central Armed Police Forces in India's National Security' was entrusted to Rohit Singh, an Associate Fellow at CLAWS. He has carried out diligent research and produced a worthy and thought provoking book.

The author provides an insightful commentary on the historical roots of some of our oldest paramilitary forces and the circumstances necessitating the creation of new CAPFs in consonance with India's external and internal security challenges. He has given an even handed account of the growth and role of India's paramilitary and central armed police forces in our country's journey through diverse challenges. He has, also contextualised the criticality of their role, now that they are designated the lynchpin of India's internal security at a time when terrorism and insurgency continue to cast long shadows over the land and its people's aspirations for a rightful place under the sun. The author has also lucidly analysed the paramilitary forces and the CAPFs capabilities to weather the present and future challenges.

The author has rightly concluded that if the country has to maximise its economic growth, enhance social peace and stability, manage China's rise and be prepared for emerging challenges, then the paramilitary forces and the CAPFs have to perform well. The author's recommendations are noteworthy and I am sure, will help the policy makers to quickly reverse the tide of insurgencies and terror in the country. I am sure this book will be a useful guide not only for the forces themselves in the discharge of their but also to those who plan their employment. The paramilitary forces and the CAPFs are key components of India's border management and internal security and this book is an important contribution to the literature on the subject. It must be read by policy makers, CAPF officers and analysts dealing with national security.

January 2013

Gurmeet Kanwal (Retd)
Former Director, CLAWS

Introduction

Historical Legacy

India is one of the oldest civilisations in the world and its landscape has been dotted with great kingdoms and large empires. Warfare is perhaps, the oldest profession in the world and the rise and fall of powerful empires have largely remained dependent on their armies. In the ancient and medieval periods of our glorious past, large standing armies were a symbol of power and an instrument of exercising control over neighbouring kingdoms and territories. The more powerful and numerically superior armies subjugated the weaker ones and extended their supremacy over the vanquished.

Ancient Indian History even after the Mahabharata period is replete with examples of large standing armies maintained by various kingdoms. These large kingdoms won over and amalgamated the smaller ones to form great empires. The Mauryan empire under Chandragupta Maurya and Ashoka was among the largest empires in the world. Its boundaries extended from the present day Afghanistan to Southern India. The Chola Kingdom in Peninsular India extended its control even across the Bay of Bengal to present day Sri Lanka, Maldives and countries of the Malayan archipelago. The armies played a pivotal role in the apparatus of these empires. Once the period of consolidating control over newly conquered territories was over, a unifying system of internal administration was established. In this apparatus, a multi-layered system of administration, which included the cabinet ministers at the ruling court, judiciary, police and *talukdars* at the village level played a pivotal role in maintaining internal stability of the empire.

From the 11th Century onwards, foreign armies began to invade and establish control over India. The Turks from Central Asia were the first to exploit the political flux in India after the disintegration of the Gupta empire. In the 14th Century AD, the Delhi Sultans were replaced by the Mughals. During the Mughal period, native Rajput rulers were required to dedicate their armies to the throne. In this system can be traced the first existence of state forces.

In the late 18th Century, the British came to India in quest of natural resources, raw materials and commodities to fuel their economy. After the battles of Plassey and Buxar, the British East India Company permanently removed the semblances of authority of the waning Mughal Empire. After the Sepoy Mutiny of 1857, the British Crown assumed control over the affairs of India.

Their nature of rule and authority notwithstanding, the British are credited with bringing India under a single administrative apparatus. They established networks of communication and rail-roads to extend control over the vast territories of the sub-continent. They introduced modern policing with the establishment of the *Kotwali* or *thanedar* system (police stations in villages) and ushered in the civil services to India. Initially, the British were heavily dependent on their army to exercise control over the subjects. Indian men were recruited primarily from the Bengal Presidency into the British Indian Army. After the Sepoy Mutiny of 1857, Indian troops were recruited mainly from the Madras and Bombay Presidencies, and organised into Regiments and Battalions on the lines of the British Army. The Indian units were officered by British officers. This changed only after 1932 after the first batch of Indian officers were commissioned from the newly established Indian Military Academy (IMA) at Dehradun. Apart from regular units, the princely states contributed their forces to the crown. These were the State Forces which were merged into the regular Indian Army post-Independence. The British utilised them in aid of the police to quell internal disturbances and uprisings.

The edifice of this system of state power continues to remain the same from the Mughal period to British India and post-Independence India, albeit with minor modifications. The legacy of our armed forces, paramilitary and police forces can be traced to the British era. A Post-Independence India continued with the established structure, re-christening a few and raising a few others.

Even today, maintaining professional and modern armies are necessary for maintaining the integrity of any nation-state. Having effective paramilitary and police forces are also essential for national security and extending good governance to the people.

India's Security Landscape

Geographical and Ethno-cultural-linguistic Context

The Indian sub-continent was formed due to heavy tectonic movements nearly 70 million years ago that caused the crashing of the Indo-Australian plate with the Eurasian Plate. The gap formed by the Tethys Ocean was completely closed by the collision of the two plates.[1] The Himalayas that are young fold mountains were formed due to the enormous amount of land crust, thrown up because of the crashing of the two plates. Since centuries, this geographical barrier along with its sub-chain, the Hindukush to the west have formed the traditional barrier to the Indian sub-continent. To the south, the Indian landmass forms a peninsula bounded by three major water bodies, the Indian Ocean in the south, the Bay of Bengal to the south-east and the Arabian Sea to the south-west. In between the Himalayas and the Indian Ocean lie straddled the vast landmass of India. It is the seventh-largest country in the world, with a total land area of 3,287,263 square kilometers. India measures 3214 km from north to south and 2993 km from east to west. It has a land frontier of 15200 km and a coastline of 7517 km.[2]

This vast landmass is bounded with numerous forests, hills, deserts and river systems. The Ganges, Indus and the Brahmaputra together form the Indo-Gangetic plain. Krishna and Godavari are the two main rivers of Peninsular India cutting across the Deccan Plateau. Due to its enormity and varied geographical features, India witnesses a great variation in climatic conditions. This could range from - 50 degrees up north in the glaciers to 50 degrees in the Western Thar desert. This variation in topography and climate has impacted the agricultural practices, customs, traditions and eating habits of the people inhabiting the Indian sub-continent. This, and contact with several communities over the centuries have led to a diverse population with different ethnic and tribal groups in India. The Census of 1961 recognised 1652 different languages spoken in the country. The eighth schedule of the Constitution of India recognises 22 languages as official languages of the country. Historically, the varied and vast demographics of India have given rise to several conflicts of interests among the people.

Troubled Neighborhood

Geography has also placed India in a troubled neighbourhood, in particular, with China and Pakistan with whom it has fought numerous wars. If the external security situation has been fraught then so has been the internal one with China fomenting the North-Eastern insurgencies in the hey days and Pakistan giving an external dimension to the Punjab and J&K insurrections. A combination of these external and internal challenges gravely impact National security putting the spot light on the role of the PMF/CAPFs.

Pilloried by Internal Conflicts

Post-Independence, India emerged as a secular, democratic republic encompassing 'unity in diversity'. However, the state continued to be buffeted by several internal conflicts with its people spread across the length and breadth of the country. Ever since its independence, India has been plagued with insurgencies in the North-East, Punjab and Jammu & Kashmir. A substantial proportion of the state's central forces and the Army have been deployed over the years to stabilise the security situation in these areas. The suppression of the militancy in Punjab and resolution of the Mizo insurgency have, perhaps been the greatest successes of the state. Both these states today enjoy relative peace and economic prosperity. The North-East, after several decades of festering conflict is also enjoying a period of relative, calm, today with the Government of India entering into negotiations with the two main Naga groups- the NSCN (IM) and NSCN (K) in Nagaland and factions of the ULFA and NDFB in Assam. Relentless operations by the security forces brought these groups to the negotiating table. The state of Manipur, though, continues to remain mired in a complex insurgency between different ethnic groups.

The state of Jammu & Kashmir is also witnessing a period of relative calm after nearly two decades of Pakistan sponsored terrorism. But, given the emerging security situation in the neighbourhood and Pakistan's reluctance to clamp down on terrorism emanating from its animosity towards India, the shadow of terror continues to loom large over the state.

Since 1993 and, especially post 9/11, the specter of urban terrorism has continued to haunt major Indian cities. This faceless terror today has become a major challenge for the state to tackle as it strikes at the very root of our secular fabric and economic progress, and so far countervailing efforts of the state have been long on diagnosis and short on treatment.

External Threats and Security Imperatives

Added to the internal schisms are the external threats to India's security. Also, many internal armed conflicts of the country have been aided and abetted by external powers. India shares a 3223 km long International Border (IB) with Pakistan. Across this Western front, India and Pakistan have gone to war three times since 1947. In 1947-48, tribal marauders from Pakistan and Afghanistan backed by the Pakistan Army invaded the state of Jammu & Kashmir and illegally occupied parts of its territory. Ever since, the two armies of India and Pakistan have been engaged in an eye-ball to eye-ball confrontation over the ceasefire line formed in 1948, to be later re-designated as the Line of Control (LoC) after its demarcation by both sides following the Simla Agreement of 1972. Since November 2003, a mutually agreed ceasefire between the two neighbours along the LoC has largely held, though Pakistan continues to push armed terrorists across this 750 km line. The Kargil conflict of 1999 was also fought along a stretch of this line. Further north of the LoC runs another un-demarcated line of 114 km along the glacial heights of the Karakoram Range. This conflict on the highest battlefield of the world has cost both the nations enormously in terms of financial human and other resources.

Further east from the Karakoram Pass to the tri-junction of India, Tibet and Myanmar in Arunachal Pradesh, India shares a 3488 km long boundary with China along the Himalayan crest line. In 1962, the two great armies of the world went to war after disputes emerged along the Eastern and Western sectors of this boundary. Along this vast frontage, the two countries are engulfed in the largest boundary dispute in the world today. Over the years, several confidence building measures have been put in place to help reduce tensions. Due to existing disputes as discussed above, the primary role of the Indian Army is to counter the external threats emerging from across the Northern and Western fronts.

Security challenges in the form of illegal migration, trafficking in human beings, narcotics, and infiltration by anti-national elements are also faced along the country's relatively peaceful borders with Nepal, Bhutan, Myanmar and Bangladesh. The length of the border with these countries are 1751, 699, 1643 and 4096.7 km, respectively. In addition, subversive elements have also made use of India's maritime boundaries to pose a security threat to India. India is separated from Sri Lanka by a narrow stretch of land known as the Palk Strait. Maldives to the West is another maritime neighbour of the country. Such large territorial and maritime boundaries pose complex and multi-dimensional security challenges to the country.

Because of the set of circumstances as narrated above, it is a no brainer that India lives in a troubled neighbourhood in South Asia, which is also the epicenter of terror in the world. Presence of weak nations (Sri Lanka, Nepal, Bangladesh, Bhutan) which are prone to insidious and sleight of hand influences by China and Pakistan, India's security acquires multifarious dimensions necessitating a greater role to be played by the Central Armed Police Forces in the foreseeable and long term future. This necessitates a look at the PMF/CAPFs and to examine how best they may be utilised to better manage National Security including by relieving the Army from its internal security burden.

NOTES

1. Plate Tectonics, Earthquake and Tsunami, Geological Survey of India, accessed at http://www.portal.gsi.gov.in/portal/page?_pageid=127,711659&_dad=portal&_schema=PORTAL
2. Department of Border Management, Ministry of Home Affairs.

1

Our Paramilitary and Central Armed Police Forces

Our PMFs in Regional Context

To begin with an opening chapter on Asia's Para Military is to put into perspective the context and role of our own PMF/CAPFs in the larger trans-national role of combating terrorism. As will be seen in subsequent analysis of various PMF/CAPFs, the common glue to different assigned roles is related to either combat terror directly, or protecting Vulnerable Areas/Points, and VIPs, etc.

Comparative figures of Para Military Forces of different West Asian countries, Pakistan and China will highlight the huge numbers of PMF that India itself has, and begs the question as to why it cannot have a lean and mean PMF machine which works towards achieving quantified tasks in a time bound manner rather than muddling along.

Unlike most of these Asian countries, India is a rare case of a democratic country having huge CAPF numbers. Other countries are largely autocratic or have flirted with democracy and dictatorship, alternately, and hence have used PMF to suppress its people.

For a democratic country like India which is truly on its way towards its rightful place under the sun, such astronomical numbers give a misleading notion and begs the purpose for which such numbers are required, until one examines the huge challenges facing this emerging power.

At 8,97,121, India has almost three times the number that Pakistan has (3,04,000) and even more than that of the People's Armed Police of China (6,50,000).[1,2] What catches the eye is that India's PMF/CAPFs are almost 60 percent the size of India's armed forces (Army: 11,29,900; Navy: 58,350; Air Force: 1,27,200).[3] And, this gap will further narrow down with the raising of additional CAPF battalions in the coming years. If these be the numbers, then can there be two questions on the need for the PMF/CAPFs to fire and deliver quickly? We all know how important regime stability is to China and in line with this aim and with an eye to the ever rising spectre of terrorism in Aisa, China, for the first time has spent more on Internal Security than on the officially declared 91.5 billion dollars it has reportedly spent on its armed forces.

Figure 1.1 below shows the Para Military numbers of Monarchical/Repressive Regimes.

• Egypt	-	397,000
• Iraq	-	386,312
• Algeria	-	187,200
• Syria	-	108,000
• Yemen	-	71,200
• Morocco	-	50,000
• Libya	-	40,000
• Iran	-	40,000
• Saudi Arabia	-	15,500
• Bahrain	-	11,260
• Jordan	-	10,000
• Kuwait	-	7,100

Source: IISS, Military Balance, 2010.

India's Security Forces at a Glance

Military: A military is an organisation authorised by its greater society to use lethal force, usually including use of weapons, in defending its country by combating actual or perceived threats.

Paramilitary force: A Force is classified as paramilitary if it has a degree of military capability. It is often integrated with the country's armed police forces.

Central police organisation: As these bodies are concerned with prevention of crime, provision of security, police training, and research & development in police matters, these organisations are compendiously covered by the expression "central police organisations."

The charts below will put into context India's security forces in the security management system of the country.

Police to Population Ratio in India

As per the Bureau of Police Research and Development, the actual police to population ratio in India is 117.09 policemen per 1 Lakh population. The total sanctioned strength of police in India is 16,82,851.

Budget

The Union Defence Budget for the Financial year 2012-13 has been pegged at

India's Armed and Security Forces

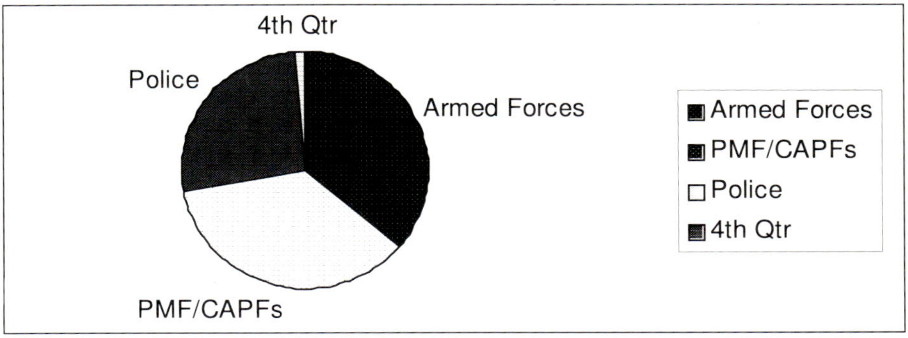

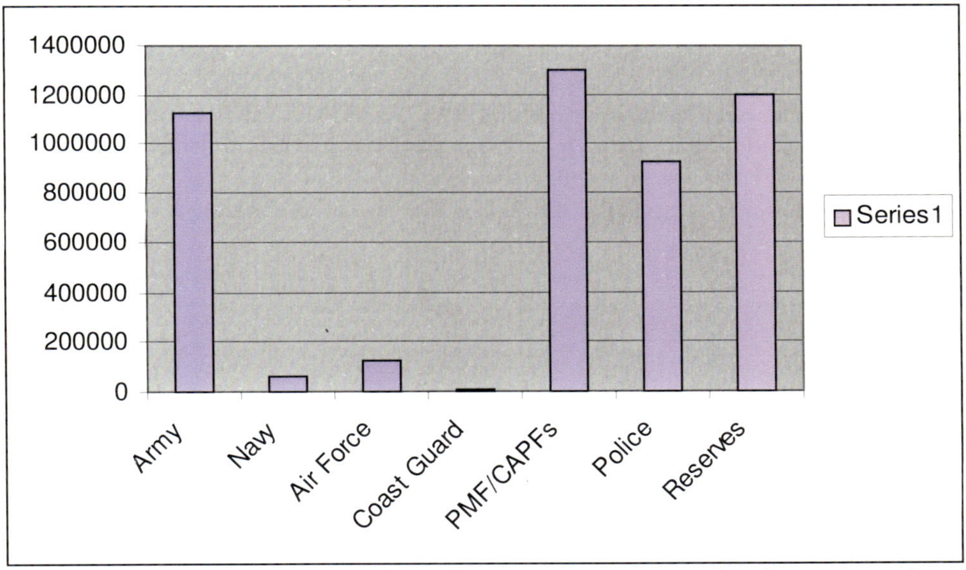

The above chart further displays the manpower strength of our Armed, paramilitary and police forces.

Rs1,93,407.29 Cr while the budgetary allocation for the Minsitry of Home Affairs stands at Rs 54,448 Cr.

Emerging Non Traditional Security threats will call for more increase in CAPF numbers which is financially neither unsustainable nor desirable. But the underlining fact remains that both Defence and Internal Security Budgets cannot grow astronomically simultaneously. The manifestation of Chinese and twin Pak/ China threat will require bigger defence budgets with a special emphasis on accelerating hardware procurement. By 2017, Chinese Defence Budget will be eight times that of India's. Therefore for India to play catch up with China, it will require to increase its defence budget substantially and in the process restrict spending on internal security. Additionally, for a heavily populated country like India, where a substantial amount of population still live below the poverty line or on low incomes, achieiving the right balance between spendings on security and other areas will always been a challenge.

Paramilitary/Central Armed Police Forces

After several classification changes, the Ministry of Home Affairs has designated the Assam Rifles (AR) as a Paramilitary Force of the Union. The other forces have been classified as Central Armed Police Forces. These include the National Security Guard (NSG), Border Security Force (BSF), Central Reserve Police Force (CRPF), Indo-Tibetan Border Police (ITBP), Central Industrial Security Force (CISF) and the Sashastra Seema Bal (SSB). The Special Frontier Force (SFF) is a Special Force which operates directly under the control of the Cabinet Secretariat. The chart below indicates their manpower strength. Previously, all these organisations were variably referred to as Central Paramilitary forces (CPMFs), Central Police Organisations (CPOs) or Central Police Forces (CPFs). In March 2011, the Government of India approved a standard definition for the term 'Paramilitary' and only those organisations which assist the Indian Armed Forces particularly closely and are led by officers of the Indian Army or Navy can be defined as Paramilitary.

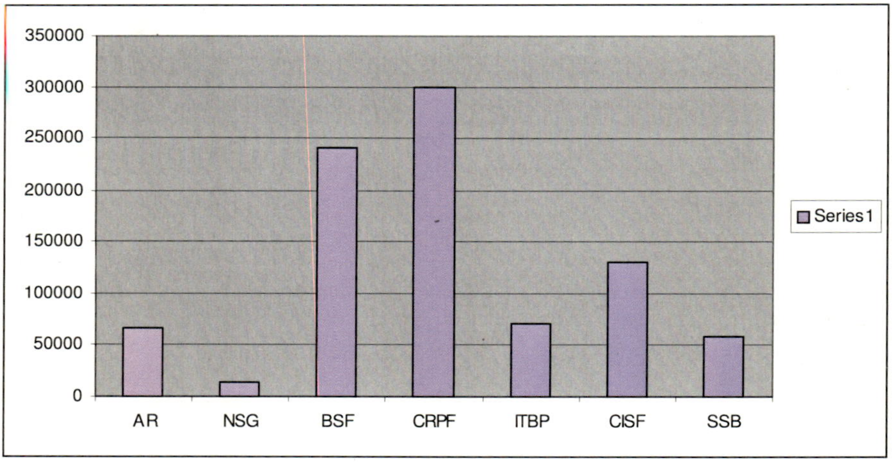

The CRPF is the largest CAPF of the country with 222 battalions and a strength of approximately 3,00,000 personnel.

Organisation	*Strength*	*No. of Battalions*
AR	66411	46
NSG	14500	05
BSF	240532	168
CRPF	300000	222
ITBP	70523	49
CISF	130155	50
SSB	75000	54

The following new raisings are sanctioned for 2012-14.

AR	1 Inspector General (IG) and 3 Sector HQs
CRPF	29 battalions (including 1 Mahila Bn), 5 Group Centre/DIG Ranges, 1 DIG Sector
ITBP	13 battalions (4 by 2013 and 9 by 2015). Creation of a Water Wing, Sub-Depot and Field Ammunition Workshop and augmentation of its Intelligence wing. Conversion of remaining 20 battalions from 4 to 6 coy pattern.
SSB	15 battalions

Source: Ministry of Home Affairs, Annual Report, 2011-12.

Our Central Police Forces

With a combined strength of 1.32 million active and 2.14 reservist troops, the Indian Armed and Paramilitary forces constitute the third largest active troops in the world after China and the United States of America.[4,5] The large numbers are justified due to the internal and external threats faced by the country and as explained in the above paragraphs.

The first paramilitary force in India was raised in 1839 when the British empire was extending its influence over the North-East. The Cachar Levies were conceived as armed police units to guard the settlements and tea estates against depredations of marauding tribals. Later, it took on border guarding roles in the North-East and was deployed to maintain law and order in other parts of the country. In 1920, this force was re-named as the Assam Rifles.

The Railway Protection Force (RPF) came into being in the year 1854 to secure the newly laid rail lines of communication in the country.

The Crown Representative Police was raised in 1939 primarily to aid the Princely States during internal disturbances. In 1949, it was re-christened as the Central Reserve Police Force (CRPF) and today is designated as the primary counter-insurgency force of the country.

The Indo-Tibetan Border Police (ITBP) and the Special Frontier Force (SFF) were raised after the 1962 Indo-China war. While the former was tasked to guard our Northern borders with Tibet, the latter comprises Tibetan refugees and are tasked for special roles across the borders.

The Border Security Force (BSF) was raised in 1968 to guard our international borders during peace-time. This force has also been used repeatedly in other

Internal Security duties since its inception. The Central Industrial Security Force (CISF) was also raised in the year 1968 to provide security coverage to Public Sector Undertakings. (PSUs).

The National Security Guard (NSG) was raised as the country's elite counter-terrorist force in the backdrop of the Punjab militancy. The Special Protection Group (SPG) was tasked with guarding the country's Prime Ministers and VVIPs in the aftermath of Prime Minister Indira Gandhi's assassination.

The Rapid Action Force (RAF) was raised as the specialised anti-riot wing of the CRPF in the year 1992. Its task is mainly to deal effectively with large scale communal riots in any part of the country.[6]

The Rashtriya Rifles (RR) was the brainchild of late Gen BC Joshi, former Chief of Army Staff as a result of the outbreak of insurgency in Jammu & Kashmir in 1990. This force today is 63 battalions strong and functions under the direct command and control of the Army.

The BSF is responsible for guarding the borders with Pakistan and Bangladesh during peace-time. The Indo-Tibetan Border Police (ITBP) remains deployed along the boundary with China. The Indian Army also maintains a permanent deployment on this border. The Sashastra Seema Bal (SSB) is responsible for the largely unheld border with Nepal and Bhutan.

As we go along, it will become apparent that the PMF/CAPF is an invaluable numerical resource, which with better capacity building and re-appraisal of role and tasks, and with some tweaking of centre – state relations and rules of engagement can adequately perform the tasks they were raised for in the first place and complement the Armed Forces' effort in being an important cog in the wheel of the National Security apparatus.

Central Police Organisations: A Corner Stone of Internal Security

The geo-strategic location of India, straddled as it is between an increasingly radicalised and unstable Pakistan to the west, and an assertive China with superpower ambitions to the north, further exacerbates our security vulnerabilities. The two-decade old state sponsored proxy war by Pakistan and various internal insurgencies have exerted a great strain on our security forces and police. The festering Left-Wing Extremism in the heart of the country has opened another front in India's many conflicts and has stretched the security forces. And, to top it all, the specter of global terrorism casts a permanent shadow on the security of the common man residing in India's rapidly emerging metros and mega-cities, greatly impacting economic security of the country.

In view of these security challenges, it is undesirable for the Indian Army to deal both with external and internal challenges as dealing will the latter may impinge on optimal operational preparedness which is its bête-noire. Hence, the importance of the central police forces.

The population of India is 1.21 billion according to preliminary figures of the 2011 Census. It is estimated that with a present growth rate of 1.41 percent, India will surpass China by 2025 to become the most populated country in the world.[7] More than 50 percent of the population is under the age of 25 and more than 65 percent is under the age of 35 years. It is expected that, in 2020, the average age of an Indian will be 29 years, compared to 37 for China and 48 for Japan; and, by 2030, India's dependency ratio should be just over 0.4.[8] This is likely to impact the future job market in the country and may lead to socio-economic unrest as a large population will compete for fewer natural and national resources for its survival. Therefore, the strain on India's police and security forces is only expected to increase, exponentially.

India, which is fast moving towards becoming a global powerhouse, will require an effective Military, Paramilitary /central Armed Police Forces and police like no other country in the world. In the event that economic growth is unable to keep pace with our growing population (not expected to stabilise before 2050), unmet aspirations of the youth will become an ulcer in India's security matrix. It is therefore essential to delve into the functioning and role of the paramilitary and central police forces of India, which are important instruments of the state for maintaining its internal coherence and stability.

Recommendations on the future role in view of present and emerging challenges will be a natural corollary to the role appraisal of the Central police and paramilitary forces.

NOTES

1. IISS Military Balance 2011. IISS Military Balance, 2009, p. 349. This document actually shows the strength of India's paramilitary forces to be 13,00,586 but that is because the figure includes Defence Security Corps, Civil Defence, Home Guards and Rashtriya Rifles.
2. Harinder Singh, Ramesh Phadke, Always in the Line of Fire, IDSA Comment, 22 Jun 2010, accessed at http://www.idsa.in/idsacomments/AlwaysintheLineofFire_220610
3. ibid (2) above
4. CSIS, Indian Armed Forces, 25 Jul 2006, http://csis.org/files/media/csis/pubs/060626_asia_balance_powers.pdf
5. The SIPRI Military Expenditure Database, http://milexdata.sipri.org/result.php4
6. Giriraj Shah, Paramilitary Forces of India, Amol Publications, pp.1-3.
7. *BBC News*, 18 Aug 2004, http://news.bbc.co.uk/2/hi/3575994.stm
8. Kaushik Basu, India's Demographic Divident, *BBC News*, 25 Jul 2007, http://news.bbc.co.uk/2/hi/south_asia/6911544.stm

2

Emerging Threats and Challenges

As India aspires to play a greater role in the Global commons, its sphere of influence and interference has also expanded. We can no longer afford to look only at our external borders to ensure our security. It is being widely recognised in strategic circles that India's immediate sphere of influence today extends from the Gulf of Aden to the Straits of Malacca. This chapter is an attempt to situate the threats and challenges that the country is likely to grapple with in the coming decades. Doing so would help us better understand the future role, deployment and tasks our Armed forces and Central Armed Police Forces are likely to undertake in the emerging security dynamics.

CRITICALITIES

There are certain regional and other criticalities emerging on the horizon which will ensure that India remains engaged in tackling them head on. Certain criticalities impinging on the role and operational philosophies of India's security forces are enumerated in the succeeding paragraphs.

Criticality 1

Terror Gravitating towards South Aisa: CAPFs need to be upto the Plate

As per SAGRA adapted from NCTC Worldwide Incidents Tracking System-WITS in a study by Abdullah Tonkan and Anthony Cordesman, 'The Iranian Nuclear Challenge: GCC Security, Risk Assessment, and US Extended Deterrence', region wise terrorist attacks for the year 2010 stood as under:

Middle East (West Asia) plus Iran	2545
South Asia	4196
Africa	658
East Asia and Pacific	560
Western Hemisphere	244
Europe and Eurasia	491

More pertinently, for India, the number of terrorist attacks have increasingly shifted from West Asia to South Asia. Again, importantly, for India is to consider the impact of the US drawdown in Afghanistan. India is the fourth highest country in the world in terms of terrorist attacks; 616 in the year 2010 to Pakistan's 2514. In so far as deaths to terrorist attacks are concerned for the same year, India stood at the fifth position, 624 to Pakistan's third position at 2475.[1]

With the terror epicenter in South Asian emanating from Pakistan, a look at the latter country's PMF security architecture will be useful, particularly, in arriving at subsequent deductions and recommendations on the employment modalities of our own PMF. As per various sources quoted by Anthony Cordesman and Varun Vira in a Net Assessment Paper for CSIS, 'Pakistan: Violence and Stability', the Para Military and local security forces operating in FATA and Khyber Pakthunkhwa along with their performance impact are: 17,000 Khassadars- poorly trained tribesman- early pickings for the Taliban; two, 4000-6800 Levies who are better trained, educated and equipped; three, 34,000-50,000 Frontier Corps, a resurgent force – with vastly improved weaponry, capacities and experience in Counter terrorism operations including joint operations with the Army. A *WikiLeaks* cable quoted US Ambassador to Pakistan, Anne Patterson, "We have created Intelligence Fusion cells of embedded US Special Forces with both SSG and Frontier Corps (Bala Hisar, Peshawar) with the rover equipment ready to deploy...through these embeds, we are assisting the Pakistanis collect and coordinate existing intelligence assets...US Special Operations Command Force are assisting the FC at the Intelligence Fusion Cell at FC Headquarters with imagery, target packages and operational planning;"[2] four, 22,817 Frontier Constabulary tasked to secure settled border areas; five, 55,000-78,000 Khyber-Pakhtunkhwa Police (KPK) ; six, 30,000 Lashkars, provided weapons by Pakistan Army.

These 200,000 plus, constitute the PMF operating in the troubled insurgency afflicted areas of FATA and KPK. The other 100,000 plus Para Military including the Razakars and Mujahid Battalions are deployed along the IB and LoC with India.

In the past year, the Pakistan PMF have shown tremendous resilience even after taking approximately 300 plus fatalities, a far cry from the 2004-05 days when some of them abjectly surrendered to the militants. Significantly, at approximately 42 percent favourable acceptability by local population, when they are operating, the Frontier Corps is second only to 48 percent acceptability of the Pakistan Army.[3] Staying ahead in favourable perception over FATA Development Authority, FATA Secretariat, Pakistan Police, Political Agent, Provincial Government, Federal Government and the US Army is no mean achievement for the Frontier Corps. It would be very important to note that 30.7 percent people vote them ahead of the Pakistan Army and other forces to take charge of security in FATA.[4]

Commenting on the FC's resurgent capabilities, Cordesman and Vira say that, "Considerable focus has now been placed on creating adequate training regimens that prepare soldiers for operations in the tribal terrain. At least three major LIC training facilities have been built at Jhari Kas, Mangl and Pabbi Hills, and new requirements mandate all incoming officers undergo LIC training. The FC has also benefitted from US and British SOF training, and monetary support." This was a far cry form post-9/11 days when the FC, the primary force tasked with guarding the FATA had, 'devolved into a backwater force commanded by the drego of the Army's Officer Corps.'[5] It is a far cry from August 2007 when 200 odd FC Soldiers surrendered to militants.

Intelligence gathering, operating in rabidly prohibitive terrain, absorbing fatalities and taking the battle to the militants are some of the important benchmarks for our own CAPFs to achieve. Hence, our CAPFs need to evolve effective measures and hone up force structures and capacity building in some of our own harsh terrain against an adversary which though wily and guileful are not as lethal and formidable as the adversaries of the Pakistani PMFs.

The PMF/CAPFs have to fire and fire quickly as the external and internal factors affecting Indian security situation, not known to be benign in the past, are poised to go on a downward spiral.

Criticality 2

External Factors

Afghanistan

The impending US drawdown in 2014 and the anticipated failure of the US' led International Security Assistance Force (ISAF) counter insurgency strategy is going to track back to India's internal security situation. There are chances of a civil conflict in Afghanistan which may impact India.

There are now considerable linkages between Pakistani Jihadi groups and their proxy home grown ones in India which can breed in 'liberated zones' or areas where the writ of the Indian state is limited.

Al-Qaida

Al Qaida, though tottering on its legs, post the Osama bin Laden killing, is diffuse and regaining ground in Iraq, Yemen, Maghreb and North Africa. Its linkages with India's foe, LeT, are strong and enduring.

Civilisational Victory

In the event that the Afghan Taliban dominates the future political structure in Afghanistan, there is every possibility that it will be regarded by Pakistani Islamists as a civilisational victory. India, a next door neighbour, may well be its next target.

Where will this malaise/ulcer breed? Obviously, exported from Pakistan in the vast ungoverned spaces, particularly of Central India and now expanding into cities, as well.

Conventional Challenges

Pakistan

The pangs of partition led to the division of India and creation of the new state of Pakistan. A distinct religious identity lay at the heart of its emergence as opposed to a secular India. Champoining the cause of its separate and distinct religious identity, Pakistan sought to megre muslim-majority provinces into its fold. Shortly, after partition, this led to the invasion of the princely state of Jammu & Kashmir and the insurrection in Hyderabad. At both places, the Indian Army moved swifly and amalgamated the states into the Indian Union. Ever since, the two neighbours, violently separated at birth, have been locked in a perpetual state of conflict which has resulted in two full blown wars and two limited ones. In fact, skirmishes and hostilities have erupted frequently along the cease-fire line in Jammu and Kashmir, where six-decades of an eye-ball to eye-ball deployment has resulted in a stalemate.

Nevertheless, the long running feud has meant that the two sides have build up their conventional capabilities to meet all challenges and to also degrade the conventional capabilities of the other side. Majority of Indian Army's field formations, air and naval assets cater to the threat from its western neighbour. All three of India's Strike Corps are tasked for driving a wedge through the Plains of West Punjab and the Sindh desert or to gain 'shallow depths' all along the western border. Similarly, all of Pakistan's Armed Forces are orbated against its' arch-rival to the East. This includes the formations presently deployed for the battle against insurgency along the countries' western borders. Due to a lack of territorial depth and perceived aggression from India, Pakistan's war doctrine has been that of an offensive-defence, to pre-empt or halt India's offensive in the opening rounds of a conflict itself.

However, over the years, the nature of this traditional conflict has undergone a shift, and the threat of war has been gradually receding due to the development and deployment of deterrent capabilities like long range nuclear-tipped missiles by both sides. Also, the successful mastering of asymmetric capabilities by Pakistan over its conventionally superior opponent has added another dimension to the conflict. By unleashing bands of terrorists, Pakistan has been able to 'bleed India with a thousand cuts' even without entering into a conventional conflict. Acting as a force multiplier, this substantial force of irregulars can also play a considerable role in the event of a conventional conflict. The increased radicalisation of the middle rung officers and men of the Pakistan Armed forces does not bode well for world security and magnifies the fear of loose nukes falling into wrong hands. The ideology of the radicalised rank and file of the armed forces, combined with the plethora of firebrand jihadist groups mushrooming in Pakistan today, poses grave threats to India and increases the threat of spectacular strikes like 26/11.

This shift in the nature of conflict from traditional warfare to a more asymmetric one, has led to the adoption of a greater and significant role for India's Central Armed Police Forces (CAPFs). The BSF would continue to play a major role in countering Pakistan's asymmetric forces along the long western borders with Pakistan. And, as their deployment becomes more permanent, they would also have to play a larger role in the event of a future conflict, complimenting the larger war efforts due to their intricate knowledge of the terrain and local conditions. The impact of Pakistan's asymmetric forces on India's internal security and the role played by the CAPFs in combating them will be discussed in the succeeding paragraphs.

China

The trade, commerce and cultural linkages between the two great civilisations dates back thousands of years. Through the accounts of travellers like Fa Hien and Hsuen Tsang, the 'middle kingdom' had long maintained an insight on happenings across the Great Himalayas, which for centuries acted as a geographical barrier preventing raiders, marauders and conquerors from moving across. As centuries elapsed, the arrival of the Turks and the establishment of the Delhi Sultanate in 1206 AD marked the decline of the indigenous kingdoms of India and heralded the arrival of outsiders. The vast northern frontiers remained largely inactive during the centuries of Mughal rule with the small peripheral kingdoms keeping local and minor aggressions in check. This inactivity was momentarily broken in the early half of the 19th century, when Zorawar Singh, a general in the Dogra Army of Maharaja Gulab Singh undertook several audacious military expeditions into Ladakh, Skardu, Astore, Taklakot and Kailash Mansarovar in Central Tibet from 1834-42 thereby extending India's reach across the Himalayan region for the first time. The British were to embarke upon several mapping expeditions across this frontier which ultimately defined India's territorial boundaries with Tibet and later the People's Republic of China.

The 'Great Game' that began in Afghanistan led to the British discovering new buffer zones to keep the expansion of their rival, the Czarist Russia in check. Russian threat to their dominion in India was perceived from Afghanistan in the west and Tibet in the North. No matter, how far-fetched this threat from Russia which lay thousands of kilometers away across Siberia, Mongolia, the Chinese hinterland, and Tibet) would have seemed, it led to the opening up of the high passes in the Himalayas and British military expeditions into Tibet to establish trade and diplomatic relations. The Himalayan barrier was breached once again after remaining dormant for many years. The Younghusband expedition of Tibet in 1903-04 led to the stationing of a British political officer in Lhasa and thus introducing a third party in the relations between Tibet and China. This further exacerbated China's difficulties in maintaining a hold over the vast and ungovernable tracts of land at its peripheries. The Chinese plenipotentiary refused to acknowledge the agreement over the Sino-Tibetan boundary reached between the representatives of Tibet and British India in Simla in 1913.

After independence, not much thought was given on defending the Himalayan frontage with Tibet as it posed no military threat to India. Also, the new-born republic of India was kept pre-occupied by an aggressive Pakistan which had sent raiders into Kashmir in October 1947 and stirred insurrections in Hyderabad and Junagadh. In 1950, Chinese troops rolled into the Tibetan plateau and merged it with the newly formed People's Republic of China. Prime Minister Jawaharlal Nehru's instant recognition of Tibet as a part of China for the first time led to the two great civilisations sharing a common border with each other. Pandit Nehru, who was by now envisaging a leadership role for India in the Non-Aligned World, also saw China as a friend and did not perceive any military threat from that country which had just achieved unification after a violent internal upheaval, and was aggressively extending its writ over its outlying areas which were previously outside its control or were very loosely integrated with it. In fact, Pandit Nehru foresaw no role for the Army in an area where 'not even a blade of grass grew'.

Minor skirmishes along the newly formed cease-fire line in Kashmir and sporadic acts of Pakistani aggression all along the western boundary ensured that India's threat perceptions remained focus on Pakistan. Resultantly, all of India's field formations were oriented, equipped and trained for defence of the plains of Punjab which was considered vital for India's security. The Northern frontiers remained largely unguarded and only had a token presence in the form of isolated pickets manned by armed police personnel. These pickets were also few in numbers and far between.

All this was to change when the People's Liberation Army (PLA) in their quest for establishing total control over a restive Tibetan population and providing depth to their lines of communications in the newly annexed province came dangerously close to the Himalayan crest line which formed the border with India as defined in the border treaties signed between the British and the Tibetans. In 1959, the discovery that the newly constructed road linking Tibet with Xinjiang, another peripheral Chinese province, passed through Indian territory alarmed even the mandarins in India. Simultaneously, China declared that it did not recognise the previous boundaries drawned by Imperial powers such as Great Britain. India now moved hastily to occupy the Northern borders, though in the absence of proper delineation and demarcation on the ground, no one knew where exactly the boundary lay on the ground. A series of moves eventually led to 'Operation Onkar' in 1961, the aim of which was to establish a string of forward posts all along the boundary in Ladakh and Arunachal Pradesh. In the absence of any logistics or other infrastructure to support troops in high altitude, this was an exercise in futility and only led to penny-packet of Infantry troops clinging on to a series of rocky outcrops in extremely dizzy heights and rugged terrain of the high Himalayas. Scant attention was paid to how even this small compliment of soldiers would be supplied or replenished at those heights. A series of such moves and patrol clashes with Chinese troops finally brought India and China to fight a bloody border war in the autumn of 1962. Humbled by a military disaster, India chose not to antagonise China and maintain a low-profile along the Northern borders. But, Indian soldiers proved their mettle and gave the Chinese a bloody nose in the face of extreme provocation during the clashes at Natu La and Cho La in Sikkim in 1967.

Ever since, not a single round has been fired along the boundary with Tibet but the two sides continue to be bogged down in a conflict as the vast boundary still remains largely undefined. In 1986, India once again looked into the Chinese eye and refused to be coyed down when the latter had moved troops across Sumdorong Chu, a narrow valley in Tawang tract, close to the area from where China had launched the major prong of its offensive in 1962. But the gains of 1986 where India had heli-lifted troops into Wangdung were soon frittered away and Chinese troops returned to occupy the same area. Once bitten and twice shy, a wary Indian government continued with its policy of appeasing China and infrastructure development along the Northern frontiers continued to lag behind.

Even as boundary negotiations continue with no concrete breakthrough, both sides exert their writ over territory by undertaking patrols which frequently violate each other's claim lines. The 1991 Border Peace and Tranquility Agreement (BPTA) and other such confidence building mechanisms have ensured that patrol clashes do not erupt into a firefight. But, in the past decade or so, China has ramped up infrastructural development in Tibet at an alarmingly fast pace. Today, an excellent network of highways link Tibet's capital Lhasa with mainland China. From Lhasa, three major highways connect the western, eastern and southern proximities of the province. A series of roads emnanting from major communication centres, further link up to the high mountain passes on the Sino-Indian border. The completion of the Gormu-Lhasa railway line (the highest railway line in the world) has further enhanced China's capability to marshal troops and logistics into the Tibetan plateau. As per estimates made by the Indian Armed Forces, the rail, road and air bases in Tibet provides PLA the capability to mobilise and sustain 34 divisions in one campaigning season (three weeks). Whether or when and in what form would this capability translate into intent is a separate matter altogether.

Nevertheless, the rapid infrastructure development in Tibet finally led to alarm bells ringing in South Block which forced a strategic shift in India's focus from the Western front to the Northern frontiers. Indian strategic thinkers widely believe that the next conventional conflict is most likely to break out in the mountains rather than on the plains of the western front.[6] This factor along with Indian military calculations of being able to tackle the conventional threat on the western front has prompted the raising of new fighting formations for the northern borders. Two Mountain divisions have been raised in the eastern sector. A proposal to raise a Mountain strike corps along with a couple of independent light armoured brigades is presently awaiting financial sanction. This shift coupled with infrastructural development (building of roads, air bases and other logistical nodes) in the Himalayan region would bolster India's defence preparedness to counter an increasingly belligerent China.

The proposal to raise a strike corps for the mountains reflects a much needed temperamental change in the largely defensive mindset of strategic planners in India. Matching China's capabilities and build dissuasive capabilities has also put modernisation plans for the Indian Armed forces back on track, although a large distance still needs to be travelled.

This shift in focus towards the northern frontiers and the building up of capabilities to take the battle into the Tibetan plateau if the need arises is likely to involve considerable resources of the Army for that theatre. Future war game scenarios may require some of our west facing formations to undertake certain tasks or act as reserves for the northern frontiers. As the two great civilisations of the world jostle for space, energy and resources to sustain economic development and meet the aspirations of their people, the northern frontier has once again emerged as a vital ground for India's security in case the jostling translates into military posturing.

Manifestation of Chinese Threat by 2017

The continuing rise of China would directly impinge on India's security calculations as an increasingly assertive China would continue its attempts to marginalise India in the sub-continent and emerge as the un-rivalled world power. By 2017, China is expected to achieve the following milestones:

- Emerge as the largest economy in the world following a decline of the US economy.
- Achieve its first Moon Landing by 2016.
- Acquire fully developed Force Projection Capabilities.
- Play a leading role as a UN Peace Keeper due to its financial clout. Resultantly, China would like to play a ledership role in major UN missions across the globe.
- Multi-National Contingents under Chinese Leadership supported by PLAN and PLAAF would extent China's strategic footprints in the world.
- Possess Modern Inventories (aircraft carriers, destroyers, frigates, submarines, Fourth/Fifth generation combat and Logistic aircrafts).

China is then likely to demonstrate its new power and capabilities by inflicting an embarrassing politio-military defeat on India. This threat could develop into a short but intense border skirmish in the mountains or into a conflict of interest in the Indian Ocean Region (IOR). Instead of attempting to play catch-up with China, India would do well to build asymmetric capabilities to counter the emerging Chinese threat.

China-Pakistan twin threat

The emerging China-Pakistan nexus has added another dimension to India's threat perceptions. Indian strategic planners now describe themselves as being confounded by a two and a half front threat scenario. The two fronts representing China and Pakistan with internal threats making up the half front. Although, China and Pakistan, recognising a common foe in India had established their relationship way back in the 1950s, it poses a far greater threat to India's security calaculations now than ever before. For nearly five decades, the contours of their relationship hinged upon Chinese military and infrastructural assistance to Pakistan. Pakistan also benefitted from China's support in the diplomatic arena. In the two wars that Pakistan fought with India in 1965 and 1971, China did little more than engaging in limited sabre-rattling on India's northern borders which did not have much impact on the outcome of battles on the western front. China's assistance to Pakistan in acquiring nuclear weapons is also well known.

After the 1962 war, China began actively supporting Indian insurgents in the North-East by providing them with arms and training. They were to later provide similar assistance in arms to jihadis battling the Indian security forces in Jammu and Kashmir. This strategy of keeping India mired in internal armed conflicts benefitted both China and Pakistan as it distracted India from preparing for conventional operations.

Today, as India has managed to douse the fires considerably in Jammu and Kashmir and the North-East, the China-Pakistan relationship has gone on an overdrive, with Pakistan emerging as a major prong in Chinese calculations to keep India in check. This has led to increased transfer of technologies and defence hardware to bolster Pakistan's conventional and nuclear capabilities to match that of India. On the political front, China is emerging as a staunch ally of Pakistan in times of its desperation when its relationship with the US is on a downward spiral, especially after the elimination of Osama Bin Laden in a raid by American Special Forces deep inside Pakistani territory. High-level state visits by Pakistani leaders and military generals to China have coincided with negative events in its relationship with the US. China has emerged as a trouble-shooter for Pakistan in the United Nations and also for rallying favourable international public opinion at a time when it is being denounced by the world community for nurturing terrorists.

Furthermore, as China emerges as a major global power, it is increasingly looking at Pakistan as a gateway for gaining access to energy resources in West and Central Asia. It is building Pakistan as a plank to cement ties with the Islamic populations of these countries. It is also dependent on Pakistan for the security of its investments in Afghanistan and fight Islamic separatists in the Uighur-dominated Xinjiang province.

To further its strategic ambitions viz a viz Pakistan, China has invested in the broadening of the Karakoram highway which links Xinjiang province to Gilgit in Pakistan's Northern Areas. This road link is also a major channel for the China-Pakistan defence trade. With an augmented capacity, this strategic over-land link would not only provide China with an access to the warm waters of Gwadar in the Arabian Sea, but would also emerge as an alternative to the choke point of Malacca for transferring energy supplies in vulnerable times of conflict. China is also investing heavily in dam projects in the Gilgit-Baltistan (Northern Areas). Reports emerged in the year 2010, that close to 10,000 Chinese construction workers including active PLA Combat Engineers were engaged for the construction and security of these projects.[7] The construction of tunnels which could be used to store ballistic missiles further highlights the importance of this region in Chinese calculations.

China's strategic ambitions and presence of troops in Gilgit-Baltistan have for the first time indicated how a two-front threat scenario could evolve in the event of a future conflict with either Pakistan or China. Gilgit-Baltistan provides an opening into Afghanistan and Central Asia from South Asia. Therein lies its geographical importance for all major regional players to gain access to locked energy resources of Central Asia. To the east of Gilgit-Baltistan lies the Ladakh region of Jammu and Kashmir. Ladakh is bound by Pakistan to the west and China to the East in Aksai Chin. It is here that India faces two of its major adversaries together on the western and eastern fronts. To the North lies the Shyok and Nubra valleys and the Saltoro ridge. India's occupation of the latter ensures that China and Pakistan do not link up at the Karakoram pass and further threaten the security of this vital sector. Similarly, the importance of this region has increased for both Pakistan and China to secure its strategic investments in Gilgit-Baltistan and provide depth to the Karakoram Highway that runs north of the Shaksgam valley which abuts the Saltoro ridge and the Siachen glacier.

Militarily, with the available logistics and infrastructure, China and Pakistan could switch forces and mount a two or maybe even a three pronged attack on Ladakh. It has also increased the possibilities of both sides coming to each others' rescue in times of a conventional conflict. It may no longer remain confined to mere military posturing. In scenario building for future conflicts this factor is now being considered more significantly. Even though these are worst-case scenarios, the possibilities remain. Whether these capabilities actually turn into intent would depend on the political conditions and geo-strategic environment prevailing in the times to come.

The development of the Gwadar deep sea port will enable the PLA Navy to acquire greater sea legs and challenge the might of the Indian Navy on both sides of the peninsula. The PLA Navy is also developing a 'string of pearls', docking and berthing facilities for its ships, all around the Indian Ocean region to enhance its blue water capabilities and be counted as a global power to reckon with. As China's appetite to consume more and more energy resources of the world increases, its navy will play a greater role in securing energy corridors and sea lanes of communications.

The last thing that India would want is to get sucked into combating the LWE cauldron, which is a likely scenario in the next four years or so if the present 'drift' situation persists. Additionally, Pakistan is likely to unleash its Jihadi proxies in any conventional conflagration; we need our CAPFs to assume potent operational capacities to look after India's vast spaces and rear areas.

Geo-Strartegic Environment

In addition to the traditional threat from China and Pakistan, India can no longer remain insulated from developments taking place in its immeditate strategic neighbourhood extending from the Gulf of Aden to the Straits of Malacca. In the coming decades, the alterning Geo-politics of this region would also impact upon India's security calculations.

West Asia

- Few US bases would be left in Bahrain and Afghanistan.
- Rise of Iran would see Iran, China and Pakistan teaming up in the region.
- Decline of Saudi Arabia.
- Rise of Turkey.
- Israel-Egypt accord may develop strains further increasing chances of a conflict.
- The Arab springs have posed a threat to monarchies affecting stability of West Asia.
- Spread of Green Shadow in Asia – The coming to power of radical elements like the Muslim Brotherhood in West Asia coupled with jihadist victories in Afghanistan would provide greater opportunities for Al-Qaeda and like-minded organisations to exploit the sentiments and spread their arc of influence across the Muslim world.
- China will attempt to lay the foundation for acceptance by South Asian Countries for Chinese access to warm water Ports in IOR viz Gwadar, Karachi, Bandar Abbas, Abadan, Dacca, Sitwe, Maldives, Chittagong, Mali, Cox's Bazaar; Yangon followed by land and rail based transportation system through the Karakarom highway.

US and European Fiscal stress means that world security architecture will see a power vaccum. India will have to step in to secure its own economic and geo-strategic interests in the region. For this, it would have to enormously enhance its force projection capabilities.

In addition to these, India has committed itself to counter several other challenges such as the threat of piracy in the IOR, gun and drug running and to collectively cooperate with world powers in the eventuality of a nuclear catastrophe or in case of an accidental nuclear launch by jihadis or the threat posed by diry bombs or RDD. India will also have to play a leadership role in Humanitarian Assistance and Disaster Relief (HADR) missions in its strategic neighbourhood. Other roles would cater towards securing Indian investments abroad, protecting transportation and energy corridors from Central and South East Asia. All this would entail a ramping up of United Nations Peacekeeping Missions undertaken by the Indian Armed forces.

Criticality 3: Internal Factors

Power Vacuum in what is euphemistically called the Red 'corridor' is a critical power vacuum. This vacuum is increasingly being usurped not only by Left Wing Extremists (LWE) but by terrorists of all hues and shades; there are growing convergences between the North East and Kashmiri insurgents coordinating with India's home grown Jihadis like Indian mujahideen, etc.

Basic Governance: There has been a systematic weakening of the state in almost 240 districts of India, now worsened by 'Centre-State' relations, arguing about where the centres rights over states jurisdiction begin and end. Corruption is rife, governance is limited, tribal rights are not restored, enabling the Maoists to get firmly embedded in these vast spaces. The weak civilian capacity is not helped by lack of a coherent military strategy and meaningful operations by the CAPFs in these regions.

Internal threats pose greater challenges to India's security due to their geographical spread and impact on population. The involvement of our own population in the numerous insurgencies of the North-East, Punjab and Jammu and Kashmir added to their complex nature, making it more difficult for the state to tackle them. Today, most of these insurgencies have been brought down to manageable levels due to relentless counter-insurgency operations by security forces. But, with the exception of Mizoram and Punjab, most of the other insurgencies continue to fester in the absence of any long-term political solution to the problem.

Current and Future Conflict Spectrum Shaping Future PMF/CAPFs Role

Just how important it is for the PMF/CAPFs to be equal to the challenging roles and tasks enshrined in its charter may be gauged by a 18 July 2011, *Indian Express* report of the Army top brass concluding that they required 60-65,000 troops to provide an effective counter to the Naxal threat. In a meeting at Lucknow on 07-08 July 2011, the Chief of Army Staff and all of the Army Commanders assessed the requirement of at least six army divisions to counter Naxal affected areas in West Bengal, Bihar, Jharkhand, Orissa, Chhattisgarh, Andhra Pradesh, Madhya Pradesh and Maharashtra. The meeting emphasised the growing clout of the Maoists buttressed by a financial corpus of Rs 1500 Crore through extortion, the meeting referred to an ISI note to General Kayani soliciting his approval to set up support infrastructure in Nepal and China to assist the Maoists. The Army Commander's meet noted the growing prowess of the naxals aided by the Security Forces' inclination in 'avoiding conflict'. The current and future conflict spectrum will be shaped also by Pakistan unleashing its potent asymmetrical 'fifth columnists'. The PMF/CAPFs will, then, be called upon to relieve the army from this threat.

Jammu and Kashmir

The rabid insurgency in the state which according to official estimates by the Government of India has claimed more than 40,000 lives in the past two decades has undergone a significant transformation. The early phase of a popular local insurgency, when thousands of youth from the state crossed the LoC to receive arms training in Pakistan and POK had lost steam by the mid-1990s. Recognising this trend, Pakistan chose to divert Pakistani fighters, primarily from its Punjab province and mujahids who had fought the Soviet Union in the Afghan jihad, to the Kashmir theatre. Clashes between groups which espoused for an independent Kashmir, and those that rallied behind Pakistan also led to the elimination of a large number of smaller outfits. The period after the Kargil war witnessed an upsurge in the number of foreign militants infiltrating into the state and resultantly, the number of violent incidents also increased. This phase, for the first time introduced the phenomenon of suicide terrorism in J&K. Small groups highly indoctrinated terrorists, most of whom were foreigners, undertook daring and suicidal raids on security forces convoys and establishments. This phenomenon lasted till 2005, though its most intense phase was in the period 1999-2002.

By the year 2004, with a tightening of the counter-infiltration grid, a cease-fire along the line of control and raising of close to 30 additional Rashtriya Rifles battalions, which were highly effective on ground, the security forces managed to gain an upper hand on the situation. Today, the state is witnessing one of its most peaceful phases ever since the insurgency broke out in 1989. Tourism and local industry are showing positive signs of revival. Security agencies estimate that not more than 300-400 terrorists are operating in the state, a huge downslide from figures which prior to 2004 mostly remained in the range of 1000-3000. A negative trend however is the advent of what has been termed as 'agitational terrorism', a spate of violent street protests which scarred the valley for three consecutive summers since 2008. A population exhibiting signs of fatigue and disdain for the gun took to stone-pelting to target the government machinery and security forces, on the instigation of separatists and elements from across the LoC. Although, the summers of 2011and 2012 have been devoid of a strife, the potential of a single negative incident sparking off mass mobilisation of people, especially in the urban centres of the valley indicates that considerable ground still has to be covered to completely eradicate the roots of the insurgency. This was again manifested in the tense situation that emerged following the accidental fire that razed the historic sufi shrine of Peer Dastageer Sahib in downtown Srinagar on 25 June 2012. Frenzied mobs took to the streets, setting fire to government vehicles. More than 50 security force personnel sustained minor injuries in their attempt to control the rampaging mobs. The violent street protests and hartals that broke out in the valley after the hanging of parliament attack accused Mohammed Afzal Guru, is yet another indicator of how fragile the ground situation is. In the two months since his hanging, nearly 23 days were lost to bandhs and curfews leading to several cancellation of bookings by tourists. Thus, despite a relative period of peace, the feeling of alienation among the valley population remains strong. Though, with an astute political management, the state government prevented the situation, which brought back memories of the burning of Charar-e-Sharif, (though under completely different circumstances) out of hand.

Even as both the central and state governments endeavour to meet the aspirations of the people, a tight security grid remains in place in the state. In addition to the regular formations along the LoC, 63 battalions of the Rashtriya Rifles, operating under 15 Sector HQs and five Counter-Insurgency forces are deployed in the hinterland. Added to this, close to 60 battalions of the CRPF also remain deployed in the Counter-Insurgency grid. To some observers, such large number of boots on the ground is unwarranted and contributes in alienating the population. Maintaining such a huge deployment is even more questionable given that only about 300-400 terrorists are now active in the state. Most of these terrorists are foreigners and the proportion of local militants has gone down dramatically. But, the security forces justify these numbers on the ground that as long as the terror infrastructure (close to 42 terrorist training camps and several hundred launch pads are operational in POK and Pakistan) remains intact across the LoC, the situation in the valley can again take a turn for the worse, depending on Pakistan's intent which is presently distracted due to its commitments in the Af-Pak region. The summer street protests also pointed towards the existence of a large number of Over Ground Workers (OGWs) and their ability to foment trouble at a short notice. In the worst-case possibility, some strategists even feared a revival of the local insurgency if the energies of the young population who had taken to the stone are not channelised elsewhere. So, despite an overwhelming improvement in the ground situation, a large number of security forces continue to remain deployed in J&K, even as fingers remain crossed on whether resurgence of pro-Pakistan forces in Afghanistan will lead to revival of terrorist activities in Kashmir as well.

North East

The North-Eastern states have also witnessed a remarkable improvement in the security situation due to splintering of major insurgent groups and sustained operations of security forces. In Assam, a large number of insurgents have given up their arms and have entered the mainstream. This led to a split in the United Liberation Front of Asom (ULFA) and National Democratic Front of Bodoland (NDFB), the two largest and influential groups operating in the state. Mass surrenders by cadres of numerous other small outfits have helped in reducing the threat in the tribal belts of Karbi Anglong and the Cachar Hills. The wiping out of insurgent bases in Bhutan in 2003 and active support by the governments of Bangladesh and Myanmar has also kept them on the run. Despite these developments, the anti-talk factions of the ULFA and NDFB are determined to carry out activities against the state and are being once again supported by China to re-group and strengthen them. Nearly two Army divisions along with the CRPF continue to aid the state government in combating the several ethnic insurgencies of the North-East. Due to a marked improvement in the ground situation, the CRPF is being encouraged to assume a more active and larger role in counter-insurgency operations enabling the Army to go into the background.

But, the recent spiraling of violence and clashes between the Bodos and muslim population in the Lower Assam districts of Kokrajhar, Bongaigaon, Chirang and Dhubri which left at least 74 people dead and more than 2 lakh rendered homeless once again highlight the uncertainities of this region of the state which is a communal and ethnic tinderbox. The presence of nothing less than 18 ethnic and sub-ethnic groups in this area is bound to increase clashes for land, space and livelihood. The presence of a large illegal immigrant population from neighbouring Bangladesh and the presence of insurgent groups backing the tribals and non-tribals further complicate the situation. Therefore, this region would still require an Army presence in the event of the NDFB reneging on the ceasefire agreement and the increasing militarisation of other ethnic groups. The security implications posed by the activities of insurgent groups in this strategically sensitive zone which connects the Chicken's neck corridor in North Bengal to the rest of the North-East India can also not be discounted. Even during the clashes in July 2012, the road and rail link passing through the Bodoland Territorial Autonomous Districts (BTAD) were disrupted for a few days and were opened only after the Army arrived on the scene.

The situation in Tripura is largely under control with negligible incidents of violence being reported from the state. The All Tigers Tripura Force (ATTF) and some smaller groups are finding it difficult to prevent their cadres from surrendering in large numbers. A sector of the Assam Rifles is deployed in the state along with the BSF which guards the state's border with Bangladesh.

The cease-fire between the two main Naga factions, the NSCN (IM) and NSCN (K), in place since 1997, continues to hold. The Naga insurgency which at one point of time was one of the most difficult to combat has now slided into an extortion racket and is marked by inter-factional clashes between the different splinter groups. The Naga peace talks have so far not been able to find a concrete political solution to the problem. Security forces, primarily the Assam Rifles (AR) are deployed in the state to monitor the cease-fire and activities of a large number of armed cadres who are holed up in camps across the state. The Nagas continue to stick to their main demand of a greater Nagaland which also includes territories in Assam and Manipur though the possibility of these armed cadres annulling the cease-fire agreement and going back to the jungles remains a distant possibility, but the same cannot be discounted altogether.

Manipur continues to remain engulfed in a complex insurgency which is divided on ethnic lines. The Hill Nagas and the valley-based Meiteis continue to lock daggers with each other. The PREPAK, UNLF and PLA are the most potent groups operating in the state today. Over the years, many other ethnic and sub-ethnic insurgent groups have emerged, further complicating the situation on the ground. No less than 35 different insurgent groups exist in Manipur today. In addition to targeting civilians and security forces, factional clashes are a common occurrence. The militants have successfully established a vicious and elaborate system of extortion and taxes to fill their coffers.

Among the North-eastern state, Manipur has the highest number of militant incidents and fatalities. With a fluid and porous border with Myanmar, the Underground groups or UGs find it easy to operate and find safe sanctuaries in that country. The AR along with small compliments of the CRPF and BSF are deployed to tackle the insurgency in the state and protect vital installations.

Urban Terrorism

The 1993 serial blasts in Bombay introduced the phenomenon of urban terrorism in India. This phenomenon was soon to engulf the metropolitan cities and later even some tier-2 cities across the country. The nature of these terrorist attacks on India's urban centers have also diversified with the use of Improvised Explosive Devices (IEDs) to carry out explosions, stand-off fire and grenade attacks. In the past decade alone, 976 people have been killed and more than 3176 injured in terrorist attacks across the country (outside J&K and the North East).[8]

The small band of terrorists armed with AK-47 rifles and hand grenades carried out a series of spectacular acts of terrorism at prominent landmarks in the cities of New Delhi, Kolkata, Ahmedabad and Bangalore. These attacks reached its high point on 26 November 2008, when ten heavily armed terrorists sailed over the Arabian sea from Karachi and struck at five different locations in South Mumbai killing 166 innocent civilians. The 'spectacular' siege of Mumbai which lasted three days sent shock waves across the world and was the deadliest terror attack in India till date. The tactics used by the terrorists in Mumbai and the publicity value of these attacks have alarmingly magnified the threat of urban terrorism in India. In fact, the phenomenon of the global jihad which has struck strong roots in the Af-Pak region and parts of West, Central and South East Asia along with North Africa poses a grave threat to the entire world.

As the interrogation of Abu Jundal, a prominent mastermind and facilitator of the attacks on Mumbai has uncovered, the threat of spectacular acts of terrorism looms large over the country. Jundal indicated of terrorists resorting to use of boats and even small aircrafts to target prominent economic and industrial installations in India. The emergence of the Indian Mujahideen (IM) following the series of blasts across India since 2005 has ominous portents for the country. The cadre base of the IM which morphed out of the radical overground outfit, Students Islamic Movement of India (SIMI) in the aftermath of the Gujarat riots of 2002. The leadership of the IM based in Karachi has close linkages with the Lashkar-e-Taiba (LeT), and has now become a primary source for the Pakistani Inter Services Intelligence (ISI) to provide logistics support for LeT and other such Pakistan-based terror groups to target India. The involvement of Indian muslims in acts of terrorism also provides Pakistan with the cover of deniability.

In addition to the jihadi terrorists, the insurgent groups in Punjab, J&K and the North-East have also carried out bomb blasts, kidnappings, etc urban centres both within and outside the geographical confines of the state in which they operate, to highlight their cause. The bomb blasts carried out by the National Democratic Front of Bodoland (NDFB) across cities of western Assam on 30 October 2008 and other similar blasts by the United Liberation Front of Asom in recent years highlight the trend of regional and local insurgent groups acquiring lethal techniques to revive themselves or as desperate measures. Therefore, India faces a complex threat of urban terrorism from a host of jihadi and insurgent groups. In the near future, the Maoists taking to urban terrorism can add another worrying dimension to this threat. The VB-IED attack on an Israeli diplomat's car in New Delhi in April 2012 is another example of un-known threats springing a surprise on us. It was the first instance of a targeted attack which bore the signatures of the Hizbollah.

The possibility of terror groups and maoists pooling together resources to carry out strikes at the behest of foreign agencies can also not be ruled out in the emerging future. Already, some coalescing has taken place between insurgent groups in the North East and the Maoists.

The police and intelligence agencies have a far-greater role in unraveling terror plots and countering the threat of urban terrorism in India. The NSG and other Special Forces will also have a role to play in terminating a spectacular act of terrorism and in carrying out covert operations to nib terror plots in the bud. The latter may even require operating outside the territorial boundaries of the country.

Internal Civil Disturbances

The struggle for Independence had seen large-scale public protests and demonstrations posing tremendous strain on the police manpower to tackle them. Ever since independence, the country has witnessed several political and social movements, and struggle for separate states or autonomous districts based on linguistics, ethnicity or regional aspirations. The Praja Mandal agitations, JP Movement were other such movements which led to large scale public mobilisation.

Added to these have been a series of communal and ethnic riots breaking out at regular intervals across the country. The anti-Sikh riots of 1984 and the ones that broke out across the country following the demolition of the Babri Masjid in 1991 and the post-Godhra riots of 2002 in Gujarat have been some major pogroms that have permanently scarred the history of post-Independent India.

All these civil movements involve mobilisation of agitated groups of people on a large scale and have the potential of turning violent. The outpouring of public frustration and anger is generally seen in the destruction of government property.

In recent years, protest movements and civil agitations have not only led to destruction of public infrastructure but disruption of the economy. The Gujjar agitations of 2008 and the road blockades in the hill districts of Manipur in which demonstrators blocked road and rail links of communications led to the disruption of trade and commerce affecting the prices of essential commodities to shoot several times, especially in Manipur. The urban landscape has also seen its share of civil movements in the form of the protests against minority quotas in universities and the Jan Lokpal Movement of 2011. Though, these movements remained largely non-violent, they did pose tremendous challenges to the police and Central Armed Police Forces (CAPFs) in tackling large crowds of people.

In the coming years, increased pressure on infrastructure in cities, and burden on resources to support a burgeoning population have the potential of public grievance and anger turning into violence, thereby putting increased pressure on the police and paramilitary manpower. Already, this outpouring of human grievances and frustration can be seen in riots breaking due to scarcity of power and water in cities. The present downslide in the economy and resultant shrinking of employment opportunities is another worrying trend which could increase the possibility of civic disturbances in the urban areas of the country. Increased signs of unrest are also being witnessed due to the re-emergence of regional aspirations of the people. The Telengana and Gorkhaland agitations have from time to time have led to the people resorting to large-scale arson and disruption of public transport systems.

While it is natural to expect civilian protests in a democratic set-up like ours, an increased frequency of civil disturbances across the length and breadth of the country does not bode well for a country aspiring to become a major world power and economic powerhouse. These fissiparous tendencies not only discourage foreign investments but also increase the burden on the government to maintain internal cohesion.

Therefore, the police and CAPFs, especially the RAF and CRPF would have to maintain effective reserves in urban centres across the country to deal with civil disturbances and enforce curfews in trying times. It should also be ensured that the services of the Army are least utilised to address these challenges in a democracy. Moreover, frequent exposure of the Army to the civil population erodes its deterrent effect for preventing mischief.

Non-Traditional threats to Internal Security

- The impact of Global warming will be felt increasingly on the already scarce natural resources of the country.
- Rising Sea levels would lead to a displacement of population from the coastal areas and increasing pressure in the interior regions.
- Water shortages will also trigger a migration of population.
- Refugee Management will become part of national security imperatives as the phenomenon of global warming can lead to large scale migration of people from countries like Bangladesh.
- Food shortages because of drought, heavy unseasional rains.
- Water Riots.
- Himalayan Region affected by retreating glaciers, flash floods, etc.

Social strife is also likely to increase due to a rising Population. Since 1947, Two India's have been added upto 2005. Another India will be added by 2020. India will comprise of 16.5 percent of the total world population by 2050.

Unemployment

Indian Labour force will incease by 32 percent by 2030. The average age of the population will be 29 by 2020. To meet the aspirations of a burgeoning young population, 250 million jobs will be required by 2020; 100 million in manufacturing, 40 million in construction, 25 million in retail. There will be fewer jobs in the agriculture sector as agricultural productivity has increased through mechanisation. This would increase the strain on already scarce resources in urban areas as more and more people move into urban areas in search for employment opportunities. The urban population in the country is estimated to reach 340 million by 2030. High levels of unemployment will increase the crime rate and could also fuel social unrests across the country

Water Conflict

10 billion cubic meteres per year of water will be required for human consumption alone in the next 10 years (more than what Bhakra Nangal can provide). In

addition, diversion of river waters in Tibet will led to a reduced flow downstream thereby affecting large chunks of our population in North and North East India.

Both Inter and Intra water conflict are predicted for India. A Classified US report has listed Ganga, Indus, Brahmaputra among the top 10 water conflict zones in the world.Beyond 2022 water will be used as a weapon of war. The World Bank has predicted Indian Cities will run dry by 2020. Since 2008, 1000 violent incidents of water conflicts have taken place in India.

The probability of a water conflict taking place with upper riparian states like China which itself is likely to be grappling with severe water shortages is further enumerated by the following statements of Chinese leaders.

Even if we do not begin this water diversion project, the next generation will. Sooner or later it will be done. —General Zhao Nangi, PLA.

The survival of Chinese Nation is threatened by Country's shortage of water. — Wen Jia Bao, Vice Premier, China Daily, Jan 1999.

Therefore, the myriad and complex level of challenges that India is likely to face in the coming years calls for an elaborate re-structuring of the national security planning apparatus in the country. The resultant policy planning would require a re-look at our priorities and dedication of substantial resources and force re-structuring to remain in vogue with the security dynamics of the 21st century world.

NOTES

1. SAGRA.
2. *Indian Express*, 21 May 2011.
3. New America Foundation Poll.
4. Vira and Cordesman, Community Appraisal and Motivation Program, 'Understanding FATA Vol. IV'.
5. Shuja Nawaz, 'Learning by Doing' as quoted by Vira and Cordesman.
6. Gurmeet Kanwal, Wars in Mountains: Capacity building needed for future conflict, *The Tribune*, 12 Aug 2011, accessed at http://www.tribuneindia.com/2011/20110812/edit.htm#4
7. Selig H Harrison, Chinese Discreet Hold on Northern Borderlands, *The New York Times*, 26 Aug 2010, accessed at http://www.nytimes.com/2010/08/27/opinion/27iht-edharrison.html
8. Pervez Iqbal Siddiqui, NIA Centre to come up in Lucknow soon, *The Times of India*, 25 April 2012, accessed at http://articles.timesofindia.indiatimes.com/2012-04-25/lucknow/31398174_1_nia-director-terror-attacks-sharad-chandra-sinha

PART I

Paramilitary Forces (PMFs)

3

Assam Rifles (AR)

Origin

Assam came under the British rule following the Anglo-Burmese War of 1826. The British explorers soon discovered rich reserves of oil, coal and tea plantations in the region. The first tea estates were opened in 1832. The British profited from the tea trade to Britain and other parts of the world. The economic wealth of the region also attracted forays by the tribals of the North Eastern region. The new British settlements, industries and plantations had to be protected from the cross-border tribal raids. As the British set about extending their administration in the region, the need for an armed force to protect its interests was felt. In order to meet the threat posed by the tribals to the tea plantations and to reduce the prohibitive cost of keeping a large number of troops in Assam, it was decided to raise a Levy or Militia body as a separate force under the civil government distinct from the regular Army and the rrmed Police. The Levy was to serve as a "Cheap semi military body"; clothed like civil police, placed on a footing better that the ordinary armed Police. It was to perform military duties and was to replace some of the regular army units in certain parts of the tribal border. It was to be officered by police officers and men were to be drawn from the civil police.[1]

Thus was raised the "Cachar Levy" comprising 750 all ranks and headed by Mr Grange, the civilian officer in charge of Nowgong (Naugaon) in Assam. The Cachar Levy was primarily employed for watch and ward duties, to protect British settlements and plantations owned entirely by the English companies and maintain law and order in tribal areas. In 1878, the British launched a series of expeditions to expand their dominance and administration to newer areas of the North East. With the adoption of this "forward policy", the task of the Levy changed from mainly defensive to positively offensive involving punitive expeditions into the tribal areas.

Since 1832 and to the present day, the Assam Rifles due to its historical role and continuous deployment in the North East Region has identified more closely with local inhabitants than any other force operating in the region. It has truly lived up to its motto of being "The Sentinels of the North East" and "Friends of the Hill People".

Adoption of the Title and Formation Sign

The force was given the title, 'Assam Rifles' in 1917 in recognition of its services during World War I. Prior to 1917, the units of the force used to write their abbreviated name on both sides of crossed khukris, e.g., Naga Hills Military Police Battalion (NHMP). Once the title changed to 'Assam Rifles' the units started writing the numeral of the battalion above the crossed Khukris. In 1992, the Force adopted the existing crest with crossed Khukris and Assam Rifles written below it. The Ashoka emblem was put above the crossed Khukris and this was approved by the government on 28 September 2001.

The formation sign depicts: Sunrise over the Himalayan snowline; crossed Khukris of the Assam Rifles; five mountain peaks representing the original Headquarter Inspector General (HQ IGAR) and the four Range Headquarters. The sun's seven rays correspond to the seven states and territories in which the force operated at that time; Assam, Nagaland, Arunachal, Mizo Hill, Manipur, Tripura and Sikkim, Ashoka Emblem.

Organisational Change

On 17 September 1947, HG Bartley, CIE, IP was appointed as the first Inspector General of the Assam Rifles and functioned directly under the Governor of Assam. This move marked the separation of the Assam Rifles from the Police. On 15 August 1948, Colonel Sidhiman Rai, MC took over as the first army officer and the first Indian Inspector General of the Assam Rifles and since then army officers on deputation from the regular army are being posted to the Assam Rifles.

The various titles of the force since 1832 were[2]:

Frontier Police – 1883
Assam Military Police – 1891
East Bengal and Assam Military Police – 1913
Assam Rifles – 1917

Role and Tasks

The Assam Rifles is designated by the GoM committee as the Border Guarding Force for the Indo-Myanmar border and is also its lead intelligence agency.

The present role of the Assam Rifles is to:

- Conduct Counter Insurgency operations in the North East and in other areas, as deemed necessary, under the overall operational control of the Army.

- During peace and "Proxy War" conditions ensure the security of the Sino-Indian and Indo-Myanmar borders.
- During war, security of rear areas in the Tactical Battle Area (TBA).
- Assist the Army in other operational tasks as required, during war and peace.
- Act as penultimate interventionist force of the Central Government in internal security situations, under the operational control of the Army, when the situation goes beyond the control of Central Police Organisations (CPOs).

Organisation

The Assam Rifles operates under the MHA but under the operational control of the Army. The present strength of the force is approximately 65,000 personnel organised into 46 battalions. The IG Assam Rifles North and South function under the direct operational control of the Army's 3 Corps at Dimapur.

MHA
↓
DG AR
(Shillong)
↓

↓	↓
IG AR (North) (Kohima) ↓ SECTOR HQs	IG AR (South) (Mantripukhri) ↓ SECTOR HQs (9,10&26)

Recruitment

In the British Period, there was no set pattern of recruitment and included men from all parts of the country. After its designation as the Assam Rifles, 70 percent of the recruits were Gorkhas while Garhwalis and Kumaonis constituted another 20 percent of the force. 10 percent of the Assam Rifles comprised the Jaruas, Lushais, Nagas and Kukis. In 1982, the recruitment pattern was broad based and made open to all Indian citizens. Recruitment rallies are conducted in every state of the country.

Initially, civil officers from the concerned districts and police officers were sent to command the Levies. From 1884 onwards Army officers were sent on deputation to command the Assam Military Police Battalions. Today, there are two streams of officers in the Assam Rifles. The first stream consists of Army officers on deputation and the second stream known as the Assam Rifles Cadre Officers comprises of re-employed Army officers and departmental promotees.

Training

The training is received at the Assam Rifles Regimental Centre at Shillong and is on the pattern of the Army.

Weapons and Equipment

Assam Rifles battalions are equipped on the lines of an Infantry Battalion with light weapons and support weapons including mortars, rocket launchers and MMGs. The standard issue is the 5.56 INSAS Rifle. In addition, battalions deployed on counter-insurgency operations are provided with the AK-series assault rifles.

History

The British Era

The task allotted to the Cachar Levy was to guard the Eastern Frontier of Assam from the Brahmaputra river to Cachar. The force maintained strong detachments of troops at Nowgong and Silchar with smaller posts all along the frontier and an Administrative Headquarters at Asaloo near Haflong. It had established 12 stockades from the foothills of the Naga Hills to the Surma Valley East of Silchar. The inter-tibal feuds of the Nagas and the almost unending incidents of violence by the tribal warriors, who raided the tea gardens, murdered British officials, transgressed the recognised boundaries or hunted human heads in the villages prompted a "Forward Policy" of punitive expeditions into the tribal areas. In this process several British officials and their escorts were killed and their bodies decapicated by the tribals. These incidents led to further punitive expeditions by the Levy in conjunction with the Army. The expeditions were also carried out to extend contact with the frontier tribes and for carrying out a survey of hitherto unexplored areas.

More than 25 military expeditions were undertaken in this period. Some of the major ones are listed below:

- Kuki operations of 1880-82 and 1917-19.
- Manipur Expeditions of 1886, 1891 and 1894.
- Lushai Hills Expeditions of 1880-90, 1896 and 1917-19.
- Abor Expeditions of 1893-94, 1911-12.
- Apatani Expedition of 1887.
- Mishmi Expeditions of 1899-1900, 1911-12.

World War I

Due to the heavy casualties suffered by the Indian Corps in the Great War, the requirement for reinforcements increased greatly. Due to the difficulties involved in calling up Gurkha reservists from Nepal, it was decided to draft volunteers from the Assam Military Police for additional reinforcements for Gurkha battalions in France, Egypt, Gallipoli, Mesopotamia, North Persia and the North West Frontier of India. About 3200 volunteers from the Assam Military Police served during World War I. Out of these, 5 Indian Officers and 237 other ranks were killed and 6 Indian Officers and 247 Other Ranks were wounded. 11 Indian Officers and 69 other ranks received various awards including three Indian Orders of Merit and five Indian Distinguished Service Medals.

World War II

The four Assam Rifles Battalions were located at their permanent stations of Aizwal, Sadiya, Kohima and Imphal at the outbreak of the war. The fifth Battalion was re-raised as the Training Battalion and was also entrusted the defence of the Indo-Tibetan border. During World War II, the Assam Rifles was employed for carrying out the following tasks:

- Furnished trained men to serve in the affiliated Gurkha battalions of the Indian Army.
- In 1941 Inspector General Assam Rifles carried out strategic reconnaissance astride the Indo-Burma border which proved valuable for conducting subsequent operations.
- Assam Rifles provided the trained nucleus of 500 men to the newly raised Assam Regiment. Most of the JCOs and NCOs who fought at Jessami against the Japanese 31 Division and won the battle honour for the Assam Regiment were ex-Assam Rifles.
- The Assam Rifles protected the vital oil installations at Digboi and Tinsukia.
- The force played a major role in the evacuation of tens of thousands of Burmese refugees during the war.
- The force functioned as elements of the much fabled and ghost-like 'V' Force on reconnaissance and harassment missions behind Japanese lines in Burma. Many of its sub-units fought alongside regular troops in the fiercely contested battles of Ukhrul and Kohima.

Post-Independence

In the post-Independence period, the Assam Rifles continued with the task of extending the administration in the North East and establishing new outposts and detachments. The most important outpost to be established by the Assam Rifles was at Tawang. This task was completed by Major Bob Khaitang, the Assistant Political Officer.[3] The Pioneer companies of the force were engaged in the construction of foot tracks, fair weather landing strips and helipads. The Assam Rifles functioned under the newly formed NEFA administration which in turn reported to the Ministry of External Affairs. The control of the Assam Rifles was passed on to the Ministry of Home Affairs while the operational control of the force continues to be with the Army. The Assam Rifles provided valuable succour to the people of the North East after the devastating earthquake of 1950.

In 1947, 10 platoons of the force were flown into Agartala to deter the Pakistani irregulars from capturing Tripura.

In 1953, the Assam Rifles provided the bulk of the forces along with units of the regular Army to contain the political unrest in Tuensang in Naga Hills. The grave threat posed by the Naga insurgency also necessitated the expansion of the force. The Assam Rifles Training Centre was established at Missamari on 01 January 1959. The Assam Rifles played a commendable role in containing the early phase of the Naga insurgency. Maj HB Rai and Sub Major Khaka Bahadur Limbu, MC of 8 Assam Rifles were awarded the Ashok Chakra for their acts of valour and bravery.

The Assam Rifles posts on the Indo-Tibet border were instrumental in guiding the Tibetan refugees and Khampa rebels to the refugee settlement established at Missamari. 5 Assam Rifles received the Dalai Lama on the Mc Mahon line at the Chuthangmu Pass and escorted him till Missamari. The Commanding Officer of the battalion, Lt Col J Dorabji was awarded the Shaurya Chakra for this task.

His Holiness donated all his weapons to the battalion and blessed them with the following words:

> "May your luck increase to the size of a mountain, may your fame be such as to cover the whole sky, may your knowledge become vast and deep as the sea, long and healthy lives to you and hope for your work for others will be a success".

1962 War

The Assam Rifles established the first posts on the McMahon Line following the forward policy adopted by the Government in 1959. The detachments at the isolated posts of Longju and Khinzamane were the first to come in contact with PLA troops in the year 1959. It was the establishment of these penny packets in the Thagla Ridge area of Tawang in Arunachal Pradesh that provoked the Chinese to forcefully evict what they perceived was transgression of the McMahon line by Indian troops. The surrounding of the Assam Rifles post at Dhola on 8 September 1962 opened the floodgates for the Chinese invasion of Arunachal Pradesh. The Assam Rifles had borne the first brunt of the Chinese attack. Five Vir Chakras were awarded within 15 days to Assam Rifles men who fought the Chinese valiantly.[4]

1965 War

During the 1965 war with Pakistan, Assam Rifles battalions filled the void in Nagaland and Manipur due to the move of Army formations to the West. It also bore the additional responsibility of manning the Indo-Tibet border and the border with East Pakistan in Tripura.

1971 War

During the 1971 war, it took over counter-insurgency operations from the Army in Nagaland, Manipur, Mizoram and Tripura.

Operation Pawan

Three battalions of the Assam Rifles (22, 23 and 26) were deployed in Op Pawan in Sri Lanka.

Jammu & Kashmir

Op Rakshak

Eight battalions of the Assam Rifles were employed in Operation Rakshak in Jammu & Kashmir from 1990-98. The conduct of these battalions was of an exceptionally high order and led to the neutralisation of a large number of militants and recovery of munitions and stores. The Rashtriya Rifles was later raised on the pattern of the Assam Rifles. The latter became an effective fighting force by 1998.

26 Assam Rifles was the first AR battalion to be inducted on 25 May 1990. The battalion operated under 31 Sub Area and was responsible for road opening tasks between Srinagar and Sonamarg. In its two year deployment, the battalion apprehended nearly 90 militants and recovered 142 assorted weapons and other ammunition. It conducted specific operations in the general areas of Kangan, Gund, Gangair, Reyil and Srinagar.

7 Assam Rifles operated under 19 Infantry Division and later under 28 Infantry Division in Kupwara sector of North Kashmir. 16 militants were eliminated in its first encounter with militants at Dudhi in Tangdhar sector along the Line of Control. In another encounter in Tangdhar sector on 4 May 1991, the battalion neutralised 72 militants in an operation which lasted 72 hours. Four RPGs, seven UMGs, 78 AK-47 Rifles, large quantities of assorted ammunition and other warlike stores were recovered during the operation. This was recorded to be the most successful battalion level operation ever conducted. In its 25 month stay, the battalion neutralised 200 militants, apprehended another 222 and effected the surrender of 74 militants. The battalion was awarded two Kirti Chakras, 01 Shaurya Chakra, 10 Sena Medals and 01 Vishist Seva Medal during its tenure at Tangdhar.

23 Assam Rifles operated from July 1994 till December 1996 in the Doda and Bhaderwah. In one of the operations, the battalion neutralised the then Deputy Provincial Commander of the Hizbul Mujahideen, Ahsan Ahmed. A HMG and

a high powered radio set was recovered from his possession. Overall, the battalion neutralised 19 militants in various operations.

18 Assam Rifles was deployed in Awantipora area of South Kashmir from November 1994 to January 1997. It was instrumental in the conduct of Road Opening Duties (ROD) on NH 1 from Jawahar Tunnel to Pantha Chowk. Later, three companies of the battalion was deployed in the CI grid under 1 Sector RR while one company was deployed at Khundru for the protection of the 21 Field Ammunition Depot. It also helped in the incident free conduct of the 1996 parliamentary elections in the state.

28 Assam Rifles operated under 11 Sector RR in Ganderbal and Kangan from May 1995 to January 1998. In one operation, the battalion apprehended 15 HM militants from Guripura village and recovered a large amount of munitions from them.

3 Assam Rifles was deployed at Mamar under 11 Sector RR from April 1997 to January 1998. Five militants were killed in an operation by the battalion in Wurapash village. One of them was later identified as a serving Major of the ISI, working as the district commander of Srinagar.

21 Assam Rifles operated under 7 Sector RR from January 1995 to March 1997. The battalion eliminated 17 militants and apprehended another 26 during its two years deployment in Kupwara.

26 and 7 Assam Rifles were awarded the COAS Unit Citation and Silver Salver by the Governor of J&K for their successful tenure in J&K.

Counter Insurgency Operations in the North East

As has been mentioned previously, Assam Rifles was the first responders when the Naga insurgency broke out in 1953. It also bore the first brunt of the Mizo insurgency when 1 Assam Rifles was surrounded by hostiles at Aizwal in 1966. After the relief of 1 Assam Rifles, more AR battalions were inducted into Mizoram. Captain Jasram Singh of 6 Assam Rifles won the Ashok Chakra for his gallantry in fighting the Mizo hostiles. Assam Rifles in conjunction with the Army has remained deployed in all the insurgency afflicted states of the North East since 1953. Presently, AR Battalions continue to remain deployed for Counter Insurgency operations in the states of Manipur, Nagaland, Assam and Tripura. One sector of the Assam Rifles remains deployed in Mizoram.

The Assam Rifles battalions operate under the operational control of the Army for counter-insurgency operations. Two divison sized force HQs commanded by Major General rank Army officers exercise operational control over the Assam Rifles Sector Headquarters which are commanded by Brigadier rank officers on deputation from the Army. The Sector HQs in turn exercise operational control over the AR battalions in their respective sectors.

IG AR (N)

Headquarter Inspector General of Assam Rifles (North) was raised at Jorhat on 15 May 1985. It moved to Imphal and assumed operational control of Manipur from 8 Mountain Division with effect from 12 November 1986. It was re-organised as 'M' Sector with an additional compliment of staff, communication resources and an intelligence unit. The op responsibility of Op Hifazat was handed back to HQ 8 Mountain Division on 28 February 1989. With the de-induction of 8 Mountain Division from Nagaland, HQ IG AR (N) moved to Zakhama and resumed the Operational responsibility of Nagaland, Manipur, Tirap and Changlang districts of Arunachal Pradesh with effect from 25 April 1990.

The operational responsibility of Manipur barring the Jessami salient was handed over to HQ 57 Mountain Division on 01 October 1992. Tirap and Changlang districts were reverted to HQ 2 Mountain Division with effect from 11 June 1993. Following the de-induction of 57 Mountain Division for Op Parakram in 2001-02, the Op responsibility of Manipur less Churachandpur district was once again assumed by IG AR (N). The HQ IG AR (N) moved from Zakhama to Kohima on 16 March 2006.

The Area of Responsibility (AOR) of IG AR (N) is Nagaland where the thrust is on facilitating the peace process. The ultimate aim is the betterment of the Naga people and to gradually bring them into the mainstream. The Cease Fire Ground Rules (CFGR) in respect of the NSCN (IM) and NSCN (K) are strictly monitored by the HQ IG AR (N) and violations reported to the Cease Fire Supervisory Board (CFSB).

IG AR (S)

Headquarter Inspector General of Assam Rifles (South) was raised on 15 September 2004 at the historic Kangla Fort in Imphal. It assumed Operational Control of all Assam Rifles units in Manipur from 01 January 2005. Presently located at Mantripukri, IG AR (S) assumes operational control over Sectors 9, 10 and 26 of the Assam Rifles responsible for carrying out Counter Insurgency operations as well as Border Guarding roles along the Indo-Myanmar border in the state of Manipur. HQ 27 Sector of the Assam Rifles moved to Churachandpur in March 2006 and was placed under 57 Mountain Division.[5]

OP Samaritan

Along with carrying out its primary task of counter-insurgency operations, the Assam Rifles has provided services ranging from flood relief, re-establish communication links, reconstructing ruined houses, clearing land slides, afford station, raising environmental awareness among the local population, constructing playing grounds, etc. Under Op Samaritan, it has also built model houses, schools, vocational training centres, bus waiting shelters, market sheds and water supply schemes, etc.

The famous and erudite anthropologist and naturalist Verrier Elwin, who was nominated as adviser on Tribal Affairs to the NEFA, had this to say as tribute to the force:

> "The custodians of law and order, the pioneers of every advance in to the interior, the guardians of our borders and, the friends of the hill people. Modestly, and without fuss, they have faced every hardship and difficulty, and thousands of villagers in the wildest areas think of them with affection and gratitude".

Critique

Performance Appraisal, Present and Future Employment

The role of the Assam Rifles has transformed considerably from that of an armed police force, expanding the reach of the administration to virgin areas and protecting its settlements to that of an effective force combating insurgency and guarding the borders. It has proved its mettle in battling insurgents and terrorists from Jammu and Kashmir to Sri Lanka and in the North East. Let us now delve into the present role and tasks and likely employment of the force in the emerging future.

Conventional Operations

Border Management

The Assam Rifles was instrumental in extending India's administration into Tawang (Arunachal Pradesh) after Independence. It was the first armed unit of the country which established military outposts on the McMahon line with Tibet. At that time the force was under the operational control of the NEFA administration which in turn functioned under the Ministry of External Affairs. The establishment of these string of posts in the Tawang sector were to later result into serious border clashes with the Chinese People's Liberation Army (PLA) and the dispute over the location of one such post on the Namka

Chu called Dhola precipitated the border war with China in October 1962. It is not to suggest that the Assam Rifles were responsible for provoking the Chinese aggression on these posts but that in fact was the larger failure of the higher direction of war. Nevertheless, Assam Rifles units did a remarkable job in manning the Indo-Tibetan border during the 1965 and 1971 wars with Pakistan and prevented China from exploiting the vulnerabilities posed by movement of certain Army formations to the Western front.

Ever since 1962, the defence of the IB and LAC with Tibet was primarily taken over by the Army and ITBP though Assam Rifles units were used as stop-gap measures to man certain portions of the border in the absence of regular Infantry battalions of the Army. With the return of Indian Army formations to their permanent locations in the North East and the raising of new mountain divisions, the Assam Rifles has more or less been relieved of the task of manning the Indo-Tibetan border.

In the present scenario, the Assam Rifles similar to the Rashtriya Rifles in the North has certain hot war tasks allotted to it in times of a conventional conflict. With its past experience of deployment along the Indo-Tibet border and the fact that their units are patterned on the lines of an Infantry Battalion, the force is well suited to perform such tasks. Being located in the theatre, the Assam Rifles is a suitable reserve available to the Army for assisting its overall operational plan in a conflict scenario. AR units can be inducted quickly in the theatre of conflict for performing secondary tasks such as protecting lines of communication, protecting VA/VPs or forming a second line of defence. The Assam Rifles personnel are parallel to regular Army troops in carrying out combat tasks. It is not only organised on the lines of the Army but its leadership also comes from the Army. The training and orientation of AR units have been closely integrated with that of the regular Army due to its long association with them. Also, AR units have proved their combat worthiness in both the world wars and in fighting the Chinese till the last round at Namka Chu in 1962.

Following the recommendation of the GoM Committee, the Assam Rifles is the designated Border Guarding force for the Indo-Myanmar border. During peace time, AR units are deployed for guarding and patrolling stretches of this border in the states of Nagaland, Manipur and Mizoram. The force has been successfully carrying out this task along with conducting counter insurgency operations in the hinterland. Myanmar being a relatively friendly country, there is no eye-ball to eye-ball deployment of forces on the Indo-Myanmar border. The International Border is also not disputed and is marked by boundary pillars. Also, due to the limitations imposed by terrain it is impossible to man every inch of this border. The primary thrust of the Assam Rifles is to intercept armed groups of insurgents moving across this stretch of the border. In the recent years, cooperation between the security forces of India and Myanmar have led to increased success on this front. Intelligence sharing and joint-operations have curtailed the activities of the numerous insurgent groups along the Indo-Myanmar border. But, despite the above measures and vastness of the frontage, this border continues to remain a hub for trans-movement of rebels, drug peddlers and arms traffickers.

Counter-Insurgency Operations

As has been mentioned previously, Assam Rifles units were among the first to be inducted into the Naga Hills in 1953 for suppressing the insurgency of the Naga Nationalist Council (NNC). Ever since, the force has played a pivotal role in containing the volatile situation in Nagaland, Mizoram, Manipur, Tripura and Assam. AR units have successfully operated under the Army to counter the insurgents. Hundreds of AR personnel have fought bravely and laid down their lives in the process. Several gallantry awards including three Ashok Chakras have been conferred on the officers and men for their acts of bravery against the terrorists.

The Assam Rifles has filled the void on several occasions and taken over the counter-insurgency grid in Manipur and Nagaland in the absence of Army formations moving to other sectors. AR units acting as reserves have also augmented the Army's strength when required in certain difficult times.

Today four sectors of the Assam Rifles (nearly 12 battalions) are deployed in Operation Hifazat in Manipur. Over the years, the Assam Rifles has played a vital role in arresting the rapidly deteriorating security situation in the state plagued by an internecine insurgency between several ethnic groups and tribes. With the establishment of IG AR (S) in the year 2005, AR has successfully taken over the CI grid in the entire state and is capable of containing the insurgency even in the absence of regular Army units. It has conducted many successful counter insurgency operations and neutralised a large number of insurgents. The presence of soldiers of local origin has been an asset and proved its value in garnering intelligence and interpreting the language of the insurgents. They are also sensitive towards maintaining peace in their native areas.

Despite the efforts of the security forces, a large number of insurgent groups remain active in Manipur, today. Over the years, the insurgency in the state has transformed into a cottage industry with the close interlinking of insurgent groups with economic activities and forced payment of illegal taxes by the population and even government agencies. Therefore, eradicating them is beyond the capabilities of the security forces alone and would require an all round effort involving all arms of the government with the requisite political and economic measures to correct the situation. The Assam Rifles units have also been actively engaging the local population with several developmental and educational schemes. It has provided the people with basic needs in areas where other arms of the state government are absent. With access to villages in the deep interiors, the force has won the hearts and minds of the hill people by building good relations with them.

Yet, the removal of the Armed Forces Special Powers Act is a major sticking point in Manipur. The involvement of some Assam Rifles personnel in some major violations such as the Manorma Devi case and some accusations of encounter killings have not helped matters much. In fact, the perception of AR personnel committing acts of excesses and human rights violations among the people of the state is fairly high. The force needs to concentrate more on this aspect and build more friendly relations with the populace. It should begin by acting swiftly against the accused personnel in cases of Human Rights violations. As the AR personnel remain permanently deployed in counter insurgency operations with no benefit of rotations to a peace station, there is a greater need for restraint and discipline in the men to prevent incidents of high-handedness.

In addition to stress-busting measures, the force should consider small family stations for the men close to sector headquarters where they can be rotated in batches for a short period for rest and recuperation and spending time with their family members.

Nonetheless, the 'Rhinoceros of the North East' is a cutting edge force available to the country for effectively fighting the numerous insurgencies in the North East. With a few new raisings of battalions, the Assam Rifles can completely take over the Counter Insurgency grid in Nagaland and Manipur and relieve the Army formation for other tasks. In the present scenario this can be successfully achieved as presently bulk of the operations in Manipur is being carried out by Assam Rifles battalions.

NOTES

1. History of the Assam Rifles.
2. Giriraj Shah, Paramilitary Forces of India, p.23.
3. Ibid (2) above.
4. Ibid.
5. Official website of the Assam Rifles, accessed at http://assamrifles.gov.in/formation.aspx

4

Special Frontier Force (SFF)

Origin

The Chinese invasion of Tibet saw a large influx of Tibetan refugees into India. These refugees were mainly settled in the Himalayan border states of Himachal Pradesh, Uttar Pradesh (now Uttarakhand), Sikkim and Arunachal Pradesh and later re-located to other parts of the country. In the late 1950s, the CIA had raised a guerrilla force comprising of Khampa rebels in Nepal. The Khampas had fled their homeland and sought refuge in parts of Nepal. The CIA provided training, resources, weapons and other facilities to the force in Mustang in Nepal. It was the Khampa rebels who had escorted the Dalai Lama during his flight from Tibet to India via the Chumbi valley.

Historically, the Tibetans were a war-waging people and had defended their homeland against raids by several invaders including the Mongols and the Chinese. Later, with the spread of Buddhist influences, the warrior streak of the Tibetan people gave way to a more peaceful orientation. Recognising the warrior streak of Tibetans, the Intelligence Bureau had conceived the raising of a special guerrilla unit comprising of Tibetan refugees in India. With the approval of the Cabinet Secretariat, this force was raised on 14 November 1962 at Chakrata, a hill town near Dehradun.[1] The primary goal of this force was to conduct covert operations in Tibet in the event of another conflict with China. A large number of Tibetan refugees were based in Chakrata which provided an ideal recruiting ground for the SFF. An initial strength of 5000 Tibetans including some Khampas were recruited. General Gonpo Tashi and Jago Namgyal Dorjee were the two Tibetan leaders of the Chushi Gangdruk who were instrumental in the forming of the SFF. In fact, the latter two were taken out of their imprisonment in India for their role in recruiting the Khampa rebels.[2] It is believed that the force received initial training and expertise in guerrilla warfare and covert operations from the CIA. The SFF personnel were equipped with American M-1, M-2 and M-3 Sub Machine Guns.[3]

Special Group

In the year 1977, a contingent of nearly 500 SFF commandos were sent to curb communal rioting in Saraswa. On completion of their task, they were joined by 500 Army personnel to receive specialised counter-insurgency operations training in Saraswa. Later only 60 SFF personnel were retained in this group. These personnel received further training in Jungle warfare and commando operations in Israel. Thus was raised the Special Group comprising exclusively of Army commandos. The Special Group was first deployed for Operation Bluestar in 1984. One Lt Col received bullet wounds while protecting PM Indira Gandhi when she visited the Golden Temple in the aftermath of the operation.

The Special Group is located at Chakrata and functions under the direct command of the IG SFF. The highly trained and specialised commando unit conducts special operations against terrorists and insurgents across the country on specific intelligence inputs. The Special group is also equipped and trained to carry out special covert operations, if required.

Command and Control

The Special Frontier Force also came to be known as 'Establishment 22'. It's first Inspector General was Maj Gen Sujan Singh, MC who had commanded 22 Mountain Regiment during World War II. Known for his unconventional thinking he had designated the unit as 'Establishment 22'.[4] Initially placed under the IB, the SFF was brought under the control of the R&AW. The IG SFF reports to the Director Security R&AW in the Cabinet Secretariat.

The SFF HQ with its Inspector General is located in New Delhi with the main centre and training facility in Chakrata.

Organisational Structure

Director R&AW
(Cabinet Secretariat)
↓
IG SFF
(Maj Gen rank officer from the Army)
↓

22 Special Group | SFF Battalions

The Special Group is comprised of officers and men from the Army's Special Forces and Parachute battalions. The SFF battalions are officered by Army officers on deputation from all arms and personnel are mainly Tibetans. 700 Gurkha soldiers also form part of the SFF.[5]

Organisational Structure of a SFF Battalion

HQ
↓
BN HQ | 4 × Aslt Teams | HQ TEAM

Equipping Profile

The personal weapons held by SFF commandos include:

- Aslt rifle (5.56 mm TAVOR)
- MP-10
- Uzi MG
- Underwater Rifle

Support Weapons

- Spas gun Franchi (shot gun)
- 20 mm cannon
- 7.62 mm PKMG
- Long Rg ATGM
- SAM
- MGL

Training

In 1964, the SFF commandos started received airborne training at the Parachute Training School in Agra. By the year 1968, the SFF had established its own airborne training facility with assistance from the Aviation Research Centre (air wing of the R&AW) at Saraswa air base in Uttar Pradesh. All SFF commandos are parachute qualified after five jumps, with three refresher jumps every year and some of them possess underwater diving skills. Most training is still conducted at Chakrata, lasting nine months and is similar to Indian Army recruit training.

SFF Personnel are Trained in Four Basic Areas

Mountain Warfare: Experts in mountain and Arctic warfare, these men are trained to survive and fight in extreme conditions. They are also known to have trained at the famed German Alpine Guides course at the Mountain Warfare School at Mittenwald and the High Altitude Warfare School at Gulmarg reaching proficiency levels that rival the best climbers in the world.

Amphibious: These troop's combat divers are the outfit's amphibious experts. In essence, it provides a comparable amphibious warfare capability to the SFF as the MARCOS provide to the Indian Navy. There is close cooperation and cross-training between its amphibious troops and the MARCOS.

Air: Air Troop is the Special Group's free-fall parachuting specialists, tasked with jumping behind enemy lines, either on their own missions or to pave the way for other squadron troops. Air Troop also employ less conventional forms of air insertion such as micro-lites and powered parachutes. For HALO/HAHO combat jumps skydivers use square-type RAM parachutes which are more manoeuverabilty also allow for softer, controlled landings than the standard round chutes.

Jungle warfare: Jungle operations are considered to be one of the toughest in the world and more men here fall to nature than the enemy. The Special Group's Jungle troopers are the masters in jungle craft. They are skilled at carrying out deep interdiction and search and destroy operations for extended periods of time.

SFF Commandos are specially trained to carry out Long Range Patrols behind enemy lines as pathfinders and also direct own aircraft fire on enemy targets.

Operations Conducted

Most of the operations of this elite special force are highly classified. In addition, the SFF has participated in the following operations, information of which are available in the public domain.

- Following reports of a possible nuclear test by China in 1964, a covert operation was launched by the CIA to place a permanent (Electronic intelligence) ELINT device on the 25,645 Ft Mt. Nanda Devi in Uttarakhand. The device, a transreceiver powered by a plutonium battery, that could detect and report data on future nuclear tests carried out by China. The mountaineering expedition to place the device on the peak was led by the famed mountaineer Lt Col MS Kohli comprising of SFF men. A similar operation was carried out by the SFF to place a device on Nand Kot. Later an operation was launched to retrieve the device from the peak as heavy snowfall had rendered it inoperative. It is believed that in the year 1969, a covert operation was launched to place an ELINT device on an unknown peak in Tibet.[6,7]
- A Task Force of 3000 SFF Commandos participated in the Indo-Pak War of 1971 in Bangladesh under Operation 'Mountain Eagle'. Prior to commencement of hostilities, the SFF was engaged in training the Mukti Bahini. In November 1971, the Task Force was deployed in Mizoram and carried out pre-emptive strikes behind enemy lines in support of the Indian Army thrust towards Chittagong. They were instrumental in destroying enemy bridges and disrupting their lines of communications. They conducted secret small missions including the operation at the Kalurghat radio station. The SFF moved into East Pakistan on 03 December 1971, they were also loaned four Indian Air Force Mi-4 helicopters. They successfully blew up Bangladesh Forces

General MAG Osmani's helicopter ride to Lt Gen Niazi's surrender ceremony in Dhaka. They also halted tactical sections of the Pakistani 97 Independent Brigade and the famed 2 Commando Battalion from infiltrating into Burma by cutting off their rear defences and flanks. 56 SFF personnel died in the operations in Bangladesh while another 190 were injured.

- Op Bluestar: SFF including its Special Group operated in conjunction with 1 PARA (SF) to gain a foothold into the Golden Temple. Assault teams of SFF and 1 PARA (SF) were assigned the delicate task of neutralising terrorists holed up inside the Har Mandir Sahib.
- Op Vijay: SFF personnel fought valiantly and some of them laid down their lives in Op Vijay in Kargil. They were also engaged in conducting certain tasks across the Line of Control during the Operation. However, no details of their participation have been made available.
- In 1984, SFF was among the first units inducted into the Siachen Glacier. The Tibetans proved to be physically fit, hardy and highly motivated and acclimatised to serve on the glacial heights, a military feet never attempted previously. Till the raising and deployment of the Ladakh Scouts, it was the Tibetan troops who were most suitably poised to survive in the permanently frozen heights upwards of 15,000 ft and maintain India's hold over the glacier.

Role and Tasks

The Tibetan troops of the SFF are most suited for employment in the high Himalayas and the Tibetan Plateau. The personnel are already well acclimatised to the harsh weather conditions and difficult terrain obtaining in this region. They possess the human spirit and endurance levels to operate for prolonged periods in the high altitude mountains and plateau. They are amenable to imbibe the lay of the land, terrain and the geographical environment is naturally friendly to them. Thus their hardy stock augmented with specialised mountain warfare and commando training provides them with the lethality to carry out special tasks during a conflict situation and in peace times as well. Their location in the Himalayan region adds an added advantage of having highly acclimatised crack troops in a state of permanent operational readiness. They can be mobilised at a short notice by air or foot in case of any contingency arising across the high mountain passes along the Northern and North Eastern Frontiers.

Recruitment

The Tibetan's sense of patriotism for the independence of their homeland and antagonism towards China is an additional motivating factor. The prime factor behind raising a Special Force from the Tibetan refugees residing in India was to exploit the advantages of their physical hardiness and emotional aggression against

China for occupying their homeland. The success of the Khampa rebels of Eastern Tibet in harassing the PLA soldiers in Tibet provided an added impetus to the raising of the SFF. Service in the SFF also offers a stream of employment for the Tibetan population in India. The recruitment base of the soldiers is their concentration centres in Ladakh, Himachal Pradesh, Uttarakhand, Sikkim and Tawang region of Arunachal Pradesh. The Tibetan Government in exile screens and selects Tibetan youth for induction into the SFF.

Conventional Operations

The SFF is organised on the pattern of the Special Forces. All personnel are parachute qualified and some even possess underwater diving skills. The force can be thus employed for Special Operations and Airborne operations akin to any other Special Forces unit. They can also be employed in any theatre of operation although they are best suited for employment in the mountains owing to the recruitment profile of the personnel and permanent location of the SFF units. In consonance to their specific role in the Northern theatre of operations, the SFF can conduct the following tasks during or preceding conventional operations:

- Small Team operations to gather information on enemy troop disposition and movement of formations in the Tibetan Plateau. The SFF commandos have the perfect cover to operate clandestinely in Tibet and can provide useful human intelligence (HUMINT) on the enemy command and control, leadership, troop deployment and movement both during peace time and in the event of a conflict.
  Their operational synergy with R&AW helps in the seamless development of this HUMINT capability. This HUMINT capability will prove extremely useful in gaining timely information in enemy troop buildup and intentions prior to outbreak of hostilities. The absence of such HUMINT capability following the Chinese invasion of Tibet in 1950 had led to a complete lack of knowledge and information on the movement of PLA divisions towards NEFA and Ladakh and their intentions which ultimately led to the debacle in October 1962. The HUMINT asset is also useful in gathering an insight into the political activities in Tibet and gauging the impact of people's protests and Chinese reprisal measures against them. This would ultimately help in the formulation of an overall picture of the political climate in Tibet which could influence military moves by the PLA.
- The information collated by clandestine HUMINT sources operating in Tibet can be used to authenticate information gathered through other sources and launch specific covert operation to suit the overall operational plan during war time.
- The information relayed by the Surveillance and Target designation

squads operating behind enemy lines can be developed to launch pre-emptive air strikes against the enemy's command and control and communication targets. These squads can also corroborate targets acquired by ELINT sources and take out air fields, helipads, landing zones, missile launch sites, etc.

- The SFF assault teams can also be launched against selected enemy troop concentrations in depth and forward zones as a preliminary to launch of own operations. The assault teams launched after the successful infiltration of the Surveillance and Target acquisition teams can also destroy the enemy's strategic assets such as missile launchers, ISR capabilities.
- The assault teams can also be employed against the enemy's leadership, communication hubs, gun positions, harbours of mechanised columns, etc to delay operations and disrupt their offensive plans. These operations may be carried out in conjunction with regular troops to suit the overall operational plan.
- In offensive mode, SFF teams operating in battalion size or as separate teams can be inserted by air or land to capture certain features of tactical importance to facilitate own offensive thrusts or occupy features which would prevent the enemy's offensive thrusts towards own territory. Airborne operations can also be launched to secure important political and communication centres in depth.
- In defensive operations, the assault teams further divided into small squads can be quickly inducted to occupy certain important passes in anticipation of an enemy movement towards the border. The SFF can hold these passes till such time that the regular forces are able to effect a link-up and occupy these passes or vital ground, etc.
- As has been mentioned previously, the SFF can be employed for carrying out effective airborne and Special Forces operations in a different geographical theatre as well. In fact, a Task Force of 3000 SFF commandos took active part in the 1971 War in the Chittagong sector. During conventional operations, it would be imperative that the SFF units be placed under the direct operational command of the Army theatre in which they would be expected to operate to facilitate their easy and seamless utilisation.

Sub-Conventional Operations

- Operation Bluestar was the first anti-terrorist operation which saw the employment of the SFF. The force was allotted the task of gaining entry into the Golden Temple complex in conjunction with the assault carried out by 1 PARA (SF). The Army Commandos, SFF and Special Group commandos were assigned separate targets.

- The Special Group, since its inception has been conducting specific intelligence based operations against insurgents and terrorists in the North East and J&K. These operations are highly classified and are carried out in extremely small teams of four to ten commandos, only. However, with the gradual stabilisation of the security situation in these areas and the availability of other Special Forces assets within the respective theatres, the frequency of these operations has gone down.
- The Special Group is a highly-trained, equipped and highly motivated specialised unit which can be employed for any type of contingency arising in the country, be it for urban warfare or rural insurgencies. They can be deployed anywhere in quick time to address specific situations such as hostage rescue, fire-assault by terrorists, hijackings, etc.
- The SFF and Special Group can also be employed for select operations against terrorist training camps, launch pads and to neutralise their leadership in distant lands.
- In the emerging security environment emerging out of the Maoist insurgency in the heartland, the force can be employed for specific commando raids and limited operations against the Naxalites if the situation gets out of hand. The employment of the SFF for a limited period for obtaining quick, decisive and specific aims can also negate the employment of the Army as the SFF operates directly under the Prime Minister's Office. The SFF can be employed in conjunction with the NSG for Special operations against the Naxalites.

The scenarios for employment of the SFF in conventional and sub-conventional operations as mentioned above are hypothetical ones which may obtain given the geo-strategic environment prevailing in the region. Without delving into the actual tactical skills, the scenarios only enumerate the combat proficiency and abilities of the SFF for employment in any theatre of operation or situation during both peace and war times.

Critique

The SFF has excellent inter-operability with the Army's Special Forces units, the Air Force and R&AW. Officered and patterned on the lines of the Army's Special Forces units, the SFF has the right leadership and command assets to maintain the level of its training, proficiency and combat edge. To maintain their invincibility and combat edge, the frequency of cross-training and joint operations with other SF units should be increased. The SFF should be included into the Special Forces resources of the country. Together with similar units of the Army, Navy and Air Force, the SFF provides a lethal and potent edge to the country's Special Operations capabilities and reach. In the emerging geo-political environment, these Special Forces will provide increased mobility, reach and maneuvrability to our force projection capabilities by land, air and sea. The SFF for obvious strategic and tactical necessities should be reverted to the Army's operational command at least during war time. Ideally, though all Special Forces assets in the country must be brought under a common umbrella.

NOTES

1. Bharat Rakshak.com, accessed online at http://www.bharat-rakshak.com/LAND-FORCES/SFF.html
2. Chushigangdruk.com, accessed online at http://www.chushigangdruk.org/history/history11.htm
3. Ibid.
4. Ibid.
5. Ibid.
6. Spies in the Himalayas, by Kenneth Conboy and M.S. Kohli, University Press of Kansas (March 2003).
7. Harish Kapadia, "Nanda Devi", in *World Mountaineering*, Audrey Salkeld, editor, Bulfinch Press, 1998.

PART II

Central Armed Police Forces (CAPFs)

5

National Security Guard (NSG)

The NSG was raised in 1984 in the aftermath of Op Bluestar and the assassination of Prime Minister Indira Gandhi. The primary mandate of the elite commando force was to carry out specific counter-terrorism operations such as hostage rescue, anti-hijacking, and the ability to neutralise terrorists with minimal collateral damage. The idea was to form a strike force, small in number to have a crushing effect on the terrorists. The NSG Act was passed by the Parliament in 1986.[1]

The charter of the force is as under:

> The NSG was set up in 1984 as a Federal Contingency Deployment Force to tackle all facets of terrorism in the country. Thus the primary role of this Force is to combat terrorism in whatever form it may assume in areas where activity of terrorists assumes serious proportions, and the State Police and other Central Police Forces cannot cope with the situation. The NSG is a Force specially equipped and trained to deal with specific situations and is therefore, to be used only in exceptional situations. The Force is not designed to undertake the functions of the State Police Forces or other Para Military Forces of the Union of India.

The NSG was modelled on the pattern of the SAS of the UK and GSG-9 of Germany. It is a task-oriented Force and has two complementary elements in the form of the Special Action Group (SAG) comprising Army personnel and the Special Ranger Groups (SRG), comprising personnel drawn from the Central Armed Police Forces / State Armed Police Forces.[2]

The primary tasks of the NSG are:

- Neutralisation of terrorist threats.
- Handling hijacking situations in air or land.
- Bomb disposal (search, detection and neutralisation of IEDs).
- PBI (Post Blast Investigation)
- Engaging and neutralising terrorists in specific situations.
- Hostage Rescue.[3]

Organisation

The total strength of the NSG is about 14500. It has two main components, namely the strike and the support elements. The strike component comprises nearly 1200 personnel and officers from the Army. They are organised into two specialised units, namely, the 51 and 52 Special Action Groups (SAG). Both these units are specialised in anti-hijacking and counter-terrorist operations. In addition, the 11 Special Ranger Group (SRG) also forms part of the NSG's strike component. The NSG has started the process of withdrawing personnel of 11 SRG deployed for VIP protection duties to augment its strike capabilities. The two support battalions are comprised of the 12 and 13 Special Ranger Groups (SRG). The force has a National Bomb Data Centre at its Training Centre in Manesar, comprising mainly of Army Engineers for Bomb detection, analysis and defusion tasks. The support component consists of personnel from the CAPFs. These men are organised into the Special Rangers Group and are mainly utilised for VIP Protection and other such duties.

Organisation
IG (Ops)
↓
↓ 51 & 52 SAG | ↓ 11, 12 & 13 SRG
↓
3 × SQNs
↓
3 × TEAMs
↓
3 × HITs

The NSG is a well-oiled machineary which is fully geared up to meet any challenge and maintains round the clock operational readiness for rapid induction. As the above chart shows, each Strike Battalion is broken down into three squadrons. A squadron is made up of three teams and three hits or sections form one team. The MP 5 Sub-Machine Gun is the standard issue of the SAG battalions. Each hit has Rocket Launchers/ Sniper Rifles and specialised equipment like Bullet-proof vests, Passive Night Vision Devices and hand-held wireless sets for communication.

Training

The officers and men on deputation with the NSG have to undergo a gruelling 13 week basic and nine weeks long advanced training. These personnel would have in any case undergone various training cadres in service with their parent units. The training process for the SAG battalions is even more rigorous. The

Organisational Structure

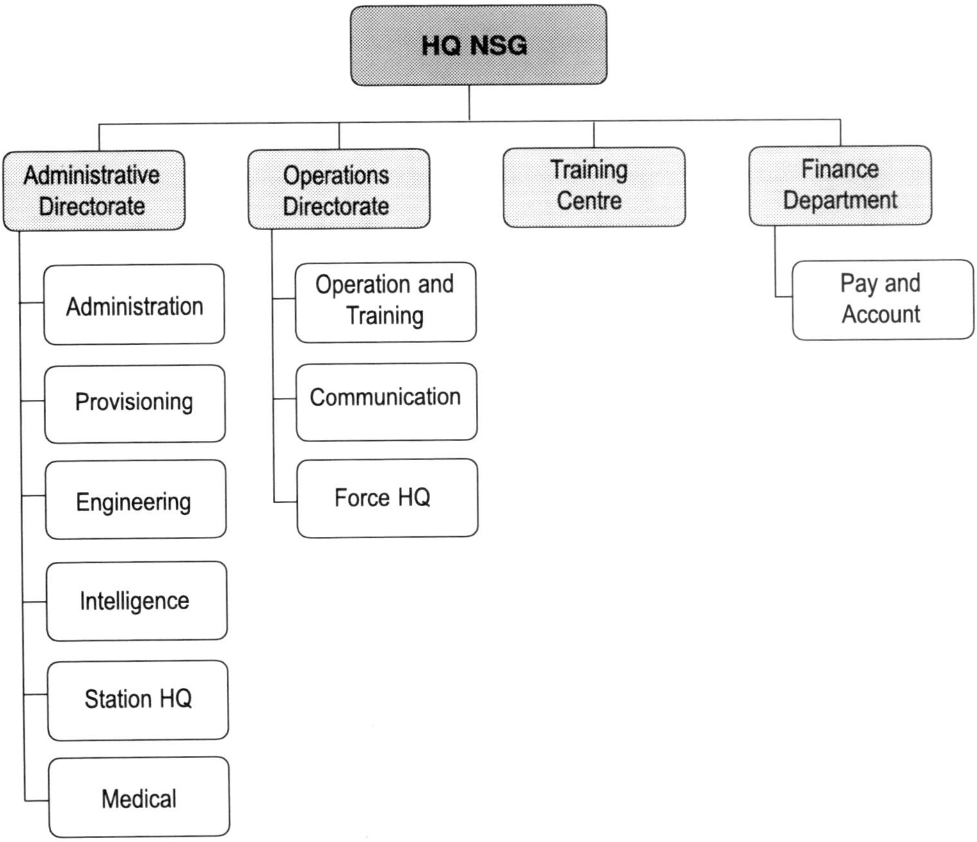

Source: Official website of the NSG.

criteria requirement for the NSG ensures that the best men from the Army's Infantry battalions and Special Forces units are sent to the NSG. Even then the rejection rate during the pre-induction training period is more than 50 percent. This indicates the tough standards set by the force. The mental robustness and physical endurance levels of the men along with their ability to survive under challenging conditions and their skill at arms are put to a rigorous test during this 13 week training period.

Those who survive these 13 weeks are then imparted specialised training in anti-hijacking drills, hostage rescue and other commando training. The training is a continuous process and the daily grind in the SAG involves physical tests/ runs and constant rehearsing of specialised drills and live firing exercises. This ensures that the men remain alert and are prepared for any contingency at all times. Survival skills and Karate training along with other methods of unarmed combat are also imparted to the commandos. The drills are continuously refined by carrying out constant mock-exercises and studying special forces operations across the world.

SAG Commandos are capable of undertaking special operations by helicopters and even carry out para-drop and under-water operations to a certain extent. To ensure high motivation levels and prevent fatigue from setting in, personnel on deputation with the NSG are turned over after completing a fixed period of two years.

Post 26/11, joint training exercises and interactions with other Special Forces units of the world have been intensified to refine own skills and procedures and to also create inter-operability with them.

Equipping Profile

The standard issue of the NSG is the MP-5 carbine and the Glock pistol. The force also uses the PSD-9 Sniper Rifle in addition to LMGs and 84 mm Rocket Launchers in use by Infantry Battalions of the Army. The SAG units are issued specialised equipment like Night Vision Devices and hand-held radio sets along with the standard Bullet Proof vests and helmets. After the Mumbai terrorist attacks, the force has gone on a massive overdrive to procure the latest weapons and equipments for specialised counter-terrorism operations. The standard weapons presently held by NSG personnel are[4]:

- Browning Hi-Power 9mm Semi-Automatic Pistol
- Glock 17 9mm Semi-Automatic Pistol
- Glock 19 9mm Semi-Automatic Pistol
- SIG P226 9mm Semi-Automatic Pistol
- Heckler & Koch M-512 12 Gauge Shotgun
- 1A SMG 9mm Sub-Machine gun
- Heckler & Koch MP5 A3, A5 and SD3 9 mm Submachine Gun
- AKM 7.62×39mm Assault Rifle
- SIG SG 551 5.56mm NATO Assault Rifle
- Mauser SP66 7.62mm NATO Bolt-Action Sniper Rifle
- Steyr SSG69 7.62mm NATO Bolt-Action Sniper Rifle
- SIG-Sauer SSG 3000 7.62mm NATO Bolt-Action Sniper Rifle
- Heckler & Koch MSG-90 7.62mm NATO Semi-Automatic Sniper Rifle

Initial Pangs and Early Operations

Soon after its raising, the NSG was plagued with petty-politics, guided by the whims of a few individuals, a brittle organisation, incapable of taking on a major mission without stumbling and an ill-equipped and demoralised force. The officers after completing their mandated two year tenures, preferred returning to their parent units. In fact, a deputation in the NSG began to be seen as detrimental to their professional growth. This led to a shortage of well-trained and experienced officers to train the men of a young force which was not yet blooded in operations.

The force was modeled on the lines of the elite commando units of the world such as the British Special Air Service (SAS), Germany's GSG-9 and the American Delta Force.

However, they could not exactly be compared to these forces at the time of raising due to a lack of blooding in operations, different operating environments and due to different control structures and equipping profiles. In fact Dr S Subramanian, a former DG of the NSG pointed out that, "The NSG, unlike the units abroad, take on every job the government asked them to under very trying and difficult circumstances."[5] Commenting on the different operating environments, he said that unlike in western countries, the local police in India is ill-equipped and are not mentally attuned to these exigencies; therefore the job of the NSG becomes even more difficult to execute.[6]

The blueprint conceived a "lean and mean" force of 12000 strong, backed by the administrative and logistics skill of 4000 bureaucrats and senior officers of the Army and CPOs. However, a force of only 3000 could be raised with a top-heavy structure of Army Generals, Brigadiers and DIGs at the force HQ in Delhi. In comparison, the German GSG-9 is only 300 strong and is led by a Colonel. In the initial days, a lack of decision making at the cutting edge level in the force was attributed to this top-heavy organisational structure.

The utilisation of the force for regular operations carried out by the Army and CPOs in Jammu & Kashmir, Punjab and Tamil Nadu further diluted the ethos of the NSG as it went against the philosophy of employment of special forces- to fight in the open. It also alerts the terrorists, thus blowing away a counter-terrorist force's main weapon—strength and surprise.[7] In the initial years, the organisation had spent recklessly on procuring training aids and importing munitions. But the apathetic state of command and control could be seen in the manner in which these resources were being utilised. An Electronic shooting range remained under-utilised as they were found to be "too expensive to maintain". A Fokker Friendship (F-27) aircraft procured for anti-hijack drills was not even assembled for use. A helidrome was used to shelter trucks and buses. The poor state of construction at its Training Centre in Manesar was exposed when rain water seeped into the quarters and even the magazine. Indigenously manufactured bullets were utilised for training as it was found expensive to import bullets from abroad for foreign weapons such as the MP-5 Carbine and PSG-1 sniper rifle. Resultantly, the firing mechanisms of weapons broke and in several instances, the effective range of the bullet got reduced. A shortage of rifles led to two commandos being dependent on one rifle. Similarly, specialised equipments such as Nigh Vision Devices were rendered ineffective due to lack of spares and batteries.[8]

In fact, as all operational decisions were taken by the Director General, after receiving the go-ahead from the Home Ministry (having been approached by the State Government) added to the delay in deploying the force at the place of contingency. One fitting example of this trend was the delay in deploying an NSG task force stationed in Madras to take out the dreaded LTTE terrorists, Sivarasan and Subha in Bangalore.

The first major operation carried out by the Black Cats was Operation Black Thunder I in Amritsar on 30 April 1986. In an operation lasting eight hours, about 300 NSG Commandos and 700 BSF men affected the capture of nearly 300 terrorists from the Golden Temple. Unlike Op Blue Star only one person was killed and two injured during the entire operation.

31 terrorists were killed and nearly 231 surrendered in Op Black Thunder-II carried out on 09-18 May 1988. The 51 SAG was divided into assault teams while the SRG effected the cordon of the Golden Temple with snipers deployed to take out escaping terrorists. The NSG operation forced the notorious terrorist Surjit Singh Penta and his men to end the siege of the Golden Temple. This operation carried out under the glare of the international and national media was touted as a huge success not only because the task was carried out while maintaining the sanctity of the Golden Temple (unlike in 1984) and also because of minimum attrition on own troops. But the force was criticised for using such a heavy force of 1000 men against a mere 46 terrorists thus belying the very purpose of commando operations.

Op Black Thunder was precisely the type of operation the NSG was raised for- taking out well-entrenched terrorists in an urban landscape with civilian population in the vicinity. The NSG was trained for carrying out specialised operations to limit collateral damage with minimum loss to civilian lives.

In January 1988, two terrorists were neutralised in Op Black Hawk, a heliborne operation carried out in the Mand area of Punjab. By the end of 1989, two companies of the NSG were deployed for regular counter-terrorist operations in Punjab. This operation code-named 'Mouse Trap' was to achieve area dominance at night in Tarn Taran district. But prolonged deployments in carrying out regular tasks already being performed by the Police, CPOs and to some extent the Army undermined the effectiveness and shock value of a crack commando outfit. It was alleged that during the three months that the NSG was deployed in Punjab, it had killed 11 men in encounters, six of whom were reportedly innocent.[9] On 6 July 1990, two NSG commandos were killed in an encounter with 15 Khalistani terrorists near an irrigation canal in Varnala in Khem Karan.

In fact, the 'take no chances' attitude had also led to the use of excessive force in an operation to neutralise just two terrorists holed up in a building in Baroda in 1991. Several rounds of ammunition and rocket launchers were used in that operation.

Major Operations

Being a Special Force, several operations carried out by the NSG have not been de-classified. Some of the major operations carried out by the force are briefly mentioned below.

- 05 September 1987 to 15 January 1988: The responsibility of guarding a high-risk terrorist code-named 'Jack' was entrusted upon the force.
- 04 August 1989: Op Mouse Trap in the Tarn Taran district of Punjab, in conjunction with Punjab Police and other security forces. NSG was able to demonstrate that it was possible to achieve area dominance at night, if the strategy and tactics were right. Ved Marwah calls this Op Night Dominance.
- 10 November 1990: NSG task force was flown to Kolkata to rescue hostages of a Thai airbus by Burmese students.
- 25-26 January 1991: The NSG was involved in Operation Ani Ben, on CI tasks in Baroda, (Gujarat) where Punjab terrorists were holed up inside a house. Two terrorists were killed and two AK-47s were recovered.
- 01 July-20 September 1991: NSG was employed along with SIT in search and strike missions after the assassination of Rajiv Gandhi.
- 25 November to 16 December 1992: 150 commandos were deployed at Ayodhya during the Ram Janambhoomi and Babri Masjid crisis.
- 27 March 1993: 52 SAG mobilised and moved to Adampur for rescue of hostages of Indian Airlines Flight IC 486.
- 24-25 April 1993: NSG Commandos stormed a hijacked Indian Airlines Boeing 737 with 141 passengers on board at Amritsar airport during Operation Ashwamedh. The hijacker, Mohammed Yousuf Shah, was killed before he could react and no hostages were harmed.
- October 1998: As part of the implementation of the Union Home Ministry's decision to conduct pro-active strikes against militants, commando teams supported by IAF Mi-25/35 helicopter gun-ships began striking at terrorist groups deep inside the mountains and forests of Kashmir. After helicopter reconnaissance were conducted to pinpoint the militants, the commandos - comprising NSG and Rashtriya Rifles personnel - were para-dropped, along with supplies, into the area to hunt the militants. They had to rely on these supplies and their ability to live off the land until replenishment every fortnight or so.
- 15 July 1999: NSG commandos ended a 30-hour standoff by killing two terrorists and rescuing all 12 hostages unharmed in J&K. The terrorists had attacked a BSF campus near Bandipore, killing three officers and the wife of another. The 12 hostages were kept locked in a room. This was the first suicide attack in J&K.
- 21 August 1999: After interrogating three captured terrorists, the Delhi

Police Crime branch confirmed that two more terrorists were hiding in a one-storied house in Rudrapur, Uttar Pradesh. Since the terrorists were considered armed and dangerous (their colleagues were arrested with over 100 pounds of RDX), the Delhi Police sought assistance from the NSG. A 16-man team arrived at the house at 4:45 am. They began their assault at 5:30 am., before first light. The first militant managed to fire at the commandos with a pistol he kept by his bedside, but was killed an instant later. The second terrorist was shot before he had a chance to fire and died 40 minutes later. No NSG personnel were injured.

- December 1999: Terrorists hijacked Indian Airlines flight IC 814 from Nepal, and landed in Amritsar, Punjab. Within minutes of landing, the Crisis Management Group (CMG), which authorizes the use of the NSG, was informed. But the CMG wasted precious hours and by the time the go-ahead was issued, it was too late. On the other hand, the NSG team on alert was elsewhere and no other team was raised during the delay. The hijacked plane took off before the NSG reached Amritsar Airport. The plane landed in Kandahar, Afghanistan where one hostage was killed. Finally, the Indian Government agreed to the terrorists' demands to release three jailed terrorists. The hostages were released and the terrorists escaped to Pakistan.
- September 2002: SAG commandos were flown to the Karnataka state in India, in an effort to catch sandalwood smuggler and forest brigand Veerappan, in the wake of kidnapping of a former minister of the state cabinet, Nagappa. They pulled out after suggesting that intelligence for the operation was inadequate. A small team was left behind to help, the hostage was eventually killed in December 2002.
- October 2002: Two terrorists attacked Akshardham temple complex in Gujarat. NSG flew in, delayed by traffic in Delhi. Op Vajrashakti is launched. They carried out assaults in which one commando was killed and another one seriously injured and in a coma, died after 18 months. But by morning the two terrorists were killed and the operation successfully completed.
- December 2002: Terrorists attacked the Raghunath temple in Jammu. NSG was ready to be flown out but called back at the last minute.
- 26-29 November 2008: Operation Black Tornado and Operation Cyclone launched to flush out terrorist and rescue hostages after multiple attacks across Mumbai. Major Sandeep Unnikrishnan and Havaldar Gajender Singh Bisht of the 51 Special Action Group (SAG) lost their lives during the operations. The NSG neutralised eight LeT terrorists and rescued over 600 people trapped in three different locations in Mumbai.

Critique

The critical elements of a Special Force or a Commando unit are shock and surprise. The men have to be specially trained and equipped to carry out operations which are beyond the capacity of other regular or police units. The objective of using Special Forces is not only to restore a crisis situation but also to deliver a delibitating blow to the enemy. The aim is to carry such swift and clinical operations that instill shock and a sense of fear in the enemy so that he thinks twice before attempting another misadventure against the nation. The invincibility and awe of the commando unit has to be upheld at all times. This is no mean task and requires a high standard of operational prowess and acumen to have an upper edge against the adversaries.

In today's electronic age, the reach of the media has made it easier and faster for perceptions to be formed. It is very difficult to maintain utmost secrecy of drills carried out during an operation under the media glare. Therefore, to maintain the 'eliteness' of special forces units, quick success is a prerequisite as perceptions are performed in a matter of minutes due to the fast dissemination of news, information and photographs over the electronic and social media. A fitting example of this was the NSG operation to neutralise the terrorists in Mumbai on 26/11. A long standoff erroneously gave undue publicity to the terrorists as also to its staying power against an elite force and contributed to their publicity needs. Such prolonged operations may dent the invincibility of an elite force and boost the terrorists' morale and provide fodder to their propaganda channels.

The NSG is one among several other Special Forces units of the country. It is the only Special Forces/Commando unit directly under the operational control of the Ministry of Home Affairs (MHA). The other units operate under the command and control of their respective services while the Special Frontier Force (SFF) is under the operational command of the Cabinet Secretariat.

Operating under the MHA, the mandate of the NSG is to operate anywhere in the country as the situation demands. For employment of the NSG, a request has to be first made by the concerned state government upon which the Centre (MHA) alerts the DG NSG for deploying the commandos. The NSG has three strike battalions (including the two SAGs) for employment anywhere in the country. The other two support battalions of the Special Rangers Group (SRG) comprising of personnel from the Central Police Organisations (CPOs) are responsible for guarding VVIPs/VIPs and other such tasks.

Analysis of Past Operations

An analysis of the known major operations carried out by the SAG battalions would bring out that the force was majorly able to achieve its objectives as per the standards expected of a Special unit. The casualty suffered in each operation has been minimal thus validating the supreme attrition ration of an elite force. In fact, the martyrs in each operation have set high standards of bravery and dare-devilry which have been recognised by the highest awards being conferred upon them posthumously, though each operation brought out its fallacies and the need to constantly correct and update operating procedures and skills.

As has been brought out earlier, the NSG conducted its first major operation (Op Black Thunder 1 and 2) with finesse and precision thus deflating the terrorist siege of the Golden Temple. The lessons learnt from Op Blue Star, decisive leadership and negotiating skills of Punjab Police and Intelligence officers ensured that the operations were concluded with minimum collateral damage to the shrine. The employment of the NSG subsequently in regular operations in Punjab was a retrograde step. If employed for a prolonged period in the initial years of its raising the force would have been equated to the levels of other paramilitary units operating there. The reverses suffered by the NSG during the operation in Khem Karan in 1990 was a reminder as to why elite forces should not be used for day to day operations thus reducing its shock effect among terrorists. In Operation Ani Ben in Baroda, the NSG was criticised for using dis-proportionate fire power including rockets against only two terrorists holed up in a building. This belied the basic concept of using special forces in such situations, which is to carry out a swift room intervention using hand-held weapons as opposed to smoking the terrorists out. On the other hand, it can also be said that the Punjab experience blooded the force and it could draw early lessons for future employment.

The common fallacy in the operations in Punjab was primarily connected to leadership issues. The force was in its infancy, though the political leadership saw it as a magic weapon in their hands to bail them out of difficult situations. The turf wars within the force HQ in the initial days also led to indecisions and a 'play safe' mentality being created. The NSG soon overcame the teething problems and proved its mettle by successfully neutralising the hijackers at Adampur and Amritsar in March and April 1993 respectively with zero civilian casualty or damage to the aircrafts.

In the turbulent decade of the 1990s the SAG commandos carried out several special operations in Punjab, Jammu and Kashmir and in the North East. These operations are highly classified and scant detail is available in the public domain. These were specific hard-intelligence based operations carried out against specific terrorist leadership targets in built-up areas. Other operations complimented the efforts of the Army and its Special Forces units, particularly in J&K. In the 1990s, the NSG was at times, specially requisitioned for carrying out swift operations in dense built-up areas of Srinagar city. Other operations would entail para-dropping from helicopters on remote mountain dhoks to flush out militants. It would suffice to say that these operations were critical for testing the mettle of the NSG in live situations and provided an opportunity to test their training skills and tactics.

Years of training in anti-hijack drills came to a naught when the NSG could not even reach Amritsar airport where the hijacked Indian Airlines aircraft IC-814 had landed for a brief moment before flying to Lahore, Dubai and eventually to Kandahar. The failure however has to be attributed to the tardy and cumbersome crisis management structure in place in Delhi at that time. By the time the NSG was alerted, the aircraft had already flown out of Amritsar. Airport authorities and police units at Amritsar's Raja Sanshi airport could have blocked the runway and prevented the aircraft from taking off. In that time-frame, the SAG's anti-hijack team could have landed at Amritsar to restore the situation. Nevertheless, the IC 814 episode highlighted the need for the anti-hijack squad to be on alert closer to the Indira Gandhi International Airport in New Delhi for a rapid deployment by air to a place of contingency.

The next major incident where the NSG's services were again not utilised was during the attack on Parliament house on 13 December 2001. The five terrorists who had attacked the Parliament were eventually gunned down by the CRPF responsible for the outer-perimeter security of the building. Though, in the initial confusion following the gunfire, NSG squads located nearby had reached the building, the NSG could not engage the terrorists as the CRPF managed to neutralise them even before they could enter the Parliament building. The services of the SAG would have been utilised had the terrorists managed to entrench themselves inside the building and prolong the standoff. In the aftermath of the Parliament attack, a Quick Reaction Team of the NSG is located close to the high security area to be able to rapidly fix the terrorists before reinforcements arrive.

The attack on Akshardham Temple in Gandhingar saw crucial time being lost in transporting the troops from Manesar to the airport. By the time the commandos arrived in Gandhinagar, the terrorists had already inflicted a large number of civilian casualties. The SAG Commandos had to be transported in civilian transport bringing out another lacuna in the rapid response procedures. In fact, the SAG could launch its operation only after midnight. However, once pressed into action, the two fidayeen terrorists were quickly eliminated. The Commandos suffered two fatal casualties during the operation.

The operation brought to fore the need to have an effective traffic management system incorporating the local police to enable a quick passage of the commandos from Manesar to the airport in New Delhi.

Operation Black Tornado in Mumbai once again exposed the time-taken in deploying for an operation. In the initial days following the operation, conflicting media reports suggested that the IL-76 transport aircraft had to be requisitioned from Chandigarh and other reports said that there was a small delay in taking off due to the time taken to warm up the engines of the transport aircraft.

Nevertheless, the attacks of 26/11 were the worst ever terrorist attack on India. The multiple and unfolding nature of the attack in a metropolitan city like Mumbai made it unique and something which the security forces had not dealt with before. Both 51 and 52 SAG were mobilised for the contingency in Mumbai. The NSG operation was handicapped from the very beginning due to lack of intelligence and knowledge of the targets and conflicting reports on the exact number of terrorists present at each location.

As the target areas (Hotel Taj and Trident) were extensive, fixing the terrorists in one location proved to be a mammoth task. The presence of civilians inside further compounded the situation. Therefore, it entailed employment of a large number of commandos to first rescue the civilians and then fix the terrorists who were constantly changing their location inside the buildings. There was a hostage situation in Nariman House where eventually commandos had to slither down an IAF helicopter to take out the terrorists after gaining an entry from the terrace of the building.

Given the uniqueness and magnitude of the situation in Mumbai, the situation was handled professionally and success achieved in preventing further civilian casualties and ultimately neutralising the terrorists. This is however not to suggest that the NSG did not draw its lessons from the operation. The force has reflected a lot on the operation and carried out brain-storming to correct its tactics employed during the operation. For instance, the action at Nariman House could have been terminated much earlier as it was a comparatively smaller building as compared to Hotel Taj. A swift and surgical operation there may also have saved the lives of the Jewish hostages inside. In fact, once the terrorists were fixed in a particular room in Hotel Trident, they were eliminated in no time.

The prolonged siege of the iconic Hotel Taj gave a lot of publicity and mileage to the terrorists. The four terrorists were finally neutralised on the ground floor of the Hotel on 29 November 2008, nearly 60 hours after they had stormed it. Given the total number of rooms in each floor and the presence of a large number of civilians, the time taken for successfully terminating the operation is justified. However, the commandos would do well to learn a few lessons from some tactical opportunities that occurred during the operation at Hotel Taj. For instance, when Maj Sandeep Unnikrishnan's squad had developed the first contact with the terrorists on the very first night of 26 November, how were the terrorists allowed to break contact and subsequently prolong the siege? The fleeting opportunity provided by identifying the terrorist location by Maj Sandeep Unnikrishnan's action should have been exploited immediately and the terrorists eliminated in no time. Secondly, when the terrorists were finally cornered on the ground floor, could the commandos have not have applied swift room intervention manoeuverabilty by eliminating the terrorists by fire and move rather than by using rockets and explosives to smoke them out? The latter tactics was justified given the thickness of the concrete walls at Hotel Taj and also due to the loss of the surprise element in the operation. So, overall the deliberate pace of the operation was justified to prevent own and civilian casualty, particularly in view of the formidable and antique edifice of the Taj infrastructure.

In all, the NSG eliminated eight fidayeen terrorists belonging to the LeT and rescued more than 610 civilians from the three locations in Mumbai. The Bomb Disposal Squad of the NSG recovered and defused a large amount of explosives and grenades from the encounter sites.

Present State of Operations

In the aftermath of 26/11, the Central Government has authorised the NSG to requisition civilian aircraft for transporting commandos in the event of a contingency.

The Centre has also increased the sanctioned strength of the NSG and created two Regional centres at Kolkata and Hyderabad and four hubs at Mumbai, Kolkata, Hyderabad and Chennai. This would reduce the time taken for the commandos to reach the projected sites of operation as contingencies arising in these cities or in proximate regional towns would be handled by these forces stationed there. These regional hubs have components of both the SAG and SRG. They have the ability to fix the terrorist location till such time as the main assault team arrives from Manesar. They would also be able to independently deal with terrorists depending on the magnitude of the situation.

Force Modernisation

The force has embarked on an ambitious modernization overdrive with the government providing sanction for the procurement of modern sniper rifles and corner shot rifles. The NSG has formulated a five-year plan which envisions raising a 2000 'new age' commando force, fully equipped and capable of operating on a self-contained basis. The plan has been made keeping in mind that a commando should be independent when he operates...his weapon, his body armour, communication devices, body wearable computer (akin to the ones used by the Navy Seals during the raid at Abbottabad) . Water and food should be with him on his body.[10] The proposed plan aimed at completion by 2015 would assimilate technology and knowledge from DRDO and artificial-intelligence organizations, as world over, expertise and transfer of technology for special forces operations are closely-guarded. With this technological leap, the NSG would acquire the capabilities to operate independently by land, air or sea. Modern equipment for bomb disposal and digital communication have been procured recently.

Training Exchange Programmes

Training exchange programmes with other special forces units of the world and agencies such as Los Angeles Police Department, Departments of Homeland Security and Defense and the FBI of USA have been undertaken. These programmes would provide a unique opportunity to acquire new knowledge and tactical expertise as also intelligence on conducting operations and on the modus operandi of terrorist organisations.

The NSG, in cooperation with the local police and members of the industry has carried out an assessment of the likely targets of terrorist attacks and VA/VPs in major cities. In addition to acquiring terrain knowledge and local intelligence, mock drills have also been carried out in some cases.

Critique

Role and Tasks

The NSG has two-distinct units, namely the SAG and the SRG. While the former is entirely comprised of Army officers and men, the latter has elements of the police and central police organisations. Officers from the Army, Police and CAPFs serve on deputation at the Force HQ and the Training Centre at Manesar. The primary role of the SAG is to undertake anti-hijacking and counter-terrorism operations. The personnel from the SRG battalions are deployed for VIP protection duties and for providing security cover during important national events such as the Republic Day Parade, etc. The two tasks, viz Special Counter-terrorist operations and VIP security are visibly distinct with the latter in a way denuding/undercutting the aura of an elite force.

Ideally, the NSG should concentrate primarily on the former responsibility as is the case with similar units worldwide. But one of the factors behind raising the NSG was to also improve VIP security in the aftermath of Primer Minister Indira Gandhi's assassination. Over the years, the MHA has reviewed the need to provide NSG cover to several VIPs under the Z category and the cover has been withdrawn, accordingly. Regardless, it is unlikely that the force can be completely absolved of this responsibility since VIPs continue to be a high-value target for terrorists and also due to the absence of a dedicated VIP protection force in the country. The Special Protection Group (SPG) is an elite VIP protection unit with very restricted numbers for protecting select VVIPs falling under the Z+ category. Also, it is highly undesirable to have a large commando force of 15,000 personnel for conducting specific operations only. It would denigrate the elite value of the commando unit and become similar to any other paramilitary force of the country. Therefore, the present arrangement with separation of units for different tasks is likely to continue with more Black Cats being withdrawn from VIP security duties to beef up the regional hubs and orient them towards carrying out other security tasks and support operations of the SAG.

Command and Control

The operational element of the NSG comprises Army personnel on deputation and the IG (Operations) is also a major-general rank officer from the Army. However, the DG NSG is an IPS cadre officer. There have been clamours in the past for the DG to be an Army officer. But these are minor issues which have been primarily resolved today and do not have much bearing on the functioning of the force.

The present structure with the NSG falling under the command and control of the MHA works well for the force as its primary responsibility is to operate in the Internal Security environment of the nation. It can optimally utilise the vast resources available with the MHA to its advantage. The expenditure is also covered under the Internal Security budget of the country thus sparing a burden on the Defence Budget. Heavy defence budgets are under scrutiny, internationally, particularly by our neighbours.

Being a paramilitary force, it also has the advantage of utilising a non-military force for difficult anti-terrorist operations which would have otherwise required the intervention of specialist military units. It is also best suited to overcome administrative, bureaucratic and procedural hurdles to operate anywhere in the urban landscape of the country and utilising the resources of police and civil agencies of the central and state governments. It also does not require special laws like the AFSPA to operate as its operations are covered under the NSG act.

Therefore, the NSG is a potent resource available with the Home Ministry to deal with specific and spectacular internal security challenges.

Operations

Anti-Hijacking

The NSG has one specially trained and equipped unit for undertaking anti-hijacking operations. In the past, the force has successfully dealt with at least two hijack situations, domestically. After the Kandahar hijacking episode, the mandate of anti-hijacking operations was expanded to include deployment of one or two personnel on board domestic carriers flying in sensitive sectors to deal with hijackers. These commandos known as 'Sky Marshalls', operate in civil clothes and merge themselves with ordinary passengers. They carry light weapons and other non-lethal weapons to immobilise a possible hijacker on board the aircraft.

The anti-hijacking drills are constantly revised and revalidated and frequent rehearsals and mock drills are conducted to test the alertness levels of the commandos. Although, globally, the number of hijacking incidents have gone down, the possibility of terrorists using aircrafts as their potent weapon has not dissipated, completely. The 9/11 hijacking introduced a completely new and lethal phenomenon of using aircrafts in suicidal missions. In fact, the unsuccessful attempt to blow himself up on an American aircraft by shoe bomber Raid the aborted attempted to bomb Glasgow airport and the foiled plot in UK to hijack multiple trans-atlantic airliners have reinforced the risk posed to aviation security by terrorists. In India, the Kandahar hijacking is still fresh in public memory which keeps the possibility alive of terrorists using an hijacked aircraft to garner maximum mileage and extracting their demands. Though pre-boarding security measures have been strengthened after the IC 814 hijacking incident, vulnerabilities and loopholes still exist especially at the airports of our neighbouring countries. Also, the possibility of an Indian aircraft being hijacked from an international destination and taken to a third country cannot be ruled out. The emergence of 'lone wolfs' or individual hijackers acting independently can also pose a challenge in the future.

In light of the above, the anti-hijacking unit of the NSG should re-visit their drills and tactical procedures to neutralise hijackers both at locations within and outside the country. Rapid deployment and the ability to stealthily storm an hijacked aircraft while it is still on ground are the vital pre-requisites in a delicate operation like anti-hijacking. The need to constantly acquire intelligence on the numbers, exact locations and weapon holdings of the terrorists is also essential. Technology should be exploited to procure equipment which can intercept communication of hijackers with their handlers, and other intrusive and eavesdropping gadgets which can provide a live picture of the situation inside the aircraft. The commandos should be equipped with light hand-held weapons with infra-red and telescopic sights for pin-point and accurate shooting to prevent casualties to hostage. Night Vision goggles and earpieces for inter-personnel communication have to be provided for squads undertaking such operations. The drills have to be immaculate and fine-tuned to quickly storm the aircraft and neutralise the hijackers. Such drills involving simultaneous entry by small squads of two or four commandos each require effective co-ordination and fire discipline on part of the commandos.

Therefore, anti-hijacking operations are highly sensitive where success and failure are often separated by a razor's edge. The force has to regularly study anti-hijacking operations all over the world to hone their skills and keep pace with tactics being employed by the terrorists.

Counter-terrorism

Other than ant-hijacking, the NSG is the primary Special Forces resource available with the Ministry of Home Affairs which can be rapidly deployed to deal with terrorist attacks of a large scale beyond the control of regular police forces. In the emerging security environment spectacular terrorist attacks can assume several forms. The number of terrorists may vary from two to 10 or even more. The mode of attack may also include light aircrafts or vessels progressing from using just motor vehicles or gaining entry by foot. The tactics and weapons used may also vary in different attacks.

Post 26/11, the target of terrorists has cast a long shadow over several iconic buildings of international and national repute and government buildings associated with national prestige. Several industrial houses, factories are also under the terror radar in addition to common public places such as modes of transportations and stations, market places, malls, religious congregations, etc. Given the high population density and surge in tier 2 cities in India, the number of targets for terrorists, where they can inflict high casualties and draw maximum mileage, have also increased.

Till 26/11, the specter of siege attacks were mainly limited to the insurgency prone areas of J&K. The attacks on the Red Fort, Parliament House, Akshardham, Raghunath Temple, Jammu Railway Station and IISC Bangalore were limited to not more than five suicide attackers being involved and the siege was not as prolonged as the 72 hour one in Mumbai.

Despite the increasing threat to our public infrastructure and government installations in cities, the precise nature of this threat can never be predicted in the absence of real-time hard intelligence. The timing and place of attack is deliberately calibrated from across the border according to the security environment and dynamics of international relations. The creation of the regional centres at Kolkata and Hyderabad and the four hubs at Kolkata, Hyderabad, Mumbai and Chennai would address the threat to urban infrastructure in these metropolitan cities and reduce the deployment time in case of an attack there or in tier two cities located, nearby.

The strike and support elements based at the hubs should have their own transport and communication resources to be able to rapidly deploy at the site of incident. Effective co-ordination must exist with local police and traffic officials to ensure grid-lock free movement of the commando force during an attack. The Regional hubs must receive intelligence available to the state police/intelligence agencies in addition to those circulating from central agencies. It should have an effective liaison with state anti-terror agencies so that if an attack takes place, all agencies are on the same grid and share intelligence and tactical knowledge. With prior interaction and developed contacts, the efficiency and time taken to deal with a crisis situation would be enhanced. Depending on the magnitude of the terrorist attack, the bulk of the strike element based in Manesar will have to be pressed into action. It needs to be seen to what extent and time-frame can the elements at the regional hubs to contain the situation. Simultaneously, the regional hubs must be reinforced with bomb detection and defusion elements. This calls for a further expansion of the numbers of the National Bomb Data Centre at Manesar so that the increased numbers can be stationed at the hubs.

Deployment in Counter-LWE Operations?

In addition to urban terrorism, the scope and lethality of red terror has undergone a drastic escalation in the recent years. The ambush on a CRPF patrol killing 76 of its personnel in March 2010 brought the scourge of Maoist terrorism to the centre-stage. Ever since, a debate has been raging in security circles on the prospects of employing the Army for operations against the Maoists as the situation becomes increasingly beyond the abilities of the CPOs and local police forces.. The Army's resources are already stretched due to prolonged deployments in counter-insurgency operations in J&K and the North East and also due to the increasing conventional threat from our neighbours. Also, special laws like the Disturbed Areas Act and AFSPA have to be brought in before employing the Army. As the spread of Naxal terror encompassed a substantial portion of the hinterland, the backlash of using Army against our own people automatically becomes a major inhibiting factor.

In this backdrop, the NSG has been re-orienting its tasking towards employment in rural insurgencies like Maoist terrorism as well. With a little tweaking and re-equipping, the strike battalions would be ready for employment in the thick jungle terrain of the Maoist hinterland. The SAG units have Army soldiers with enough CI experience from J&K to the North East. The employment of NSG would also negate the possibility of using the Army and give unnecessary filip to the propaganda mills. There will be no need to pass special laws like the AFSPA.

But the objective of employing Special Forces in countering the maoist menace should be only to create shock and awe. The commandos should only be used in specific intelligence-based operations against well entrenched hideouts and cause attrition of the Maoist leadership. The commando tactics such as insertion by air or by slithering down helicopters, stealthy small team actions inside dense jungles and deep penetration of maoist hot beds would provide an upper hand to the security forces and take the maoists by surprise. They would be increasingly kept on the run and impose a fear psychosis among the cadres. Besides keeping the leadership unhinged and unbalanced. It would also boost the morale of security forces deployed in anti-naxalite operations.

The employment of commandos has to be selective and limited in nature. Prolonged employment would take away the shock value and using them for regular operations like laying ambushes, etc for a prolonged period would be highly detrimental. In this the NSG should also take a leaf out of its own experience during the Punjab insurgency. Nevertheless, the NSG is an effective response option available with the government for selective operations against high profile Maoist targets. The NSG can operate from secret bases in the Naxal areas for a limited period and eventually fall back upon its regular locations. The Air Force assets can be utilised for insertion and exit iperations.

Rapid Deployment and Streamlining Procedures

In all NSG operations, the primary handicap has been the time taken to reach the place of incident from its base near New Delhi. The creation of regional hubs has addressed this lacuna to a certain extent but given that the assault force may still have to be reinforced from Manesar, there is a need to further address this issue. For one, an effective traffic plan must be in place to transport the commandos from Manesar to the airport at Palam in New Delhi. A Standard Operating Procedure must be in place with built-in direct communication between NSG and local and traffic police of Delhi and Gurgaon. Similar arrangements have to be put in place at the dis-embarking destination. Helicopters can also be stationed at Manesar to further reduce the time taken to reach the airport. But this may not be a cost effective method given the number of helicopters that may be required to ferry troops and equipment and time will still be spent in flying the helicopters to Manesar and then to the airport. Embarkation and dis-embarkation from the helicopters will take its own time.

The security bureaucracy also imposes its own restraint in reacting quickly to a situation. A lot of time is spent between obtaining the request for employment coming from the state governments and the final authorisation from the Home Ministry. Therefore, the DG NSG should be suitably empowered to ready his forces for deployment on the basis of an evolving situation and the likelihood of the requisition of NSG's employment. Although the Centre has now authorised the NSG DG and IG to re-quistion civilian aircrafts from domestic carriers to transport troops, it would be better that transport assets of the Indian Air Force are exclusively stationed at Palam airport for the NSG. Such assets should not be diverted for VIP duties or other tasks.

Critique

- The NSG is a lethal and elite commando force of the country to deal with special and extra-ordinary situations emerging in the urban landscape of the country. With right-sizing of forces and equipping with all the latest weaponry and equipment, the potency of the force is being further enhanced.
- The strike component of the NSG should not be expanded beyond a certain number of say 3000 to maintain the high training equipping and operating standards as also the exclusivity or elite nature of the force. Deputation of personnel from the Army ensures that seasoned and well experienced officers and men are available for the dedicated tasks required to be performed by the unit.
- Given the volatile security situation in our immediate neighbourhood and the phenomenon of urban terrorism the scope for deployment of special forces like the NSG for internal security situations remain high. This aspect will acquire greater import post the US drawdown in Afghanistan and likely increase in terrorist threat. Though the frequency and nature of such interventions cannot be predicted, it is expected to remain low for the next one to two years, at least. Also, given the stabilising security environments in J&K and the North East and due to the availability of ample Special Forces and Infantry resources of the Army, the employment of NSG in operations there is unlikely. Therefore, it may not be an entirely bad proposition to utilise the force for selective operations against the Maoists. This would keep the force relevant and

provide an opportunity for realistic testing and evaluation of its own skills.

- The role of VIP security has to be further reduced over a period of time so that the support element of the NSG can be strengthened. Is there a case for raising a separate force for providing VIP security ? This again needs to be viewed in the light of the number of interventions the NSG may be involved in the future. Also, common training and other facilities makes the two elements of NSG mutually inter-dependent on each other.
- There is a need to streamline procedures to enable effective and quick deployment of the NSG as it is a rapid response force to avoid delays. Rapid deployment can be achieved with the available resources integral to the Home Ministry and air assets of the Air Force which can be made available in no time. There may not be a case for the NSG to have a separate air wing of its own though the same can be looked into.
- The SAG has to refine its tactical skills employed for operating in an urban environment where minimising civilian casualty and preventing collateral damage are critical requirements. The tactics of smoking the terrorists out as employed in an insurgency environment cannot be replicated in cities where the time taken to end a siege only provides more publicity to the terrorists. Therefore, the crack commandos should have the right weapons and equipment to complement swift and decisive tactical maneuvers with precision firing to neutralise the terrorists. This no doubt imposes a high-degree of risk to personal safety but then these are high-value operations where the national prestige is at stake. The commandos possess the requisite room-intervention and hostage rescue capabilities but the leadership has to be bold enough to employ such tactics rather than be risk averse by executing deliberate operations which is time consuming and fire power predominant.

NOTES

1. Giriraj Shah, Paramilitary Forces of India, pp. 240-248.
2. Official website of the NSG, www.nsg.gov.in
3. Bhashyam Kasturi, Vital Stats, Force, January 2012.
4. Ibid (3) above
5. Ibid (1) above.
6. Ibid.
7. Ibid
8. Ibid
9. Ibid
10. Counter-Terrorism: NSG to raise new-age commandos, *The Tribune*, 16 October 2011, http://www.tribuneindia.com/2011/20111017/haryana.htm#1

6

Indo-Tibetan Border Police (ITBP)

Indo-Tibetan Border Police Force was raised on 24 October 1962 following the Chinese aggression in NEFA and Ladakh. It was raised as an integrated guerrilla cum-Intelligence-cum-fighting force of the Union. The force was to indoctrinate and train the local population for resistance against the enemy in border areas.[1] The primary role of the force is to guard the Indo-Tibet border areas. Initially, four battalions (two each in Himachal Pradesh and Uttar Pradesh) were raised. They were accorded sanction under the CRP Act of 1949 and the CRP rules of 1955. The ITBPF Act was finally passed by the Parliament in the year 1992. The responsibility for the raising and training of the force was entrusted to the Director Intelligence Bureau (IB). Following this, a Joint Director of the IB was appointed the Special DG of ITBP.[2]

Today, the ITBPF is deployed in guarding our Northern Borders from Karakoram Pass in Ladakh to Jarep La in Arunachal Pradesh. The deployment along the 3,488 Km Sino-Indian Border is often stretched in penny packet deployments of section and platoon strength. The nature of deployment generally implies prevention and control of trans-border crimes, detection and prevention of infiltration and border violations, handling minor skirmishes and incursions. The function of the ITBP is to maintain vigil on the Northern Borders and promote a sense of security among the local populace. The defence of the country is primarily the task of the Defence Forces and the ITBPF will be in supporting role.[3] The operational commitment of the force encompasses counter-insurgency operations in J&K and the Naxal affected areas, internal security duties and protection of banks and some threatened VIPs. Currently, five battalions of the force are deployed for anti-Naxalite operations. The ITBP can be requisitioned by the Home Ministry to restore and preserve order in any area in the event of a disturbance.

Organisational Structure

The force is led by a DG rank officer who is supported by Addl DGs, IGs and DIGs. The force is divided into four operational frontiers and one training and L&C zone led by an IG rank officer. The frontiers are further divided into sectors which in turn control the battalions on the ground.

The six ITBP Frontier HQs are located at:

- Northern Frontier – Dehradun
- North West Frontier – Chandigarh
- Eastern Frontier – Shillong
- Special Frontier – New Delhi
- Training Zone – New Delhi
- L&C Zone – New Delhi

The Sector HQs are located at:

Dehradun	Bareilly	Ladakh—Leh	Shimla
Amritsar	Delhi	Itanagar	Gangtok
Tezpur	Bhubaneshwar	Lucknow	Almora
L&C Sector—Chandigarh			

Org Structure at Bn Level

An ITBP Battalion is led by a Commandant and has six companies plus an administration and support company. The sanctioned strength of an ITBP battalions is 1450.

BN
(Shillong)
↓

↓	↓	↓
ADM COY (Dy/Asst Comdt)	6 × COY (Dy/Asst Comdt)	SP COY (Dy/Asst Comdt)

↓
3 × PLs
(Inspector/Sub Inspector)

Recruitment

Originally, each ITBP battalion wes to consist of a company of Tibetans. They were consolidated into a single battalion and later discharged to the SFF.[4] ITBP battalions were raised by recruiting Kumaonis and Garhwalis for the UP Sector, Sikhs, Jats and Dogras for the HP Sector, Assam tribals for NEFA and East Pakistan refugees for North Assam. In the year 1976, a large number of Emergency Commissioned Officers from the Army were inducted into the ITBP. This increased the operational efficiency of the units.[5]

Training

ITBP's major training centre was raised in 1976 in Mussorie. It imparts training to officers, sub officers and holds promotional courses. The ITBP Academy has been given the status of 'Centre of Excellence' by the Government and is now on the path of modernisation of its training infrastructure.

The ITBP has recently established a CIJW School at an altitude of 6000 ft at Mahidanda in Uttarkashi district of Uttarakhand.

The Basic Training Academy of the ITBP is located at Bhanu in Panchkula district of Haryana. Basic Training Centre chisels and shapes new entrants at the levels of Constables and Head Constables and turns them into a combat soldier capable of performing border management tasks as well multidimensional tasks like Counter Insurgency Operations and Internal Security. The Training Centre has specialised in the training of 'Instructors' in Drill, Weapons, PT and Judo and therefore also attracts trainees from State and Central Police Forces. It also conducts in-service training of section level commanders, besides having a separate wing for training of dogs and horses and its handlers and riders.[6]

Mountaineering and Skiing Institute, a premier Institution of the country on Mountaineering and Skiing was established in 1973 as a Winter Craft Wing of the Force. In 1990 it was re-christened as Mountaineering and Skiing Institute. The Mountaineering and Skiing Institute imparts specialised training to the members of the Force in Mountaineering, Skiing, Survival in High Altitude, Rescue Operations and River Rafting. Specialisation of the Institute in these disciplines attracts trainees from Central and State Police Forces, including Defence Forces. It is a matter of pride that the Institute conducts pre-Antarctica induction training for the Indian Expedition in Snow/Ice Craft and Survival Techniques in High Altitude.[7]

The training for ITBP lays special emphasis on high altitude warfare and survival training skills keeping in view the deployment zone of the force. These include[8]:

- Expert use of weapons.
- Commando operations and clandestine tactical mission including clandestine air insertion by day or night, catches, demolition including improvisation in field of explosives, their deification/neutralisation.
- Rock climbing, mountaineering, skiing and snow craft.
- 'Living off the land' including the knowledge of survival techniques in snow bound mountains and high altitudes.

The personnel are also extensively trained to[9] :

- Meet the challenges of surprise attack and infiltration taking advantage of the terrain.
- Carry out guerrilla role/act as stay-behind parties in case any part of

our territory is over run by the enemy or when defenses are by – passed by the enemy.

- Carry complimentary role to the Army on the outbreak of hostilities after attriting the first onslaughts of the enemy forces to gain time for our main defences in battle preparation and provide early warning in time, strength and direction of attack/ threat line.

Equipping Profile

The 5.56 mm INSAS Rifle is the standard issue of ITBP battalions. Other weapons include:

1 × 5.56/7.62 LMG per section
1 × 51 mm Mortar per platoon
8 × MMGs per battalion
1 section of (6 × 81 mm Mortars)
1-2 × 84 RL per Bn
1-2 × UBGL per Bn

Role and Tasks

In the year 1974, a working paper was submitted to the Government following which a reorganization of the force took place. During this period 96 per cent temporary posts manned by the ITBP were converted into permanent ones.[10] The re-organisation was implemented in 1978 and additional ITBP battalions were raised. In addition to re-structuring the training institutes and battalions, four specialist battalions for telecommunication, service and supply group, transport and support were created. The role of the force was clearly defined.

The Committee of Secretaries, Government of India outlines the various roles of the ITBP:

(a) To keep vigil on ingress routes and prevent border violations in co-ordination with other security forces.
(b) To provide a sense of security to the population living in border areas.
(c) To control trans-border traffic, crimes (including smuggling) and unauthorised civilian ingress and egress, in co-ordination with the Intelligence Bureau (IB).
(d) To provide protection and all facilities to the IB to enable it to carry out, its assigned tasks, both in peace and war.
(e) To function under the operational control of the Army as may be required in sensitive areas.
(f) To function in a similar role to that of the BSF in a war situation.

The war time role of the ITBPF is as enumerated below.

(a) Holding ground in less threatened Sectors so long as the main attack does not develop in that particular sector and it is felt that the local situation is within the capability of the ITBPF to deal with. The ITBPF units can continue to remain deployed in a particular sector even in a war situation, to release the Army for offensive tasks. In the event of a major attack developing which is not within the capacity of the ITBPF to deal with, the Army can be expected to either reinforce the ITBPF with Artillery or other support, or relieve the ITBPF from its role in a particular sector.

(b) Protection of vital installations particularly airfields against enemy commandos/para troopers or raid. This role can be entrusted to the ITBPF units, which are placed under the Army's operational control.
(c) Providing extensions to the flanks of main defence line, by holding strong points in conjunction with other units.
(d) Limited aggressive action against Para-military or irregular Forces of the enemy within the overall plan of the Armed Forces.
(e) Performing special tasks connected with intelligence, including raids-These are the tasks, which might be entrusted to ITBPF units by the Army in a war situation according to local necessity. It would, however, be expected that the state of training and equipment of the particular ITBPF units would be kept in view in assessing their adequacy for the tasks.
(f) Acting as guides in an area of responsibility where routes are known—this is a task, which the ITBPF should be able to perform.
(g) Maintenance of law and order in enemy territory administered under the control of the Army—The ITBF could be used to supplement the civil police in a situation where civil police is not readily available.
(h) Provision of escorts.
(i) Guarding of prisoners of war camps.
(j) Assistance in control of refugees.
(k) Anti-infiltration duties in specified tasks: this is an important responsibility which will have to be performed by security forces.

Achievements

- The ITBP is a multi-dimensional force. Presently, the battalions of ITBP are deployed on Border Guarding duties from Karakoram Pass in Ladakh to Jarep La in Arunachal Pradesh covering 3488 Km on the Indo-Tibet border. The ITBP holds posts ranging from an altitude of 9000 to 18500 ft in the Himalayan region. Being a mountain trained force, its officers and men are professionally trained mountaineers and skiers. The border posts manned by ITBP are exposed to high velocity storms, snow blizzards, avalanches and landslides, besides the hazards of high altitude and extreme cold, where temperature dips up to minus 40 degree

Celsius. The force conducts long and short range patrols to keep an effective vigil on inaccessible and unmanned areas on the border and LAC. To maintain optimum operational efficiency of troops, periodical tactical exercises are conducted independently as well as jointly with Army. Some of the important exercises conducted were 'Ex Abyas', Ex Tarang', 'Ex Swabhiman' and 'Ex Gaurav'.

- ITBPF battalions are also deployed on CI Ops/IS/VIP security duties at Chamba-Doda border in J&K and with VIPs in Delhi and Srinagar.
- The ITBP battalions played a limited role in Rajouri, Poonch and Reasi areas of J&K during the 1965 war. They were instrumental in the defence of Gool Police station and instilling a sense of confidence among the population of the border districts of Rajouri and Poonch during the war.
- During the peak of the Punjab insurgency in Punjab, six ITBP battalions were guarding as many as 169 branches of banks having currency chest.
- The ITBP is responsible for the conduct of the Annual Mansarovar Kailash Yatra since 1981. It provides communication, security and medical cover to the Yatris from Gunji to Liplulekh pass in Uttarakhand. It is also deployed for protection of yatra routes during the Amarnath Yatra in Jammu and Kashmir.
- The ITBP was deployed for securing the IX Asian Games in Delhi in 1982. The force is regularly engaged for the peaceful conduct of assembly and general elections in the country.
- ITBP is providing outer perimeter security to the Rashtrapati Bhavan in New Delhi. ITBP Companies have also been engaged in protecting the Indian Embassy in Colombo (Sri Lanka). Presently, ITBP Commandos are providing security to the Embassy of India in Kabul, Afghanistan and the Indian consulates at Jalalabad and Kandahar since November 2002. Besides, two companies of ITBP provided security for BRO workers engaged in the construction of the Delaram-Zarang road in Western Afghanistan since July 2004.
- ITBP has also excelled in UN Peace Keeping Operations. The force personnel have been deployed in Angola, Namibia, Bosnia & Herzegovina, Mozambique and Kosovo. Presently, one company of ITBP is deployed in UN Mission in Congo since November 2005. A National Centre for UNCIVPOL training has been setup at ITBP Camp, Tigri, New Delhi for providing systematic training to Indian Police officers for deployment in UN Missions.
- As the force is extensively deployed in the Himalayan region, the force is the first responders for disaster relief operations. It has established eight Regional Response Centres in Himachal Pradesh, Uttarakhand and North East. It also trains personnel for Radiological and Chemical/

biological emergencies. It has established a National Centre for Training in Search, Rescue and Disaster response at Bhanu, Haryana. ITBP performed commendably in providing rescue and relief during the Alaknanda tragedy in the Chamoli district of Uttarakhand in 1970, the earthquake in the remote areas of Himachal Pradesh in 1975, Bhagirathi floods in 1978, missing Army Patrol in a blizzard in Ladakh in 1981, havoc caused by the avalanche in Lahaul and Spiti in 1979.[11] It was also among the first to respond during the flash floods in Leh in August 2010 and the Sikkim earthquake in September 2011.

- The force has excelled in mountaineering, adventure sports and dare-devilry. It has successfully scaled more than 158 Peaks in the Himalayan Region including three on Mount Everest. Its skiers have been national champions, who have done India proud in the Winter Olympics. Its river rafters have created international records in rafting through the turbulent white waters of the mighty Brahmaputra, the Ganges and the Indus. It was the first CPMF Contingent to win the Best Marching Contingent Award at the Republic Day Parade in 1998, 1999, 2000 and 2011.

Critique

- The ITBP is performing its task as the designated border guarding force for the Indo-Tibet border since its inception in October 1962. But, unlike the bulk of the deployment of the BSF on the Indo-Pak border in the West, the deployment along the Northern Borders with Tibet has a sizable deployment of the Army due to the undecided nature of the border. Due to the large size of the border (3,488 km) and volatile nature of the boundary dispute with China, it is not possible for a Paramilitary force to independently guard the border just as the BSF mans the International Border between India and Pakistan. Also, the strength of the force is not large enough to cover all the passes and gaps along the IB and LAC with Tibet and Xinjiang. Post the 1962 border conflict with China, it was a deliberate government policy to maintain a forward posture of paramilitary forces (ITBP) on the IB with China and keep the Army in the rear. It was feared that a forward deployment of the Army would antagonise the Chinese and lead to further tensions with them.
- The ITBP is majorly deployed along the IB in the Middle Sector with Tibet in the states of Himachal Pradesh and Uttarakhand. Due to the terrain configuration and inclement weather conditions, the ITBP is deployed in penny packets along the IB. The distance between two pickets is quite extensive at places. Adhering to the provisions of the Border Peace and Tranquility Agreement (BPTA) between India and

China and other Confidence Building Measures (CBMs), there is no eyeball to eyeball deployment between the Border Defence Regiments of the PLA and the ITBP. Both sides send out long range patrols to maintain surveillance along the border. On the Indian side, the deployment of the ITBP at places is quite far-removed from the boundary due to limitations imposed by terrain and non-existence of developed lines of communications. Under these conditions and deployment a large number of border passes remain unheld during peace time. The deployment of ITBP thins out along the Tibetan border in the states of Jammu & Kashmir (Eastern Ladakh), Sikkim and Arunachal Pradesh. In these sectors the Army is majorly deployed with isolated pickets manned by ITBP in between.

- The ITBP is performing a commendable job of border-guarding in a high altitude region under difficult operating conditions. A lack of infrastructure development since 1962 imposes further stress on keeping the logistics and supply lines open to its forces. The MHA has sanctioned a sum of Rs. 1,937.00 crore for constructing 27 new roads to link ITBP BOPs in the states of J&K, Himachal Pradesh, Uttarakhand, Sikkim and Arunachal Pradesh. The 804 Km of ITBP roads would enhance the operational capability of the force along the Indo-Tibet border.[12] The ITBP personnel are well trained and equipped for performing their job in the Himalayan region. The men are best suited for that geographical area and the force has gained enough experience and expertise in conducting operations in a harsh mountainous region over the last four decades. ITBP is among a select lot of armed forces which has remained deployed in altitudes upwards of 15,000 ft for such a long period on a permanent basis. The ITBP personnel, therefore, possess adequate mountain warfare and survival skills to endure in operations at such high altitudes. They would prove to be a valuable asset to the Army in carrying out its operational tasks and providing intelligence in the event of a conflict or heightened state of deployment.
- In the light of the dynamic and emerging security situation along the Northern frontiers after China's massive and rapid military infrastructure development in the Tibet Autonomous Region (TAR), there is a need for building greater inter-operability between the ITBP and Army both at the strategic and tactical levels. The ITBP is a potent force available on the ground to augment and enable the Army's expanding deployment profile all along the boundary with Tibet. Conducting regular tactical exercises and firing practices with local Army units and sub-units, the potency and training capabilities of the ITBP should be further enhanced.
- As per the description of their war-time tasks, the ITBP units can be

split into smaller platoons and sections to hold certain un-held passes and cover infiltration routes. They can also act as guides and pathfinders for offensive Army formations. ITBP elements can be re-grouped to augment the Army's rear area guarding roles and deployed for guarding prisoner of war camps, VA/VPs, airfields and drop zones, etc. They can be deployed for keeping the lines of communications open during hostilities and fetching supplies for Army units deployed in the forward zones. The ITBP companies/platoons should be expected to carry out tasks within the battle plans of an Infantry battalion or Brigade.

- Theoretically, it was thought that the ITBP should man the entire frontage with Tibet as the PLA's paramilitary Border Guarding units are deployed on the other side and not their Army. But the PLA's rapid mobilisation capabilities coupled with large pockets of dispute and an un-resolved nature of the border, India has been forced to maintain the Army's presence as the first-line of defence along majority of the border. Also, as has been mentioned previously, the ITBP does not possess the requisite numbers and resources to maintain presence all along the border from the Karakoram Pass in Ladakh to Jarep La in Arunachal Pradesh.

  This problem is further manifested by certain incidents in the late 1990s where PLA troops entered into confrontations with ITBP personnel in Arunachal Pradesh. A few years back, another experiment to replace an Army Battalion with an ITBP one from a particular sector back-fired when PLA troops increased their incursions into that sector following the withdrawal of the Army battalion. Such incidents, therefore, have reinforced the need of not lowering the guard against an increasingly assertive and belligerent PLA.

- In pursuance of its primary border-guarding task along the Indo-Tibet frontier and during peace-time and expected tasks in support of the Army in conflict scenarios, the ITBP should be exclusively deployed in that theatre and concentrate on its primary task only. The force personnel should be withdrawn from conducting other tasks such as protecting VIPs, deployment in the protection of some Indian embassies and assets abroad, deployment for conduct of elections, deployment for anti-Naxal operations and other such tasks. The rotation of ITBP personnel and battalions for rest and recuperation should be more frequent. The battalions or companies should be rotated between their forward deployment posture and training centres or sector HQs in the foothills. These stations at the foothills should be developed as peace-stations for ITBP personnel with adequate facilities for re-creation and living quarters for their family members, etc.

  The above aspects and the emerging security environment along the

Sino-Indian border highlight the need to take a re-look at the deployment pattern of the ITBP and calls for building greater synergy with the Army. Even during peace time, the ITBP is dependent on the Army's lines of communications and logistics support in certain sectors. The role and tasks of the ITBP are integrated into the overall battle plans of the Indian Army during hostilities. But in keeping with the uncertain nature and timing of breakout of hostilities, it would be prudent to keep the ITBP units under the operational control of the Army even during peace time. Some analysts have suggested bringing the ITBP under the complete control of the Army. But given the turf wars and other factors, such an arrangement is neither feasible nor desirable.

NOTES

1. Giriraj Shah, Paramilitary Forces of India, p. 209.
2. Ibid.
3. Role and Tasks of ITBPF (Chapter 1).
4. Ibid (1) above, pp. 210.
5. Ibid (4) above.
6. Official website of the ITBP, accessed at http://www.itbp.gov.in/btc.htm
7. Ibid (6) above, accessed at http://www.itbp.gov.in/msi.htm
8. Ibid (1) above, pp. 213.
9. Ibid (8) above.
10. Ibid (1) above, pp. 211.
11. Ibid (1) above, pp. 218.
12. Ministry of Home Affairs, Outcome Budget 2011-12, accessed on 31 March 2012 at http://mha.nic.in/pdfs/OB(E)2011-12.pdf

7

Border Security Force (BSF)

Origin

Even two decades after India's independence, the defence of the country's international borders during peace time was undertaken by Armed Police Battalions of the respective states. This was a primarily ad-hoc arrangement and relied on the setting up of isolated border posts and patrolling undertaken by the Armed Police. In April, 1965, Pakistan captured a few areas in the Rann of Kutch in Gujarat. This exposed the vulnerabilities of the existing system of border security. An emergency committee of the Cabinet recommended setting up of a more robust Border security unit under the control of the Central Government. By this time, Pakistan had re-organised its Border guarding forces more or less on the lines of the Army.[1]

On 1 December 1965, BSF took over the responsibility of guarding the country's international borders. 25 Armed Police battalions of Gujarat, Rajasthan, Punjab and Madhya Pradesh were amalgamated to form the BSF.[2] These battalions were organised on the pattern of the Army in terms of organisation, training, weapons and equipment holdings. Some of these battalions had fought gallantly in the skirmishes before the 1965 war and also during the war. The BSF benefitted from absorbing nearly 448 Emergency Commissioned Officers from the Army.[3] The leadership provided by these officers was instrumental in the shaping and orientation of the BSF in the initial years. Two sector HQs for the Western and Eastern sectors were raised. The Sub-Sectors were located at Jalandhar, Jodhpur, Jammu, Srinagar, Bandipora, Kadamtala and Shillong. Concurrently, 12 reserve battalions of the BSF were raised and the five India Reserve Battalions of the time were amalgamated into the BSF.[4]

Organisation

The Border Security Force is one of the largest paramilitary units of the world and operates under the control of the Ministry of Home Affairs.

Currently the force has 2,40,000 personnel and is organised into 168 battalions.[5]

The force operates under the Director General with its Force HQ in Delhi. The primary branches of the Directorate General of the Border Security Force are headed by an IG rank officer. These are:

- Operations
- Administration
- Provisioning
- Communication
- Accounts
- Training

The BSF Frontier HQs are located at:

- Kashmir Frontier: Srinagar
- Jammu Frontier : Jammu
- Punjab Frontier: Jalandhar
- West Bengal Frontier: Kolkata
- Assam Frontier: Shillong (responsible for BSF battalions in Assam, Meghalya and Mizoram)
- Tripura Frontier: Agartala (responsible for BSF battalions in Tripura, Manipur and Nagaland)

The Frontier HQs are commanded by an IG rank officer and has 2 or more sector HQs headed by a DIG rank officer. Every BSF Sector has three to six battalions under its command.

Organisational structure at Battalion level

BN
↓
HQ COY | 7 × SERVICE COYs

The sanctioned strength of a BSF battalion is 1154 personnel. Each battalion has a HQ + 7 Service Companies. The sanctioned strength of a Company is 137.

The BSF also has seven Regiments of Artillery made up of 105 IFGs (Indian Field Gun).

Equipping Profile

5.56 mm INSAS Rifle – standard issue.

2 × 5.56/7.62 LMG per section

1 × 51 mm Mortar per platoon
8 × MMGs per battalion
1 section of (6 × 81 mm Mortars)
1-2 × 84 RL per Bn
1-2 × UBGL per Bn
Some BSF BOPs also have RCL (recoiless) anti-tank guns.

Role and Tasks[6]

BSF is the designated border guarding force for the Indo-Pakistan and Indo-Bangladesh border.

The role of the BSF is:

(a) To promote a sense of security among the people living along the borders; and
(b) To prevent trans-border crimes, unauthorised entry and exit from India, smuggling and other illegal activities.

The peace and war time tasks of the force are:

(a) Peace Time

(i) Promote a sense of security amongst people living in the border areas by providing protection to life and property against depredation from across the border.
(ii) Prevent smuggling and infiltration as also to deal with minor intrusions and incidents of firing from across the border.

(b) War Time

(i) Perform duties within the overall plan of Army formations.
(ii) Holding ground in less threatened sectors.
(ii) Provide guides and escorts.
(iii) Protecting vital installations, VAs/VPs.
(iv) Anti-infiltration duties.
(v) Assistance in control of refugees.[7]

In addition, the Union Government can use the force for various internal security duties from time to time. Presently, 12 battalions of the BSF are deployed for anti-naxal operations in the states of Chhattisgarh and Orissa.

Deployment

The BSF has the onerous task of guarding vast frontage of the country's international borders with Pakistan in the West and Bangladesh in the East. The length of the boundary along which the force is deployed in various sectors in given below.

(a) Indo-Pak Border

(i) Jammu & Kashmir: 214 Km.
(ii) Punjab: 547 Km.
(iii) Rajasthan: 1035 Km.
(iv) Gujarat: 512 Km.

(b) Indo-Bangladesh Border

(i) West Bengal: 2188 Km.
(ii) Assam: 270 Km.
(iii) Meghalaya: 421 Km.
(iv) Tripura: 861 Km.
(v) Mizoram: 306 Km.

Legal Powers

To perform its tasks effectively, the BSF has been given legal powers under the Cr.PC., Customs Act, 1962, Passport Act, 1967, Dangerous Drugs Act, 1930 and Opium Act, 1978. It can exercise jurisdiction over these provisions within a belt of 80 km in Gujarat, 50 Km in Rajasthan and 15 Km in the states of Punjab, West Bengal and Assam.

Training[8]

Border Security Force, one of the largest Para-Military forces in the World, is a versatile force, which is responsible for guarding round the clock, vast and volatile borders not only against trans-border criminals but also against heavily armed trans-border terrorism as well. Though guarding the borders is the prime commitment, security forces remain heavily and decisively involved in the interior as well in combating insurgency and militancy in various parts of the country. Because of its friendly and human face, BSF remains the much sought after force for combating and containing serious law and order situations in the trouble prone States. And in case of hot War, BSF works as a force multiplier and contributes substantially towards over all war efforts of the nation as a credible front line Force.

By virtue of this unique dual role, the Border-men more commonly known as "PRAHARI" is required to be a perfect policeman during peace and a professional soldier during War. Management of borders (International Border), restoration of law and order situation in the interior and fighting a conventional/ unconventional War are the three challenging assignments which a border-man is required to carryout. In short, these fundamental essentials make the "Training Trilogy" of BSF. Professional proficiency of any Force is directly related to the standard of training of that Force and it is primarily due to this commitment that BSF refuses to compromise on its training assignments irrespective of handicaps and heavy orders. BSF believes in sweating during peace to ensure that it does not bleed during war or war like situation.

Major Training Institutions

For organising and carrying out "Basic Fundamental" training and "In Service Professional Training", we have three (03) main training Institutions, (05) Special Training Schools and (11) STCs/BTCs spread across the Country. Three main training Institutions are:

(i) BSF Academy Tekanpur is situated on Gwalior-Jhansi Highway at a distance of 30 Kms. from Gwalior (MP). This is the alma mater of border-men.

(ii) Training Centre and School (School of Excellence for Counter Insurgency and Commando Type Specialised Training) is located at Meru, 12 Kms. off Hazaribagh town. Meru Camp Hazaribagh is the craddle of specialised type training like Commando and counter insurgency.

(iii) Central School of Weapons And Tactics (School of Excellence for Small Arms) is located on the out-skirts of Indore on Bijasan Road, Here, we refine and sharpen the shooting skills of our 'PRAHARIES'.

Training Institutions for Special Training

Besides above mentioned three training institutions there are five training schools for special training:

(a) Central School of Motor Transport (CSMT) Gwalior

In order to maintain a high standard of functional efficiency and road worthiness of MT fleet in the Force, the Central School of Motor Transport popularly known as CSMT, was set up at Sagar (MP) in Jan'1963. Initially the School was under the supervision of MP Police and was taken over by BSF in Feb'71. This school continued to function at Sagar upto 18/11/1979 before shifting to its present location in Tekanpur. Spread over an area of 60 acres, this school of Motor Transport has developed as a prestigious Institution. School has been recognised as a "Centre of Excellence" by the Ministry of Home Affairs. Motor Training imparted in CSMT includes:

(i) Driving and Maintenance course.

(ii) Motor Vehicle mechanic course.

(iii) Auto Electrician course.

(iv) Fleet Management course (Officers)

(v) BSF Recovery driver course.

(b) National Training Centre For Dogs (NTCD) Gwalior

The National Training Centre for Dogs (NTCD) is a premier Training Institution run by BSF on behalf of MHA. The NTCD breeds service dogs, trains dogs and their handlers for BSF, other Central Police Organisation and State Police Organisations. The dogs are trained in basic obedience, narcotics and explosive detection, tracking, guard duties and patrolling. The dogs trained by NTCD have an enviable record of service. Some of the achievement at a glance:-

(i) "HEARO" proud product of NTCD, ensured a seizure of more than Rs.100 crores for Bombay Customs.

(ii) "SONU", another proud product of NTCD, effected a seizure of 2.2 crores of high-grade hashish in 1997 at Delhi Airport.

(iii) Similarly 'SUKKA' seized 14 kgs of high-grade hashish valued of Rs.1.40 crores for Delhi Customs.

(iv) "FANTA" was instrumental in detecting 10 Kgs of RDX during Amarnath Yatra in 1993. Thus played a major role in averting what could have led to a major tragedy.

(c) Signal Training School-I Tigri Camp New Delhi

The Border Security Force, Signal Training School-I is located at Tigri Camp, New Delhi adjacent to Khanpur on M B Road.

(d) Signal Training School-Ii Yelahanka (Bangalore)

The STS-II BSF is located on Chaklate-Bangalore road near Yelahanka, 21 Kms off Bangalore town.

(e) 'G' Training School New Delhi

The BSF 'G' Training School is located at block 'C', Ist floor, Pushpa Bhawan (Madangir) in South Delhi.

Subsidiary Training Centres and Basic Training Centres

In addition to main Training Institutions, BSF has (11) Subsidiary Training Centres/Basic Training Centres. Basically these are the breeding and training centres for various field formations. Coverage and establishments in 2 tiers:-

(a) STCs Covering Border States

- STC BSF Hamhama (Kashmir)
- STC BSF Udhampur (Jammu)
- STC BSF Kharka Camp (Punjab)
- STC BSF Jodhpur (Rajasthan)
- STC BSF Baikunthpur, Siliguri (Bengal)
- STC BSF Chura Chandpur, Manipur (Assam, Manipur, Meghalaya and Nagaland)

(b) STCs/BTCs covering Hinterland

- STC BSF Tekanpur (Gwalior)
- STC BSF Yelahanka (Bangalore)
- STC BSF Hazaribagh (Jharkhand)
- BTC BSF Hazaribagh (Jharkhand)
- BTC BSF Indore (MP)

These are the nodal training Centres where 400-500 recruits always remain under training, thus training approximately 5000 recruits every year.

Past Operations

During the 1965 War, the erstwhile Armed Police Battalions performed certain rear areas protection tasks in the state of Jammu & Kashmir. Eight such battalions were responsible for protecting vital lines of communication and bridges from the Pakistani infiltrators. Notable among these were defending Shamsa Bridge on Sonamarg-Drass road and Wayne bridge in Kupwara. 2nd Battalion of the Punjab Armed Police suffered casualties in action with the infiltrators in Kargil. 1st Battalion of the Punjab Armed Police fought in the RS Pura sector and received two gallantry awards. 29th Battalion of the Punjab Armed Police received seven gallantry awards during fighting at the Hussainiwala sector in Punjab. Thus, the newly embodied BSF battalions in December 1965 had a rich repository of combat experience.

1971 War

In the western sector, BSF battalions were responsible for holding ground against enemy advances particularly in Tulel valley of Gurez sector. It repulsed the infiltrators at Budil Pir Pass and Rupi Pass, both situated at altitudes over 15,000 ft. on 3/4 December 1971.

In Punjab, BSF battalions not only bore the initial brunt of the Pakistani attack but were instrumental in capturing some enemy posts such as Ranian and the recapture of Raju Motham post. A BSF company gave an excellent account of itself in the battle of Burj where Assistant Commandant Wadhwa fought and died gallantly. Head Constable Ajit Singh of the BSF company charged at an LMG and killed its crew in a daring assault.

In Rajasthan, BSF was responsible for holding ground and also made some notable advances along with the Army. The role played by elements of the BSF company during the battle of Longewala is legendary.

In the Rann of Kutch, BSF battalions captured Chadbet, Nagarparkar and Virwah from the enemy.

The role of the BSF in the Eastern sector is however more remarkable. It was instrumental in providing intelligence, logistics, training and other support to Mukti Bahini units even before the war. It operated along side Mukti Bahini elements in Dinajpur, Kurigram, Rajshahi and Syhlet. BSF units often provided flank protection to advancing columns of the Army and were engaged in the defence of captured areas, and mopping up of stray Pakistan Army elements.[9]

The BSF suffered casualties of 127 dead and 392 wounded during the war. 94 personnel were taken PoW by the enemy. In recognition of its gallant role in the war several gallantry awards including one Maha Vir Chakra, one Vir Chakra and 46 Sena Medals were conferred on BSF personnel.

IS Duties

The BSF has been deployed to contain several insurgencies in the North East and J&K. In the 1970s, BSF was deployed in Nagaland. It functioned along with the Revolutionary Government of Nagaland (RGN) in its ranks. Several operations against the rebels were led by the former RGN cadres. Later, the BSF absorbed several rebel cadres of the RGN and other Naga insurgent groups in its own ranks. Some of them even rose to the rank of Commandants in the BSF.

Jammu & Kashmir

BSF battalions have been deployed in the state of Jammu & Kashmir since 1965. In 1981, additional BSF battalions were moved to the state to augment the Army's deployment on the Pir Panjal and Shamsabari Ranges and in the Kargil sector.[10] The BSF moved in to support the police and CRPF who were overwhelmed by the worsening internal security situation in 1989. By the year 1993, the BSF strength for Counter Insurgency operations in J&K rose to 30,000. The BSF replaced the CRPF which took over the task of protecting vital installations.

The BSF played a crucial role in establishing the writ of the state in Srinagar city which was virtually taken over by militants in the heydays of the insurgency. It took over bunkers from the CRPF and increased its presence in the militant strongholds of downtown Srinagar, areas where the Police and CRPF could not access earlier. This process was started when 69th Battalion of the BSF moved into Rainawari. Under a strong Inspector General, Ashok Patel, the BSF started to increase the tempo of their operations against the militants rather than simply reacting to their actions. More bunkers were established in the city and the frequency of cordon and search operations increased. Gradually, the 'G' or the Intelligence branch of the BSF established its sources in the city. Mating of human intelligence with accurate signals intelligence led to the capturing of key militant leaders in small team post-dusk raids. In one such operation in April 1990, the BSF captured three key JKLF leaders including Yasin Malik. Yasin Malik, later fled from a Srinagar hospital with the connivance of the police and hospital doctors. In June 1990, the BSF eliminated the former Deputy Commander of the Hizbul Mujahideen in an encounter in Srinagar city. By 1991, the BSF had moved into all the key towns of the Valley, viz, Anantnag, Bijbehara, Baramulla, Sopore and Bandipore.[11]

The BSF took many casualties during the intense phase of the Kashmir insurgency in the early 1990s. But, it played a crucial role in re-establishing the writ of the Indian states in the urban centres and towns, which had been virtually 'liberated' by the militants. It also assisted the Army's operations by carrying out effective road opening tasks and securing the lines of communication. With its domination of towns, the Army could concentrate its operations in the rural areas. The role of the BSF in Srinagar city has been most exemplary and the force had established an effective CI grid in the city by the mid-1990s and led to the decline in violence levels there. One of the major successful operation, again highlighting the effectiveness of its 'G' Branch was the elimination of the dreaded Jaish-e-Mohammed (JeM) commander for Kashmir, Ghazi Baba along with four other militants in downtown Srinagar. The operation, led by then DIG K Srinivas, was meticulously planned for weeks in advance which led to the pin-point identification of Ghazi Baba's hideout in North Srinagar's congested Qamarwari locality. Ghazi Baba was one of the masterminds of the December 2001 attack on the Indian Parliament.

Till October 2007, the BSF neutralised 2749 militants and apprehended 9798.[12]

In the year 2003, the BSF began the process of handing over CI commitments in Jammu & Kashmir to the CRPF. By 2005, the BSF had completely withdrawn from Srinagar city and in 2007 from most other towns of the valley. Since 2009, the counter-insurgency responsibilities of the force have been completely taken over by the CRPF.

In addition to manning the 213 Km long International Border in the state, BSF platoons occupy certain posts along the Line of Control (LoC) under the Army's operational command. A few BSF companies are also deployed to augment the second-tier in some places.

Presently, the BSF deployment n J&K is operationally divided into two Frontier HQs at Jammu and Srinagar.

North East

BSF was invariably rushed in to assist the state police and CRPF in containing the insurgencies that engulfed Nagaland, Mizoram, Manipur, Meghalaya, Tripura and Assam. BSF companies were deployed as stop-gap arrangements to contain the violence in worst hit districts. Eventually, with the induction of the Army, BSF was relieved from insurgency hit areas. The role played by the force was noteworthy in bringing down the levels of violence in Assam in the early 1990s.

The present deployment of the BSF in the North East is as under.

Assam and Meghalaya Frontier

This frontier was created on 26th April 1971 as North East Frontier in the wake of uprising of Mukti Bahini in Bangladesh. Later on North East Frontier was bifurcated into two separate frontiers i.e. AMM&N and TCM in June 1983. AMM&N Frontier was further renamed as AM Frontier on 6th may 2006.

The Assam and Meghalaya Frontier is responsible for 577 kms of International border with Bangladesh. This includes 134 kms in Dhubri district of Assam which includes 57.1 kms of riverine border in the mighty Brahmaputra and 443 kms of land border in Meghalaya state. One battalion is deployed in Nagaland for counter-insurgency duties.[13]

Assam

Following the large scale violence against Hindi-speaking people in 2007, 25 companies of the BSF were deployed in the worst-hit districts of Dibrugarh, Tinsukia, Shivsagar, Nalbari, Darrang, Kamrup, Bongaigaon, Goalpara, Kokrajhar, Lakhimpur, Dhemaji and Sonitpur.

One battalion of the BSF was also deployed in Guwahati for the smooth conduct of 33rd National Games.

Manipur

The BSF was de-inducted from counter insurgency operations in Manipur in the year 2003. However, the force had to be re-inducted in 2004 following the deteriorating situation in the state following the killing of Manorma Devi by Assam Rifles personnel.

Presently, four battalions of the BSF are deployed for counter-insurgency operations in the valley districts of Imphal East, Imphal West, Thoubal, Bishnupur and Churachandpur town.

Mizoram and Cachar Frontier

Mizoram & Cachar Frontier became operational at Silchar from 1st Nov 2006. Before this, it was functioning in Kashmir Valley as an adhoc I S Duty Ftr Baramulla with its HQ at Singhpura Baramulla. As Baramulla Ftr, it had Baramulla, Kupuwara and Bandipura Sectors under its command, and was deployed on the Line of Control and also engaged in counter insurgency operations in Baramulla & Kupuwara District of Kashmir Valley. After making notable achievements in accomplishing these tasks, this HQ moved to its present location Silchar and has been renamed as Mizoram & Cachar Ftr.

Mizoram and Cachar Ftr has three Sectors namely, Cachar, Mizoram and CI Ops Manipur, under its command. Its area of responsibility is spread over three states of Assam, Mizoram and Manipur. In Mizoram and Cachar, the troops of this Ftr are guarding India's border with Bangladesh. Troops deployed in Manipur are engaged in counter insurgency operations. BSF troops deployed in these three states are performing their duties with highest degree of dedication and commitment.[14]

Tripura Frontier

Four Armed Police battalions of the state police were merged into the BSF in the year 1966. These battalions were organised into a BSF sector HQ at Agartala. This sector HQ was under the IG BSF in Kolkata. On 01 Nov 2006, a separate frontier for Tripura was created. The Tripura Frontier of the BSF is responsible for conducting counter-insurgency operations and guarding the Indo-Bangladesh border in the state.

The areas of responsibility and deployment of other BSF Frontier HQs are briefly mentioned below.

North Bengal Frontier

North Bengal Frontier with its HQ at Kadamtala was raised on 1st April 1988, carving out of erstwhile West Bengal Frontier covers an area of responsibility of 885 kms along Indo - Bangaladesh border including 33 kms of Dahagram Angarpota enclave in the northern part of West Bengal State. The borders of this Frontier are spread in the Districts of Uttar Dinajpur, Darjeeling, Jalpaiguri and Coochbehar. The Land Custom Station (LCS) Fulbari and Immigration Check Post (ICP) Changrabandha are located in this Frontier area. BSF also maintains the Tinbigha Corridor connecting the Bangladesh Enclave Dahagram and Angarpota in this Frontier.[15]

South Bengal Frontier was raised on 23 April 1988. BSF battalions in this sector are deployed in the 24 Parganas district of West Bengal along the Indo-Bangladesh border.

Jammu Frontier

This frontier was raised on 1 January 1981. Initially when the Jammu frontier was raised in 1981 two sectors i.e. SHQ BSF Jammu and SHQ BSF Rajouri were placed under Jammu Frontier. During the year 1992 when the militancy in J&K was at its peak , SHQ BSF Doda was raised under Ftr HQ Jammu. The Sector was further bifurcated into DIG IS Duty Doda and DIG IS Duty Kistwar.SHQ Kistwar was functioning as an adhoc HQ, which was Shifted to CI(ops) Rajouri. Late in 31st july 2004 sector Sundarbani has been raised in place of CI (Ops) Sector Rajouri. And Doda was later shifted to CI (Ops) Ramban in March 1997.[16]

Punjab Frontier

The first Sector of Punjab Frontier was raised on 1st Dec 1965 with its HQ at Jalandhar. 10 Battalions of PAP which were embodied into BSF were deployed on International Border of Punjab w.e.f. 2nd Oct 1966.

This frontier HQ at Jalandhar is responsible for guarding the Indo-Pakistan boundary in the state of Punjab. The BSF keeps a vigilant eye against drug and arms traffickers along this stretch of the border. It has a water wing and a mounted wing for patrolling the riverine and areas along the border having tall elephant (Sarkanda) grass.

Water Wing

For effectively guarding riverine areas, the Water Wing was created with its HQ at Jalandhar. Water Wing assists BSF troops in negotiating rivers, creeks and streams. Water Wing actively participates in disaster management. Water Wing also plays a crucial role in border domination efforts of Border Security Force.

Mounted Wing

Large tracts of the International border of this frontier are covered with thick Elephant Grass (Sarkanda). The tall and thick Elephant Grass hinders visibility and negotiability in the border areas. To overcome this problem, a Mounted Wing was raised during Jan 1967. Since then, this Wing had been actively involved in border domination. This Wing had also participated in various National and International events and has won many laurels and medals.

Border Fencing

Punjab border has always been a favorite target for infiltration of terrorists, arms, ammunition and contraband goods from across the border. To overcome this problem, a fence was erected on India's border with Pakistan, to check cross border terrorists movement. This border fencing has been illuminated with border fencing lights (BFL) so that complete border of Punjab is illuminated throughout the night and trans-border activities are kept under watch.[17]

Rajasthan Frontier

Frontier HQ of Rajasthan and Gujarat was established on I Nov 1971 at Jodhpur. During May 1972, one new Sector i.e. Bikaner Sector was raised. Later, on Ist April 1989 one more Sector HQ was established, at Jaisalmer and Sector Headquarters at Jodhpur was shifted to Barmer. This frontier guards the 1075 Km stretch of the Indo-Pakistan border in the state of Rajasthan.[18]

Gujarat Frontier

Gujarat Frontier was carved out of the Rajasthan and Gujarat Frontier in the year 2004. It was operational w.e.f 1 April 2004. The frontier is responsible for guarding the Indo-Pak border from Barmer in Rajasthan to Sir Creek in Gujarat, a distance of 741 Km. It has three sectors at Barmer, Gandhinagar and Bhuj.[19]

Critique

The BSF closely resembles the Army in terms of organisation, training and weapons profile. Augmented with an air wing and select number of field artillery guns, the BSF is a potent central force at the disposal of the government for tackling difficult situations. The initial shaping and orientation of the force was done by able and experienced hands of Emergency Commissioned Officers from the Army. The newly formed BSF battalions benefitted from the rich combat experience which these officers brought with them from the Army and helped organise and train the men on the pattern of an infantry battalion. Since its raising in 1965, the force has proved its worth as a first responder in internal security situations which were beyond the control of the state police and in some occasions even the CRPF.

The BSF gave a fairly good account of itself in conducting minor tasks and defending some posts in the 1971 Indo-Pak War. Their prior deployment along the border with the erstwhile East Pakistan was useful in providing intelligence and other aid to offensive Indian Army formations during their thrust into Bangladesh. The BSF also aided the efforts of the Mukti Bahini before the outbreak of conflict.

Given the organisation pattern, weapons profile, training and experience gained due to a continuous deployment on the International Border with Pakistan, the BSF in the eventuality of a conventional war is expected to play a major role alongside the Army instead of withdrawing the Border Out Posts (BOPs). The BSF battalions would form part of the Army Order of Battle and fight along side regular battalions. Earlier, the practice was of infantry companies replacing BSF from the BOPs during War. As the BSF holds the border permanently, they are useful in providing intelligence on the terrain and enemy dispositions even during a conflict. With modern weapons, improved training and orientation with the terrain, BSF men are expected to fight shoulder to shoulder with the Army, at least in defensive battles. The practice of BSF companies holding on to their BOPs would relieve Army manpower for limited offensive tasks within a particular sector. By holding on to BOP, BSF is expected to force the enemy to launch attacks to capture them. Any such determined attacks on a BOP reveals the enemy intention in the area which are important planning considerations for the defence of a locality, area or zone. Thus, the BSF is a very core component of the Army plan in its defence of strong points, nodal points in the vast deserts of Rajasthan. By holding on to select BOPs the BSF also ensures that maximum ground is covered and defended from the enemy's offensive and these select BOPs then from the launch pads/bases for offensive operations across the IB. Similar to the ITBP in the mountains, the BSF will function under the Army's operational command to carry out secondary tasks during battle. In addition, it can also be expected to carry certain primary tasks such as defending a post or a key feature from enemy attack.

During peace time, the BSF has the arduous responsibility of guarding more than 6000 Km of the country's international borders with Pakistan in the West and Bangladesh in the East. Given the hostility of our western neighbour and pressure of illegal migrants and anti-national elements from the east, a permanent deployment on both the borders is necessitated. The earlier practice of armed police units from the respective state governments was not found adequate to cover the vast international borders of the country. Therefore, the formation of a Border Guarding agency under the direct control of the Central Government was a step in the right direction. And, since 1965, the BSF has been able to maintain the sanctity of the International Boundaries during peace time. The

Army due to its role during war time can not be expected to permanently guard the non-disputed borders and the BSF has proved to be a force multiplier in maintaining the country's territorial integrity. Also, the Army is already overstretched on the disputed boundaries with Pakistan and China and in prolonged deployments in Counter Insurgency operations in J&K and the North East.

To further improve border management, the Government of India has sanctioned the construction of an additional 509 BOPs (383 along Indo-Bangladesh border and 126 along Indo-Pakistan border) at an estimated cost of Rs. 1,832.50 crore. There already exist 802 BOPs on Indo-Bangladesh border and 609 BOPs on Indo-Pakistan border. Construction of these additional BOPs will provide all necessary infrastructures for the accommodation, logistic support and the combat functions of the BSF troops deployed on the Indo-Bangladesh and Indo-Pakistan borders.[20]

By now, the BSF deployment is well organised into sectors, both along the borders with Pakistan and Bangladesh. The BSF men cover the ground well with adequate knowledge of the terrain and local conditions prevalent along the border. Years of deployment have helped them gain enough knowledge on the behaviour pattern of the local population and the border guarding agencies on the opposite side. The BSF has well adjusted to the varied terrain conditions along the border. The western border with Pakistan is dotted with tall Sarkanda grasses and agricultural fields interspersed with rivers and marshes in the Jammu region and Punjab to the deserts, shrubs and sand dunes in Rajasthan. In Gujarat, the barren landscape of the Rann of Kutch and waters of the Sir Creek adds to the unique terrain configuration of India's borders. The eastern border with Bangladesh is marked with marshes, flooded rice fields and rivers.

Due to the vastness of the frontiers and vagaries of terrain, it is not possible to cover every piece of ground. The distance between two BOPs varies from sector to sector. The gaps are covered by foot and mobile patrols. Most sectors in the Jammu region and Punjab, today, have roads running parallel to the border fencing to facilitate mobile patrols. Camel patrols are common in Rajasthan and Gujarat. The water wing of the BSF patrols the Sir Creek and riverine borders with Bangladesh in West Bengal. The induction of modern sensors, thermal imagers have augmented the surveillance capability of BSF battalions.

The completion of the border fencing and flood-lighting of the Indo-Pakistan and to a certain extent the Indo-Bangladesh border has improved surveillance capabilities and made the borders less porous. Yet, anti-national elements device ingenious methods to penetrate the fencing. Due to the vagaries of the terrain and demographics on both sides of the border, zero-movement of people is not possible. In the coming years, the government should invest in procuring new technologies to improve surveillance and prevent illegal activities and movements of anti-national elements along the borders. Mini-radars, underground sensors, hand-held UAVs should bolster the surveillance capabilities at the battalion level on the ground.

The daily trans-movement of Bangladeshi immigrants on the eastern border is beyond the control of the BSF alone. Due to the high population settled on both sides and the huge length of the border encompassing five states, it is practically impossible to track down every infiltrator. The governments of both India and Bangladesh need to adopt economic and political measures to curb illegal movement from Bangladesh.

The BSF has proved its mettle in counter insurgency operations from Nagaland to Jammu & Kashmir. Like all central forces, it has remained periodically deployed in all the insurgency affected states for Internal Security duties. Its deployment has had a salutary effect in many places during a difficult period when the effectiveness of the police or other Central Police forces had waned. Adhering to the recommendations of the GoM Committee, the BSF should be totally withdrawn from counter insurgency deployments. It has been withdrawn from all CI tasks in the state of Jammu & Kashmir. The process should also be completed from Nagaland and Manipur where a few BSF battalions still remain deployed in place. The BSF should not have been deployed for anti-naxalite operations in tandem with the CRPF as a force accretion measure. Its deployment in the Naxalite belt should be avoided in bits and pieces. If deployed, it should have been in full force, where it would have been more effective and would have had a salutary effect, as it had on the J&K militants when the local police had floundered.

In the end, the BSF has a chronic and a serious issue of peace to field rotation of its battalions due to prolonged deployments along the international border. A solution to this problem can be found by maintaining a balance of tenure at the borders and in towns and cities. The number of family stations should be increased. More facilities such as residential houses, schools, etc should be opened up at the locations of sector HQs close to the border. The personnel deployed at the BOPs could be rotated for months to spend time with their families at these locations. The withdrawal of BSF companies from the Line of Control in J&K and from CI duties in the North East and Left-Wing Extremism affected areas could free up more units for peace stations.

The force needs to adopt better and more welfare and stress relief measures for its personnel who are deployed permanently along the country's long and vast borders. Better pay and allowances coupled with more promotion avenues among the ranks and secondary employment avenues for them would go a long way in increasing efficiency and motivation levels of the personnel. In the officer cadre, more avenues of promotion for direct entry officers should be created beyond DIG level and the force DG should be a BSF cadre officer rather than an IPS cadre officer.

Year	*Militants/ Extremists Killed*	*Militants/ Extremists Appr*
1990	433	905
1991	647	1099
1992	524	2224
1993	442	1919
1994	327	1315
1995	194	1036
1996	127	932
1997	128	499
1998	162	223
1999	247	262
2000	284	221
2001	334	295
2002	334	299
2003	213	160
2004	129	148
2005	147	130
2006	68	53
2007	42	39
2008 (Nov)	29	28
Total	**4811**	**11787**

NOTES

1. Giriraj Shah, Paramilitary Forces of India, p. 37.
2. Ibid.
3. Ibid.
4. Ibid, p.38.
5. Official website of the Border Security Force, accessed at http://bsf.nic.in/introduction.htm
6. Ibid.
7. Ibid (4) above.
8. Sourced from http://bsf.gov.in/Pages/Training.aspx
9. Ibid (1) above.
10. Official website of the BSF, accessed at http://sgr.bsf.gov.in/intro/index.htm
11. L.N. Subramaniam, CI Operations in Jammu & Kashmir, accessed at http://www.bharat-rakshak.com/MONITOR/ISSUE3-2/lns.html
12. M.D. Sharma, *Paramilitary Forces of India*, p. 134.
13. Official website of the BSF, accessed at http://am.bsf.gov.in/introduction.htm
14. Official website of the BSF, accessed at http://www.bla.bsf.gov.in/intro.htm
15. Sourced from http://nb.bsf.gov.in/HISTORY.html
16. Sourced from http://jmu.bsf.gov.in/History.htm
17. Sourced from http://www.pb.bsf.gov.in/introduction.htm
18. Sourced from http://raj.bsf.gov.in/_private/Intro.htm
19. Sourced from http://guj.bsf.gov.in/history.html
20. Ministry of Home Affairs, *Outcome Budget 2011-12*, accessed on 31 March 2012 http://mha.nic.in/pdfs/OB(E)2011-12.pdf

8

Central Reserve Police Force (CRPF)

Origin

The origins of the CRPF can be traced to Neemuch, a small town in Mandsaur district of Madhya Pradesh. The first battalion of the force was raised here on 27 July 1939. Owing to the prevailing political fervent in the Princely states of then British India, it was felt that a Crown Representative force should help maintain law and order. The Prajamandal Agitations in the Princely states after the AICC Resolution of 1939 further intensified political unrest in the states. The Crown Representatives Police was raised to avoid involvement of the Provincial Government's forces in the affairs of the Princely States.

This force was originally organised and trained on military lines and made self sufficient in all respects. It was designed to operate in detachment under the overall superintendence and control of the Political agent. The force was not meant to replace or supplement the Civil Police, but was to undertake duties usually performed by the Army when acting in aid to Civil Power. Its very name, the Crown Representatives Police, indicated its distinct identity. Initially only one battalion was raised and Major JF Peart was its first Commandant. The battalion had seven other gazetted officers, 30 subordinate officers, 100 Head Constables and 870 Constables in its rolls. The composition was a mixed one and included Hindus, Muslims, Christians and a few British elements.[1] The CRPF retains this mixed composition till date.

The CRP came into prominence with its swift handling of the Hur menace. With the arrest of their leader the Pir of Pagaro, the Hurs of Khairpur had gone on a rampage and had killed the Nazim of the State Police. The CRP detachment restored order in Khairpur by July 1943. Detachments of this battalion helped maintain law and order in the states of Charkhari and Indore, Balasinore in Baroda Agency and Kishangarh.

Between 1946-47, detachments were sent to Rewa, Pataudi, Dujana, Datia,

Charkhari, Kothi (Nowgong), Loharu, Ratlam, Ajmer, Deoli, Rampur, Rajkot, Junagarh, Chamba and Virahi to maintain order.[2]

Post-Independence

The force faced disbandment as the need to maintain a reserve force ceased with the lapse of British Paramountcy over the Princely states.[3] However, Sardar Patel recognised the need to maintain a reserve force to deal with unrest and maintain law and order.[4] Consequently with the "Central Reserve Police Force Act" of Parliament, the Crown Representatives Police became the Central Reserve Police Force (CRPF) with retrospective effect from 15 August 1947. The Act made CRPF an "Armed Force" of the Union. It was presented with the "President's Colours" on 19 March 1950.

In 1947, the force took a leading part in the operations in Kathiawar states of Manawardar, Bantwam Sardargarh, Mangrol and hastened the process of their merger with the Union. It also assisted the Indian Army during Operation Polo to liberate Hyderabad in 1948.[5] In the 1950s, the force was deployed in various anti-dacoity operations all over the country especially in Pepsu and Chambal ravines of Madhya Bharat. It was deployed for the suppression of communal violence in Rampur.[6] From 1955 companies were deployed to maintain law and order in J&K and the Naga Hills. It was also deployed against the Razakars in Hyderabad and Telangana. Six companies were deployed in Maharashtra to tackle the threat posed by the Samyukta Maharashtra Morcha in the year 1956.[7] The CRPF was also engaged in border guarding duties till the BSF and ITBP were raised in the aftermath of the 1965 war. In the immediate aftermath of independence CRPF units were independently deployed at Barmer, Gadra, Road, Jaisalmer, Jodhpur and Kutch. They patrolled the borders on camels and jeep and even on foot. These units foiled all Pakistani attempts to establish contact with the states of Junagadh, Mangrol and Hyderabad, then known as the 'Kutch Corridor".[8]

Hot Springs, 1959

On 21 October 1959, a CRPF patrol of 20 men led by Dy SP Karam Singh was ambushed by Chinese troops at Hot Springs in Eastern Ladakh. The Chinese attacked them from a hill top killing 10 personnel while the rest were taken prisoners. This was the first major incident with the Chinese troops on the borders that precipitated the Sino-India war of 1962. 21 October 1959 is marked as Police Martyr's Day every year.[9]

Sardar Post, 1965

In 1965, the CRPF had established two posts namely Sardar and TAK posts in the Great Rann of Kutch on the borders with Pakistan in Gujarat. On 9 April 1965, the Pakistan Army had launched a brigade sized attack on the posts. Sardar

Post held by the 2nd Battalion of the CRPF withstood the attack for nearly 12 hours and inflicted 34 casualties on the Pakistan Army. Five CRPF men died in this attack and 19 were taken prisoners.[10] This action brought out the gallantry of the men. The Sardar Post incident marked the culmination of hostilities by Pakistan that ultimately led to the Second Indo-Pak War in September 1965. During the war, CRPF battalions were deployed for protecting Vital Installations and bridges in J&K in addition to keeping the lines of communications open. Many attacks on bridges by the raiders were repulsed by the CRPF.

During the period 1957-60, 133 Pakistani infiltrators were liquidated by the CRPF in J&K.[11]

The 9th Battalion of the CRPF fought a rear guard action during the withdrawal from NEFA. The force was among the first troops to be moved forward when the Chinese withdrew from Kameng and Siang Divisions. It was extensively deployed in other parts of NEFA to maintain law and order.[12]

1971 War

Two CRPF battalions were deployed in the Western sector and three in the Eastern sector. The CRPF was entrusted with the task of guarding PoW camps set up at Ranchi, Ramgarh, Sagar, Agra and Gwalior. It also provided security to the Bangladeshi refugee camps during that period.[13]

1965-1988

In November 1969, CRPF was deployed in culling large scale communal violence in Gujarat. Induction of two battalions in Kerala nipped in the bud the Naxalite movement taking roots in the state. The battalions also successfully combated Naxalism in Andhra Pradesh. 95 Companies of the CRPF was deployed to maintain law and order during President's Rule in West Bengal due to the Naxalite uprising in the state from 1969-71. Five battalions were deployed in the 1971 War. The CRPF battalions organised local defence at several places in the Akhnoor-Samba belt in the western sector and guarded air fields in the eastern sector. During 1972-73, 12 battalions were deployed in Andhra Pradesh to meet the deteriorating law and order situation emerging due to the Telangana agitation.

In the year 1973, the CRPF played critical roles in the merger of Sikkim state with the Union of India and was instrumental in restoring normalcy. It recovered arms and ammunition looted by the Sikkim Congress agitators. The force also provided protection to both the Chogyal and Chief Minister Kazhi L Dorji.[14] In 1974, the force played a major role during the railwaymen's strike of 1974. CRPF officers were co-opted as sector and sub-sector commanders in various co-ordination committees all across the country to guide and conduct the movement of trains. CRPF battalions were deployed during the Chhatra Sangarsh Samiti agitations in 1974 and for the peaceful conduct of assembly elections in Gujarat in 1975. 1n 1974, 10 CRPF battalions were deployed in Bihar during the JP Narain movement. By their prompt action on 18 and 19 March 1974, Patna was saved from large-scale mob violence. In two major operations, 19 Naxalites were killed by the CRPF in Masaurhi and Bhojpur. The force lost four personnel in anti-naxalite operations. It assisted the state police in arrested nearly 1,151 naxalites and anti-social elements and seized 85 fire arms and 482 rounds of ammunition during that period.[15]

CRPF battalions were deployed in Mizoram when the Mizoram National Front Rebellion started. In January 1975, CRPF battalions captured two of the five killers of three senior police officers in Aizwal. In 1979, a battalion operating under the operational control of the Army brought about the surrender of 15 fully armed MNF insurgents. It subsequently led to the recovery of a large number of arms and ammunition. In 1977, CRPF was instrumental in the conduct of general elections.

More than 13,000 people were rescued during devastating floods in West Bengal in the year 1970. In the year 1975-76 battalions played an active role in providing succor to flood victims in Bihar. A 45 m breach in Poonpoon river was plugged by CRPF men which prevented flood waters from reaching the capital city of Patna.

The CRPF played a role during the Delhi riots in 1974 and the anti-reservation stir in Gujarat in 1985.

Punjab

The CRPF was first inducted in Punjab in the year 1981 during the agitation over the Union Territory of Chandigarh. From 1983-1993, Punjab remained a prime theatre of action for the CRPF. Initially, the CRPF was outmatched by the terrorists in weaponry, training and tactics.[16]

In the year 1984, more than 100 companies of the force were deployed in Operation Blue Star under the operational control of the Army. The force lost 35 personnel in the year 1985-86 to terrorists. In the year 1989, 39 CRPF men were killed battling the terrorists in Punjab, In 295 encounters, nearly 313 terrorists were killed and around 1000 apprehended. In other parts of the country the CRPF killed 57 extremists and apprehended 2900. 16 CRPF men were martyred and 124 injured in these operations. During this period one battalion was deployed to maintain peace in the Darjeeling Hills of West Bengal.[17]

Two battalions of the CRPF and a Mahila Company were as part of the Indian Peace Keeping Force (IPKF) in Sri Lanka. Constable T Mohan of 35 Battalion was posthumously awarded the Vir Chakra for his gallant role in defending Jaffna Fort in an attack by the LTTE.

Peace Keeping Battalions

In the early 1980s, three Peace Keeping Battalions (PKE) were raised. In addition to the normal strength of a duty battalion, these battalions consisted of 244 engineering personnel. The PKE repaired houses of both hindu and muslim rioters in Meerut in 1982 while the doctors and nurses provided medical relief to the affected people. The PKE repaired and rebuild houses, bridges and places of worship in Nowgong district of Assam. The PKE medical teams worked round the clock during the Bhopal Gas Tragedy in 1984. The PKE were disbanded in three phases between 1987 and 1994 but its model was later re-instated in the raising of the Rapid Action Force.[18]

Mahila Battalions

To deal with the increased participation of women in crime, the first Mahila Battalion was raised in 1986. It gave a good account of itself during the riots in Meerut. The second mahila battalion was deployed during the IPKF operations in Sri Lanka and was instrumental in the recovery of a large quantity of arms and ammunition.[19]

Role and Tasks

The Central Reserve Police Force (CRPF) is an armed Force of the Union of India, with the basic role of striking reserve to assist the State/Union Territories in Police operations to maintain law and order and contain insurgency. Its role is that of a catalyst in maintaining law & order, and returns to barracks once this objective is achieved. The force is also being used for various police duties in various States.

Broad gamut of duties performed by the CRPF are:[20]

- Crowd control
- Riot control
- Counter Militancy/Insurgency operations.
- Dealing with Left Wing Extremism
- Overall co-ordination of large scale security arrangement specially with regard to elections in disturbed areas.
- Protection of VIPs and vital installations.
- Checking environmental de-gradation and protection of local Flora and Fauna
- Fighting aggression during War time
- Participating in UN Peace Keeping Mission
- Rescue and Relief operations at the time of Natural Calamities.

7.5 percent of the Force is deployed for the security of VIPs mostly in North-Eastern States, J&K, Bihar and Andhra Pradesh which include Governors, Chief Ministers, Ministers, MPs and MLAs of J&K, Assam, Arunachal Pradesh, Manipur and Nagaland, Tripura and Mizoram. CRPF is also providing security (Static guard) at the residence/office of Prime Minister of India, various Union Ministers and MsP and other dignitaries.

17.5 percent of the Force is deputed for guarding the important installations of Central and State Governments mostly in insurgency affected areas which includes Secretariats, Doordarshan Kendras, Telephone exchanges, Banks, Hydroelectric projects, Jails etc. CRPF is also deployed for the security of Parliament House.[21]

10 Companies of CRPF are deployed for the security of three sensitive shrines i.e. Krishna Janma Bhoomi, Shahi Idgah Masjid complex (Mathura), Ram Janma Bhoomi- Barbi Masjid complex (Ayodhya) and Kashi Vishwanath Temple-Gyanvapi Mosque (Varanasi). Four Companies of the Force are deputed for the security of Mata Vaishno Devi Shrine, Katra, Jammu (J&K).[22]

Organisational Structure

Today, the CRPF has a strength of 222 battalions which includes:

Executive Bns: 187
Disaster Management (NDRF) Bns: 02
Mahila Bns: 03
Rapid Action Force (RAF) Bns: 10
Signal Bns: 05
CoBRA Bns: 10 (4 under raising).

It also has 1 Special Duty Group and 39 Group Centres (1 under raising), 14 Training Institutions, 4 (100 bedded) Composite Hospitals, 17 (50 bedded) Composite Hospitals, 7 Arms Workshops and 3 Central Weapon Stores.[23]

In addition, the GOI has sanctioned raising of 31 battalions (including 1 Mahila Bn), 6 Group Centres/DIG Ranges and 2 IG Sectors for the year 2011-12 onwards. CRPF has become the largest Central Para Military Force (CPMF) of the country.[24]

Force HQ

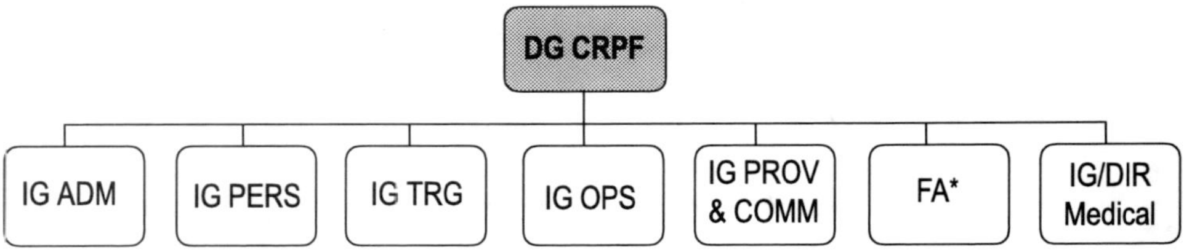

* Financial Advisor

Operational Ranges

For Operational Control, the force is divided into:

3 × Special DG Zones

J&K Zone: Jammu
NE Zone: Guwahati
Central Zone: Kolkata

↓

1 × ADG Zone
Southern Command: Hyderabad

↓

17 × IG Sectors**

↓

1 × IG CoBRA

↓

48 × DIG Ranges

The 17 operational Sectors are located at:

Sector	*HQ*
Srinagar	Srinagar
Jammu	Jammu
IG (Ops) Kashmir	Srinagar
Central Sector	Lucknow
Eastern Sector	Kolkata
Manipur & Nagaland	Imphal
NE Sector	Shillong
Northern Sector	New Delhi
Southern Sector	Hyderabad
Western Sector	Navi Mumbai
Bihar	Patna
North West Sector	Chandigarh
Rajasthan	Jaipur
IG (Ops) Jharkhand	Ranchi
IG Special Sector	Raipur
IG CoBRA	New Delhi
IG RAF	New Delhi
IG Ops (NES)	Jorhat

Organisational Structure at Battalion Level

BN

↓

↓	↓
HQ COY	7 × SERVICE COYs

The sanctioned strength of a CRPF battalion is 1154 personnel and that of each company is 137. However, the effective strength of each company varies from 65-80 personnel.

Equipping Profile

5.56 mm INSAS Rifle – standard issue.
9 mm CMG
2 × 5.56/7.62 LMG per section
1 × 51 mm Mortar per platoon
1-2 × 84 RL per Bn
1-2 × UBGL per Bn
AK-47/74 Rifles are issued in sector store.

Training

In the early days, officers and men were trained at their battalions only. As the force acquired a multi-dimensional profile, a need was felt to open training institutes and academies to impart basic recruit training before the men proceeded to their respective battalions. Some seats in Army courses were also reserved for CRPF officers. The CRPF has institutes for specialised training; the wireless operators were trained by the Directorate of Coordination, Police Wireless. The first training institution of the force came up at Neemuch in 1960. The first Recruits Training Centre, first established in Barwaha (MP) was shifted to Neemuch. The Internal Security Academy was established at Mt Abu in 1975. It is the primary training academy of the CRPF today and imparts basic training to directly appointed gazetted officers and runs various courses like the Vertical Interaction Course, Human Rights, Communal Riots and Counter Insurgency for IPS and CRPF cadre officers. The training facilities of the CRPF has expanded over the years and today it has the following training institutions across the country:

Internal Security Academy (Mt Abu)—1
CRPF Academy (Neemuch)—1
Central Training Colleges—4
Recruit Training Centres—5
Counter Insurgency & Anti-Terrorist School (CIAT)—1
CTC (T & IT)—1

Growth of the CRPF

Year	*Number of Battalions*
1939-47	01
1949	02
1959-61	09
1962	14
1965	17
1971	70
1985	83
1988	93
2010	218

Source: RSD Dogra, 'Nation Keepers: CRPF'.

125 battalions were raised in 22 years indicating the rapid growth of the organisation. This period of over two decades also saw the eruption of various forms of internal schisms in Assam, Punjab, Jammu & Kashmir and the spiraling of the Maoist insurgency since the year 2000.

A separate post of Inspector General, CRPF was created in 1963. In 1971, with the strength of the CRPF reaching 70 battalions plus a Signals Battalion, the need to create a full-fledged Directorate General was felt. Mr VG Kanetkar became the first DG of the CRPF in the year 1971. He was assisted by three Deputy Directors and one Wireless Advisor at the Headquarter.[25]

Org Structure at Battalion Level

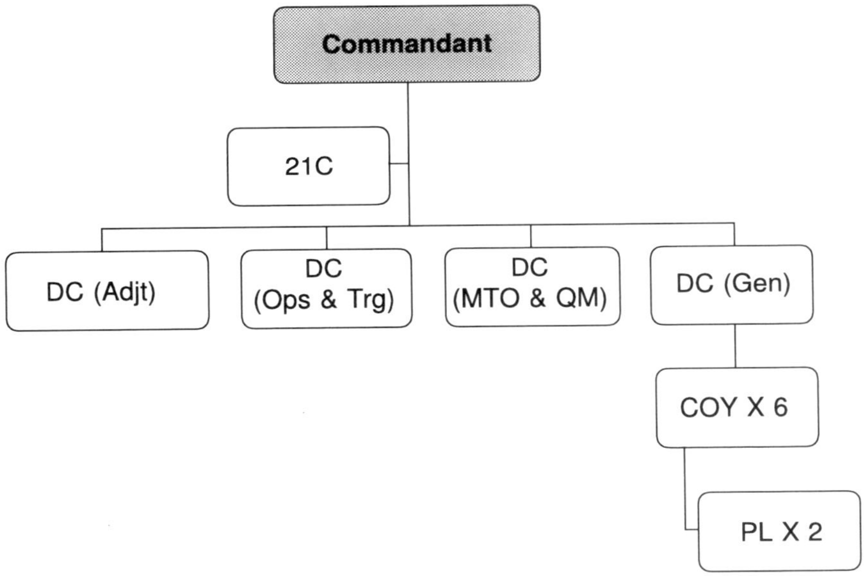

The total sanctioned strength of a CRPF Bn is 1154. A CRPF Battalion has HQ plus 7 companies each headed by an Assistant Commandant. The strength of one Coy is 133 personnel. Actual operational strength of each company is 76.

Budget

Actual Expenditure on CRPF during the period 2000-01 to 2010-11

Year	*Expenditure (in crore)*
2000-01	1653.25
2001-02	1894.42
2002-03	961.13
2003-04	2087.78
2004-05	2516.96

Year	*Expenditure (in crore)*
2005-06	3228.03
2006-07	3642.40
2007-08	3911.69
2008-09	5557.82
2009-10	7587.56
2010-11*	6167.10

* As on 31.12. 2010.

Counter-Insurgency Operations

Nagaland

The CRPF was inducted along with regular Army battalions in Nagaland in 1956. Today, the force is playing its part in the integration of the state into the National mainstream.

Assam

The CRPF was first inducted in Assam in 1957. From 1960 onwards, the strength of CRPF deployment was gradually increased to counter language riots, ethnic conflicts, foreigners issue and the agitations of the All Assam Students' Union. By the 1980s, the CRPF had to grapple with the full-blown militancy of the ULFA and NDFB. The presence of Naga, Kuki and Cachari rebels in the eastern and southern parts of Assam further worsened the security situation in the state. Presently, with a considerable half of both ULFA and NDFB entering into ceasefire agreements with the Government, the security situation in the state has stabilised to a great extent. But the CRPF has taken a frontline job in maintaining peace in the state and is extensively deployed for carrying out operations and other tasks independently. It has more or less withdrawn from static duties of providing security to government buildings, etc.

Manipur

The CRPF has remained deployed since November 1962 to tackle the myriad insurgencies of Manipur. The valley and hill based insurgent groups, prominent among them being the People's Liberation Army (PLA), People's Revolutionary Part of Kanlgleipak (PREPAK) and the NSCN (IM) have let loose a reign of terror since the 1960s. The CRPF had to move in to restore the edifice of the state and assist the besieged state police. The city Police Control in Imphal was jointly manned by the CRPF and the police. At one point in time, seven out of nine entry points to Imphal were manned by the CRPF. The force had set up 40 posts in the state capital to maintain control. After the jailbreaks of 1980, 1981 and 1982, the CRPF also took over prison security in the state.[26] The CRPF had to pay a very heavy price to keep the roads and highways open and enable the state police to regroup themselves in Manipur.

Mizoram

The Mizo National Army (MNA) of Laldenga struck across the then Lushai Hills district on 28 February 1966 and proclaimed an independent state of Mizoram. The Army and CRPF were rushed in and they eventually gained an handle on the situation and the insurgents were pushed into the jungles. In 1975, the CRPF took over the security of Aizawl town and was successful in nabbing three killers of top police officers in Aizawl on 13 January 1975. The CRPF maintained a strong presence with regular patrols in all parts of the town. It guarded all vital installations and sensitive spots including the residences of the ministers and top officials. Eventually, the security forces gained an upper hand and Mizoram returned to peace with the signing of the Rajiv Gandhi accord in 1986.[27]

Tripura

The continuing influx of refugees from Bangladesh upset the ethnic balance of Tripura and gave rise to a tribal insurgency. By the year 1998, the original tribal inhabitants were reduced to a mere 25 percent of the total population from 70 percent at the time of Independence. The Bangladeshi immigrants usurped most of the jobs and businesses in the state. The CRPF was first deployed in the state in 1965.[28] It took over some BOPs from the Army during the 1971 war. The CRPF continues to remain deployed in the state for the protection of developmental and infrastructural projects. The tribal insurgency, especially of the All Tripura Tigers Force (ATTF) is on the ebb but the influx of immigrants continues to pose a challenge to the state.

Arunachal Pradesh

The CRPF first stepped into the land of the rising sun in 1958 and has since maintained a presence of about five to seven battalions in the state. These battalions are deployed in the insurgency-hit districts of Tirap and Changlang besides augmenting the state police for guarding prisons and performing regular policing roles to prevent ethnic conflicts and controlling other law and order problems in the state.[29]

Jammu & Kashmir

The first CRPF battalions were inducted into the state in the 1960s. They were employed for the protection of bridges and other vital installations during the 1965 war. At the outbreak of insurgency in 1988-89 additional CRPF battalions were inducted into the state. They were deployed to maintain law and order and enforce curfew and prohibitory orders in towns especially in Srinagar city. With the worsening of the situation, more central forces such as the BSF were deployed. Areas of responsibility were divided between the two central forces. With the induction of the Army for counter-insurgency operations, the CRPF primarily took over protection duties such as guarding VA/VPs and sensitive installations like airports, telephone exchanges, transmitter and relay stations, government buildings and residences of officials, state ministers and reinforcing the local police. The CRPF along with other security forces was responsible for conducting parliamentary elections in 1996 and 1998 and the Assembly elections in 1996. In the year 1998, the CRPF raised a battalion comprising of surrendered militants.

The force was not employed in direct counter-insurgency operations against militants. This task was mainly performed by the Army and the BSF to some extent. Implementing the recommendations of the GoM on Defence formed after the Kargil war, Army and BSF formations previously engaged in counter-insurgency operations were deployed to guard against intrusions along the LoC and the IB. The counter-insurgency grid in the hinterland was filled by the CRPF. It began taking over responsibility of Srinagar city from the BSF in the year 2003 and Sopore town in 2006.

Present Deployment Pattern

Today, CRPF companies are incorporated within the AOR of RR units in the hinterland. In addition to performing CI tasks, they continue to guard VA/VPs in the state. CRPF has replaced the Army and BSF in all major towns of the state. They are increasingly being co-opted in operations against militants. Most of the operations in built-up areas are being conducted jointly between the RR, CRPF and Special Operations Group units of the J&K Police with the CRPF engaged in establishing the outer cordon of villages during operations. The Road Opening task on NH 1A between Jammu and Srinagar has been taken over by the CRPF. The CRPF plays a vital role in the safe conduct of the Annual Shri Amarnathji Yatra by securing the roads, tracks and camps between Jammu and Pahalgam/Baltal during the duration of the yatra.

70 battalions of the CRPF are deployed in the state of J&K. Out of these 15 are deployed in Jammu division and 27 in Srinagar city. The remaining 28 battalions are deployed for counter-insurgency operations across the state.

After the first summer agitation of 2008, a re-appraisal of the CRPF deployment has taken place with more battalions being deployed for law and order duties especially in Srinagar city. Today, 30 percent of the CRPF strength in J&K is deployed for performing law and order duties like crowd control, enforcing prohibitory orders, etc. Another 32 percent of the force is engaged in providing protection to vital installations and performing static guard duties. 18 percent of the force is deployed for counter-insurgency operations. They are deployed in company strength at different locations and support the operations of the RR and Jammu and Kashmir Police. 12 percent of the battalions are employed in training while 1 percent is held in reserve. The remaining 7 percent of the force conduct Road Opening tasks, mainly on NH 1 from Banihal to Srinagar.

Counter-Insurgency Operations

Ever since 1989, quantum of the CRPF battalions were engaged in static guard duties and protecting VA/VPs. Though they had engagements with militants who attacked or fired at their posts or during convoy movements, deliberate direct operations against militants was fairly limited. Eight battalions of the CRPF replaced the BSF from downtown areas of Srinagar in November 2003. By 12 September 2005, the responsibility of Srinagar was completely assumed by the CRPF. The government raised 50 additional battalions for the purpose of deploying CRPF for counter-insurgency operations. The process took two years as security agencies had concerns with the ability of the CRPF to directly take on militants. Now, they were engaged in conducting routine naka checking/ frisking, house to house searches and occupation of small pickets in streets, mohallas and markets; duties previously performed by BSF battalions.

Assuming responsibility of Srinagar city was not an easy task as the phase of *fidayeen* or suicide attacks had not yet waned. The militants launched attacks on CRPF posts and the stand-offs, sometimes continued for days. In some instances in Srinagar and Sopore, Army troops had to be called in to neutralise the holed up militants. But eventually CRPF got blooded in these operations and achieved the capability to neutralise the *fidayeens*. The CRPF was also able to thwart *fidayeens* from storming their camps and eliminate them before they managed to gain entry. To cite one example, two suicide attackers were eliminated as they attempted to storm a CRPF camp on the banks of the Dal Lake on 11 October 2007. In the last suicide attack on 06 January 2010 in Lal Chowk, the CRPF eliminated the two *fidayeen* terrorists after a 22 hour long operation. Significantly, no army support was requisitioned for this operation. This indicates that the force has achieved specialised capabilities to directly take on well motivated and equipped terrorists, at least in built-up areas of Srinagar city.

Not many anti-terrorist operations have been conducted ever since the force assumed responsibility of the CI/CT grid in Srinagar city. The BSF on the other hand conducted operations based on information and also regular cordon and search ones. Some analysts are of the opinion that as the CRPF is not conducting operations against the terrorists in built-up areas of the city, it has turned into a safe-haven for terrorists, especially their leaders. One example cited is the fact that the recently killed LeT Commander for North Division, Abdullah Uni used to frequent Batmaloo locality in downtown, frequently on his motorbike from Sopore town. Other factors for a lack of direct operations in the city could be attributed to the fact that as suicide attacks have been negligible and there is a visible improvement in the security situation, a number of hard measures such as frisking of people, conducting house to house searches, barricading/checking of vehicles were withdrawn to provide succour to the people. Also, the Special Operations Group of the J&K Police has developed the intelligence network and capability to conduct specific operations within city limits. In one such operation on 10 March 2011, the police had gunned down two JeM militants including its Chief Operations Commander for the valley. The CRPF can assist the police in such operations. The BSF, in the year 2003 had notched up a major success by eliminating the then JeM commander in Kashmir, Ghazi Baba in an operation in Qamarwari locality of the old city. Densely populated and congested by-lanes of the old city are preferred hideouts for terrorists facing the heat elsewhere in the valley. Three JeM militants were killed in an operation by the Rashtriya Rifles in Maloora locality of North Srinagar on 21 October 2011 reinforcing the fear that terrorists continue to frequent the city for seeking hideouts. Prolonged stay in Srinagar city provides them the time and ability to plan major strikes both within and outside the state.

Another reason for a lack of CI/CT operations attributed to the CRPF is that the summer agitations since 2008 have taken away the focus from conducting operations to crowd control measures. Information is also difficult to come by due to the increased hostility of the people ever since the agitations began. Also in the post-agitation phase, a number of CRPF posts and pickets were removed from congested localities to prevent them from being besieged by protesters. Whether this has helped the militants by design or default to acquire safe sanctuaries is difficult to say, but it cannot be entirely ruled out either. In the overall picture though, the residual strength of terrorists operating in J&K has gone down tremendously over the past six to seven years and the terrorist strength within the city would have gone down as well. In any case precise human intelligence is essential for conducting operations in built-up areas. The CRPF's intelligence wing is in primary stages of inception and the information flowing through IB/MAC is seldom specific in nature.

Elsewhere in J&K, the 28 battalions employed in the CI/CT grid are deployed in company strength, co-located with RR units. All posts on major roads, towns, market places, vital installations like power houses, telephone exchanges, etc have CRPF deployment. Across the valley, CRPF companies conduct regular combing operations and are effecting recovery of arms dumps and apprehension of OGWs and militants during naka checking. Sometimes these operations are undertaken independently or with the SOG. CRPF personnel are also conducting joint operations with the police and RR. They are responsible for providing the outer cordon during operations in villages. In some instances crowds prevent the operation party from extricating from the encounter site or organise protests after the operation is over. The CRPF outer-cordons play a role in dealing with such situations after the Army's assault parties have withdrawn. Overall, the CRPF is playing a complimentary role in the CI/CT grid in J&K. Their deployment relieves the RR manpower from towns and VA/VPs so that they can conduct area domination and intelligence-based operations against terrorists. In some places, the CRPF companies provide ROPs in roads leading to Army camps.

The CRPF is also responsible for conducting Rail opening tasks in the

Kashmir railway from Anantnag to Baramulla. The CRPF has performed this task exceedingly well and has effected recovery of IEDs on railway tracks preventing major tragedies.

Law and Order Tasks

The Amarnath Shrine board agitations that broke out in the summer of 2008 brought to fore a new dimension to the security situation in the state. Organised protests that often broke out after Friday prayers in downtown Srinagar engulfed the entire valley within a month or two. The state was brought to a virtual stand-still with blockades and strikes in the Jammu division as well. The Jammu-Kashmir divide had virtually stalled all economic activity in the state. The road blockade in Jammu shot up prices of essential commodities in the valley. The ability of violent crowds bringing the entire valley to a stand-still at a time when militancy was at its lowest ebb took many by surprise.

The CRPF due to its large-scale deployment in Srinagar city and major towns of the valley bore the brunt of these protests. They along with the state police were often deliberately targeted by the stone-pelting crowds. The strategy was to provoke the security forces into opening fire and cause civilian casualties. These incidents added fuel to the fire and provoked large-scale protests. As the CRPF personnel were largely oriented for counter-insurgency tasks, they dealt with the protesters with force and opened fire in self-defence. Often the men facing an overwhelming number of violent protesters resorted to firing in panic. Due to lack of training and panic, the protesters were often shot in upper parts of the body resulting in fatal casualties.

The CRPF or the state police cannot be blamed entirely for causing the casualties among protesters. In many instances small pickets of less than 10 personnel or a vehicle were surrounded by the mob in an attempt to lynch the men. In such situations, the security forces were faced with no choice but to open fire in self-defence. To avoid an open confrontation, CRPF personnel were deliberately withdrawn from potential trouble-spots whenever a protest was anticipated. This strategy, however was only partially successful as in the absence of security forces, the mob indulged in large-scale arson and ransacking of government property. Eventually, such crowds had to be dealt with forcibly, Many CRPF men were seen throwing stones at the protesters portraying a brutal face of the security forces. But such steps were spontaneous in the heat of the moment and in the face of extreme violence and abuses hurled by the protesters including women.

The psychological impact of street protests on the securitymen can be gauged by the high figures of injuries suffered by them. Between, June 2008 to September 2010, nearly 1552 CRPF personnel suffered injuries in stone-pelting incidents in the Kashmir valley. Many of the personnel were left disfigured or with broken limbs.[30]

In retrospect, it can be said that the street protests if handled more delicately would have kept the civilian casualties low and prevented the situation from going completely out of control. But such a reaction was expected from an already over-stretched and stressed out force when faced with a new form of challenge which the violent street protests presented. Militants fired from within the crowd provoking the security forces to open fire. The 'Muzaffarabad Chalo' rally was violently broken on the Baramulla-Uri road after militants from within the large crowd fired at and shot dead the Hurriyat leader Maualna Shaukat Aziz who was leading the march to the line of control in Uri.

Today, the CRPF is better poised to tackle street protests. The task of the 28 CRPF battalions in Srinagar city has been re-oriented from counter-insurgency to law and order duties. The force has procured equipments such as helmets, batons and other riot-protection gear to deal with mob violence. Its personnel have undergone specialised training in crowd management. Mahilla companies of the force have also been deployed to deal with women protesters. Special emphasis is being laid to isolate and arrest the instigators and mob leaders before the protests assume a violent form. Maximum restraint is being exercised in opening fire or causing unprovoked or accidental death to civilians especially children. (The death of a 17 year old boy, Tuffail Matoo, who was accidentally caught up in a street protest had snowballed into a violent summer of protests in the summer of 2010). 3504 CRPF personnel have suffered injuries while tackling street protests in Kashmir in the three years since 2008. This is a huge number and could have easily led to bitterness and a breakdown of morale among the personnel. But the CRPF leadership has taken corrective measures and prevented such a situation from arising.

Counter-LWE Operations

The growth of Left-Wing Extremism (LWE) in the Indian hinterland necessitated deployment of central forces to contain the situation. The CRPF was first deployed from 1969-71 to stem the first tide of LWE in India. Despite being suppressed brutally the rebellion continued to fester in the most backward and remote interiors of the country for decades. Lack of governance coupled with rampant corruption and exploitation of tribals kept the pot boiling, waiting to erupt one day. The early 1990s saw the regrouping of armed Naxal units operating mainly in the northern part of Andhra Pradesh. Concurrently, the Maoist movement continued to flourish in parts of West Bengal and Bihar where it assumed the form of a caste struggle between upper classes and the oppressed dalits or backwards.

As the armed groups grew in strength and began inflicting casualties on local police forces, deployment of central paramilitary forces became necessary. Initially, this deployment was reactionary and followed deployment of paramilitary companies in areas where a major naxal attack occurred. The paramilitary companies attached to a district headquarter of local police stations acted more or less as a deterrent to prevent more attacks. The Indian state's distraction with major insurgencies in J&K and the North-East and increased tensions with its western neighbours kept focus away from the brewing storm in the remote interiors of the country. This lack of attention from both the central and state governments, intelligence agencies and security forces provided the movement space and time to grow from strength to strength and assume the militant form it does today. Lack of development and jobs in the afflicted areas provided a steady stream of recruits to the Maoists. With procurement of modern and sophisticated weaponry from abroad, expertise in making IEDs/landmines and training in guerrilla warfare the Maoist fighters were in a dominant position to overcome the state police forces and pose a formidable challenge to the paramilitary forces as well.

Today, LWE afflicts 230 districts of the country in the states of Andhra Pradesh, Maharashtra, Chhattisgarh, Orissa, Jharkhand, Bihar and West Bengal. A few districts in Madhya Pradesh, Uttar Pradesh and Karnataka are partially affected by LWE. Out of these 230, the Central Government has declared 32 as worst-affected districts. The Red Corridor from Nepal in the North to Andhra Pradesh has become a compact zone providing enough transit routes and safe zones for the armed guerrillas to operate and recoup. In the next phase of their operations, the Maoists aim to spread their Compact Revolutionary Zone (CRZ) to districts of peninsular India as well.

Deployment of CRPF

The state of Andhra Pradesh continued to face challenges of LWE soon after the movement was initially suppressed in 1971. Due to a resolute political and security strategy, the state was able to contain the situation to a great extent by the latter half of the 1990s. And in the year 2004 it lifted the ban on the People's War Group to facilitate a ceasefire. The state now claimed to have successfully brought the situation under control in its northern districts bordering Maharashtra and Madhya Pradesh (later Chhattisgarh). Ever since more than 3000 civilians and security force personnel have lost their lives to Maoist violence. However, from the security point of view, the armed Maoist groups only shifted their base into these bordering states and later spread out into the forest belts of Orissa and Bihar. Therefore, the scope of the movement enlarged in terms of its geographical spread and casualties. It also swelled the number of armed maoist cadres.

As the Central Government realised the gravity of the situation, more and more paramilitary companies were deployed in these areas. Initially, the deployment was from a mixed batch of companies from the BSF, CRPF, ITBP, SSB and CISF. After the CRPF was designated as the primary counter-insurgency force of the country, this deployment has been streamlined and today 76 battalions of the CRPF are deployed for anti-naxal operations across the so-called 'Red Corridor'.

The most worrying factor in the fight against naxalism has been the adverse casualty ratio inflicted on the security forces. The attrition rate has always favoured the security forces operating in J&K and the North East.

Operational Challenges

The CRPF had little experience in directly taking on militants in J&K and North-East as bulk of their forces were deployed in conducting static guard duties, protecting VA/VPs limited road-opening tasks and enforcing curfews etc.

Lack of Experience in Conduct of CI Operations

India's Paramilitary forces have had a fair share of experience and success in deployments in urban areas of J&K and the North-East. The army has always dominated the hinterland with the CPOs engaged in protection duties. With the exception of the BSF, they have rarely operated independently in a grid-pattern or launched combing or seek and destroy operations in forests and mountains. But they have now been pitch forked into exactly this pattern of deployment in the fight against Naxalism. The area of operation is vast with dense forest coverage.

Therefore, with no previous experience it was naïve to expect them to achieve quick success in this theatre of low-intensity conflict where the Naxalites are not only indigenous to the area but have organised and entrenched themselves for at least two decades before the first *Khaki* jackboots arrived on the ground. Due to such inexperience in conducting CI operations, the CPOs were unable to adjust to the ground situation. Faced with serious command and leadership deficiencies, they are carrying out offensive operations. By and large they tend to operate in large groups and are sitting ducks to Maoist ambushes. They lack the skills and experience to conduct cordon and search operations, area domination patrols, surgical operations against a specific target and laying ambushes and counter-ambushes. Since offensive operations have suddenly become the essence of present and future operations a realisation they are slowly getting around to.

Raising New Battalions and Counterinsurgency Training

Prime Minister Manmohan Singh identified Naxalism as the gravest Internal Security challenge facing the country. As the CRPF was earmarked as the primary counterinsurgency force, its modernisation and expansion received a fillip. Today, most of the CRPF battalions are well equipped with modern weaponry and gear. As the CPOs took more and more casualties at the hand of the Naxalites, a need was felt to enhance their counter-insurgency training. The Counter-Insurgency and Jungle Warfare School at Kanker, Chhattisgarh was the first training school to be established. The School has provided training to thousands of State Special Police and Paramilitary forces. More such schools are being raised across the Naxal-affected states.

Inadequate CI Training

Since the year 2006, several field formations and Infantry Regimental Centres of the Indian Army's Central, South-Western and Western Commands have been imparting a six week pre-induction training capsule to CRPF and State Police force companies prior to their induction in Counter-Naxalite operations. Nearly 48,000 CRPF and police personnel have been given some form of training by the army. However, the army feels that the CPO leadership does not take this training capsule in a serious manner. Companies are sent in isolation for training. A battalion seldom turns up together as a complete unit. Even the companies which eventually arrive are pooled together from men from different units and companies.

The IPS officers do not feel motivated enough to attend the training capsules. The personnel are sent without any pre-training orientation. The fitness levels of the men are so poor that a bulk of the six week period elapses in bringing them in a shape to receive the training. Administrative issues pertaining to the sharing of finances between the MHA and MOD has been recently sorted out with the MHA agreeing to foot the bill for training of its personnel. The absence of a young officer cadre seriously impairs the ability of the rank and file to imbibe meaningful and motivated training and to provide continuity. The personnel are reluctant to go through the hard grind of live firing, rigorous field craft and vigorous platoon level tactics. A notable shortcoming is in their psychological domain where they perceive aggressive offensive operations as a taboo. But they are now shaping up to take on the type of operations required to tackle the LWE insurgency.

Deployment in Naxal Areas

Once deployed, CRPF and other CPMF Companies are placed under the supervision of the district SP who then directs them into operations. Companies are attached with different police stations/posts and occupy government buildings such as health centres and schools in villages. The Paramilitary is not organised into sectors with each battalion having a dedicated area of responsibility. Therefore, the very nature of deployment precludes a serious attempt at operating against the Maoists. The deployment pattern sets forth a defensive mindset whereby different CRPF companies are positioned over a widespread area in a piecemeal fashion. There is no cohesiveness of the force.

Coupled with a severe disconnect with their officer leadership who are not present on the ground, the paramilitary men are in the process of shedding their 'bunker mentality.' Till very recently, the Maoists did not have to strain much to keep the areas around the CRPF posts under their control. They attacked these isolated posts at will and decamped with a substantial amount of weaponry. And when the forces moved out for an operation with a lack of knowledge of the area and terrain they were sitting ducks for Maoist ambushes. The forces deployed in such operations incurred severe casualties by flouting the basic rules of counterinsurgency operations by moving in large numbers or in a single file or moving without flank protection, using vehicles on dirt tracks/ unmetalled roads, returning by the same route after conducting an operation.

A majority of the CRPF companies hence deployed in a piecemeal manner were sitting ducks for the armed Naxal squads who dominated the villages and forests and carved out a 'Liberated Zone'. Unlike in J&K or the North-East where the area was dominated by the Army, here the Maoists constantly launched attacks on the CRPF posts and convoys. In fact, bulk of the casualties were inflicted by IEDs during administrative movement of vehicular convoys.

Post-Dantewada Ambush

The Chintanlar ambush is a classic case of how not to conduct a counter-insurgency operation the lessons of which the CRPF cadre has done well to assimilate. In fact, the case-study of this ambush, can be taken as a template of how an inexperienced CRPF was conducting regular operations in LWE affected areas. The ambush initially shook the morale of the force and led to a temporary suspension of major operations. The Government of India after studying the recommendations of the EN Rammohan Committee (appointed to carry out an assessment of the CRPF operations) has overhauled the force's deployment in LWE areas. More CRPF battalions have been deployed but they continue to operate in a piecemeal manner. On the ground, the security forces have had some major successes in which the Naxals have suffered some serious reverses. In some operations, the CRPF has inflicted more attrition on the extremists and suffered fewer casualties themselves.

Commando Battalions for Resolute Action (CoBRA)

The Government of India in the year 2008 decided to raise 10 specially trained and equipped battalions for counter-insurgency operations and jungle warfare. These specialised battalions have been raised as part of the CRPF. Six of these battalions were raised in Naxal-affected districts of Jagdalpur (Chhattisgarh), Koraput (Orissa), Hazaribagh (Jharkhand), Gaya (Bihar) and Bhandara (Maharashtra). Four more battalions were provided to the states of West Bengal, Jharkhand, Uttar Pradesh and Assam. The CoBRA battalions are meant for offensive operations against the naxalites and insurgents.

They are especially trained and equipped for carrying out active operations like cordon and search, combing operations, etc. The personnel have received specialised counter-insurgency training in the Counter Insurgency and Anti-Terrorist schools set up in various states. The CoBRA battalions are equipped with sophisticated weaponry such as the AK Series rifles, rocket launchers and 51 mm mortars. The operational performance of the CoBRA battalions have been by and large successful though they have at times been relegated to performing tasks such as protection of polling booths during elections, etc.

CoBRA battalions are also better organised than regular CRPF battalions. A CoBRA battalion has six companies and each company is divided into three teams. Each company is led by a Deputy Commandant. Each team is led by an Assistant Commandant and has 39 personnel in it.

The CoBRA battalions are staffed by officers having a younger age profile. There are 25-30 officers in each CoBRA battalion as compared to only 14 in a regular CRPF battalion. These factors, ie a younger age profile of officers and a high ratio of officers ensures that the battalion maintains high standards of operational efficiency and morale while operating in a challenging and fluid counter-insurgency environment. Presently, nine CoBRA battalions are deployed in the LWE theatre and one in Karbi Anglong district of Assam.

The table below displays the present deployment of CRPF and CoBRA battalions in the LWE grid.

State	*CRPF Bn*	*CoBRA Bn*
Chhattisgarh	17	02
Jharkhand	18	02
Orissa	10	01
West Bengal	07	01
Maharashtra	07	01
Bihar	06	01
Andhra Pradesh	03	NIL
Madhya Pradesh	02	01

Appraisal

The 222 CRPF battalions deployed across the length and breadth of the country are performing various tasks from counter-insurgency operations to crowd control and static duties at vital installations, etc.

Counter-Insurgency Operations: The CRPF has always been among the first responders in the North East and J&K to prevent the situation from deteriorating further. The CRPF has played a tremendous role in keeping the peace in these trouble-torn corners of the country. But a role appraisal of their deployment pattern over the decades, highlights that their primary role has been in support of the Army in carrying out counter-insurgency operations. Once the CI Grid was taken over by the Army and BSF in some areas, the role of the CRPF has majorly been to guard vital installations, provide security to VIPs and other government buildings and carry out limited road-opening tasks in select areas. The force has had very little experience in taking on militants directly, or conduct operations such as cordon and search, raids, laying ambushes or neutralising militants holed up inside a built-up area.

However, the CRPF today is independently controlling the CI grid in the urban areas of J&K, including Srinagar city. Their performance has been satisfactory. But given the overwhelming presence of the Army/RR units on the line of control, second-tier and in the hinterland, and a tremendous decline in the number of militants operating in the state, is the CRPF in a position to completely replace RR units from J&K?

Or will the militants gain an upper-hand if the RR is replaced from even selected districts? Are the CRPF battalions combat-worthy enough to carry out tasks performed by the Army for more than half-a-century now? These are the questions the CRPF hierarchy has to pose to itself to justify the faith the Indian Prime Minister has posed in them by declaring them to be the CI force of the country.

So what are the judging parameters by which any force should be able to carry out effective counter-insurgency operations and does the CRPF meet those requirements?

The troops in a fighting unit should possess the requisite training in handling firearms, fitness and motivation levels and a sense of bonding and camaraderie between themselves.

Although the troops possess basic knowledge of weapons and fitness levels, this training is not continuous and evolving. The training at the battalion level has to be more rigorous and practical. Due to their recruitment and deployment pattern, the bonding and camaraderie between men is not as strong as it is in an Infantry battalion. Their stretched and isolated deployment over a vast area and under a different command set-up further inhibits collective training and bonding. The organisational structure is mostly similar to an Infantry battalion. But by and large principle, the CRPF battalions do not possess the same levels of efficiency, drills and orientation as the infantry/RR battalions.

The force should be combat-ready by carrying out intensive training and collective-firing exercises prior to their deployment in a CI area.

The peace to field rotation of CRPF battalions is very uncertain and frequent. In fact companies are repeatedly deployed from one difficult area to another. The men get very little time to carry out basic firing leave alone intensive training of battle-inoculation, etc.

The force should be an effective fighting unit with troops possessing adequate fitness levels and training to endure in a difficult and dynamic operational environment. In addition it should be equipped with all the

latest gadgetry, equipment and state-of-the-art weapons for taking on highly motivated and well-trained militants.

The CRPF today, barring some deficiencies which can be over-come, have the equipment and weaponry almost similar to an infantry battalion for conducting counter-insurgency operations. But the fitness levels and specialised CI training of their men is lacking. The specialised training can however be imparted at the Army's Corps Battle Schools, provided battalions undergo this training as a collective-unit. Counter-Insurgency operations are essentially a junior leaders's battle. The proficiency of section and platoon level training has to be of a high standard. The CRPF is accustomed to operating in large numbers as against in section strengths of 10 and 15 which is critical in CI ops. Their ability to fire and move, withstand withering fire, counter-ambush, and endure casualties etc is not developed enough to withstand the demands of a challenging CI environment. The dis-connect between the officer and men compounds this problem further. Also, the men now need to be motivated enough to perform rigorous tasks such as night ambushes and participate in prolonged operations. Though it has to be admitted, that the CRPF is increasingly measuring upto assigned tasks in their deployment in LWE-affected areas to a great extent, now.

The unit should be battle-hardened with enough combat experience with the troops being able to endure in a fire-fight.

As has been brought out earlier, the CRPF units have had very little experience in direct operations against militants. This is not to infer that the CRPF has not been able to combat militants when attacked but the ability of their men to endure under fire is limited since they not participated in too many fire-fights with the militants. On a regular basis, invariably succumbing to IED attacks which is an indirect attack, in any case.

The unit should be deployed in a grid-pattern under a single command and control set-up.

The CRPF companies are assigned to different districts and police station areas. In some cases, this deployment stretches for hundreds of kilometers. Ideally, all the companies should be deployed in the same geographical grid under the command and control of its battalion commander and sector HQs. In addition, their experience in conducting routine activities such as cordon and search, combing operations, laying-ambushes is fairly limited.

An appraisal of its deployment pattern indicates that the CRPF has been performing the following major tasks:-

- It is the designated Counter Terrorism force of the country.
- It has been used in some form or the other in Counter Insurgency operations.

- Protection of Rear Areas and Lines of Communication/Logistics mode.
- Vulnerable Areas /Points, Very Important People protection.
- Law and order duties.

A careful analysis of the above would indicate that the bulk of the CRPF deployment has been in the protection of rear areas, vulnerable areas/points, protection of VIPs. The force has been deployed in various internal disturbances obtaining all across the country.

The Road Ahead

As one evaluates the CRPF's performance since its raising, it is evident that the force was raised as a striking reserve by the Central government to be deployed in unfolding internal security situations across the country. In that the force has lived up to its expectations and has performed its tasks at difficult times.

In addition to the Army, the government has used nearly all the Central Police Organisations in Counter Insurgency duties at some point or the other. This is despite the fact that these forces were neither raised for this purpose nor did they possess the requisite training, weaponry, skills and the motivation to endure in Counter-Insurgency duties. Nevertheless, they did carry out supplementary roles with success.

After being designated the primary counter terrorism force by the Central Government, more than half of the total number of CRPF battalions are deployed in Counter Insurgency operations in Jammu and Kashmir, North East and in LWE affected areas. As has been mentioned earlier, 28 out of the 70 battalions in J&K are deployed for Counter Insurgency operations (excluding Srinagar city). The CRPF companies operate within the grid of Rashtriya Rifles units. With the general improvement in the security situation in the state and the residual strength of militants having come down to 400-600, this trend is likely to continue. But, despite that due to lack of combat experience and inadequacies at the structural level which have been highlighted in the preceding paragraphs, the CRPF is not in a position to independently take on the CI/CT role in J&K, which is why the Government of India in its latest budget has gone on to increase the budget outlay for RR battalions, whereas, one should have seen reduction in their numbers. Clearly, the CRPF is yet to fill in the breach. Fortunately, with experience, they promise to be on their way.

Similarly, in Assam, peace has returned with violence levels coming down drastically with factions of the ULFA and NDFB entering into ceasefire agreements with the Centre. Although the Army remains deployed in the state, the CRPF has taken over bulk of the CI tasks and is performing an effective role. Whether or not it will be able to keep the peace, if the Army is relieved of its CI role in Assam needs to be seen. Also, there can be no guarantee that militants return to the path of violence if the talks break down or the anti-talk factions gain strength with external support and an increase in cadre strength.

The only area where the CRPF has performed a direct Counter-Insurgency role has been in the LWE affected states of the Indian heartland. Judging by its high attrition rate in anti-naxalite operations and no visible improvement in the ground situation or a severe denting of the Maoist operational capabilities, its performance is as yet on the learning curve with a promise to be there in the short to medium term.

Presently, despite the fact that more than 170 of the total 218 battalions are deployed in CI areas, (though not all of them would be performing CI roles) and it being the designated Counter Insurgency force of the country, the CRPF is to travel some distance, yet to assume and discharge the onerous but distinguished mantle of the designated counter insurgency force of the country. The force continues to be in a massive expansion and modernisation mode. So what should be the future role of the force ?

Given India's burgeoning youth population and rising regional aspirations, the demand for creation of more employment opportunities, sharing of resources and forming of new states are expected to rise. The recent Telengana agitation and the economic blockades in Manipur are an indicator of this rising trend. The Gujjar agitations in the years 2007 and 2008 have also highlighted the vulnerabilities of people's angst having a spill-over effect on the country's economy and global image. As India moves towards being an economic power house, it can ill afford to be held back by these developments which can dent its global image and prevent foreign investment from coming into the country.

The CRPF as a strike reserve is the best suited force to be deployed for potential law and order situations which may develop more frequently in the coming decades. For this, CRPF battalions have to be deployed in or around major second and even third-tier cities across the country. It can be effectively deployed along with the RAF units to counter public agitations obtaining due to political, economic, industrial or social reasons. The CRPF will continue to be utilised for the smooth conduct of assembly and general elections and major events such as Commonwealth games, etc. However, the CRPF has its work cut out in assuming independent charge of CI operation in J&K.

Recommendations

- The CRPF units would, therefore continue to be rotated between field areas and peace stations. The field area tenures in J&K, North East and in LWE-affected states should be a fixed two and half to three year tenure. At present deployment of some battalions stretch beyond this period imposing tremendous strain on the men. Their turn-over periods in peace stations should be increased and the number of peace stations should also be increased. An additional 29 battalions of the CRPF are being raised. This would ensure that at least half of the battalions are deployed in a peace station at any given period of time.

- The concept of CoBRA battalions should be done away with. All CRPF units should be similarly equipped and trained to perform both CI tasks in field areas and law and order duties in peace stations. All CRPF battalions should be equipped and trained on the pattern of the CoBRA. Specialised CI equipment and weapons can be held as sector stores and taken over by units being inducted in CI areas.
- Adequate training facilities should be created at the peace stations where the men can be oriented and trained with capsules for CI operations prior to their field deployment.
- Pre-induction training should be provided to the CRPF units at the Army Corps Battle Schools in J&K and NE. The Army can create similar training facilities to impart such training in the Naxal affected areas.
- Despite the above, the CRPF will be fully-blooded in CI operations only after it has operated effectively along side the Army in operations such as raids ambushes, combing operations, etc. On the job training in conducting ROPs, security of COBs, etc, daily routine need to be imparted. Given the general improvement in both J&K and Assam, the Army can co-opt larger components of the CRPF already deployed there in conducting such operations. The experience and combatisation thus gained by the CRPF would also prove effective in LWE areas. Specialised training in handling communications and countering IEDs should also be imparted. The CRPF's proposal of recruiting retired PBORs from specialised arms such as the Engineer Corps is a step in the right direction. In fact, officers leaving the army after 5/10 yrs should be given an option for lateral transfer into the CRPF to enhance their CI experience and training. Jawans leaving the army after 10 years of service may also be recruited as section commanders in the CRPF.
- The critical area that needs to be addressed is at the cutting edge, i.e. at the battalion level. The age profile of officers has to be lowered. More young officers have to be recruited as platoon and company commanders. These officers should be trained at the IMA/OTAs and also serve some time with Infantry battalions. The latter proposal has already been implemented.
- The CRPF battalions should operate under their own command and control structure at the battalion, range and sector levels. The officers who are directly recruited into the CRPF should be eligible for promotion upto the highest (DG) level. The top posts (DIG and above) should be filled by CRPF cadre and not IPS officers. This would boost the morale of the force at the cutting edge level.
- Adequate recreational and family welfare facilities like residential quarters for families, education for children (CRPF schools exist in the country),

medical facilities for men should be enhanced. Gladly, actualization of these infrastructures have been conceived at the time of writing.

The table below lists the force's operational achievements since 2001. However, it may be noted that the number on militants killed may also include those killed in joint operations with the army and police.

Table 1

Year	*No. of Operations*	*Militants*		*Seizures*	
		Killed	*Apprd*	*Arms*	*AMM*
2001	198	229	149	318	14114
2002	207	178	107	281	12827
2003	93	86	92	167	12361
2004	118	96	160	168	7831
2005	132	151	301	219	11575
2006	124	152	517	277	10746
2007	90	101	249	182	11665
2008	65	103	221	162	15663
2009	53	74	123	143	11107
2010	43	87	161	224	20981
2011	14	27	57	63	3018
Total	1137	1284	2137	2204	131888

Table 2: Operational Losses of CRPF in J&K

Year	*No. of Operations*	*Own Force Losses*			
		Killed	*Injured*	*Arms*	*AMM*
2001	198	28	152	0	0
2002	207	45	112	1	60
2003	93	09	44	0	0
2004	118	31	103	1	30
2005	132	21	110	0	165
2006	124	09	199	1	35
2007	90	17	151	2	150
2008	65	10	826	4	120
2009	53	11	513	4	120
2010	43	05	1586	2	60
2011	14	00	40	0	0
Total	1137	186	3836	15	740

NOTES

1. RSD Dogra, 'Nation Keepers: Central Reserve Police Force', APH Publishing Corporation, 2004.
2. Ibid.

3. Giriraj Shah, 'Paramilitary Forces of India', Anmol Publications, 2004.
4. Ibid (1) above.
5. Ibid (3) above.
6. Ibid (1) above.
7. Peacekeepers of the Nation, Central Reserve Police Force, Vanity Books, 1998, p. 38.
8. Ibid (7) above.
9. Ibid (1) above.
10. Ibid (3) above.
11. Ibid (7) above, p. 67
12. Ibid (7) above, p.69
13. Ibid (7) above, p.70
14. Ibid (7) above, p. 71
15. Ibid (3) above.
16. Ibid (7) above, p. 77
17. Ibid (3) above.
18. Ibid (7) above, p. 51.
19. Ibid (7) above, p.52.
20. Official website of the CRPF, www.crpf.gov.in
21. Ibid (11) above.
22. Ibid (11) above.
23. MHA Annual Report 2010-11.
24. Ibid (11) above.
25. Ibid (1) above.
26. Ibid (7) above, p. 91.
27. Ibid (7) above, p. 97.
28. Ibid (7) above, p. 99.
29. Ibid (7) above, p. 99.
30. Kashmir turmoil takes heavy toll on CRPF jawans, The Tribune, 22 September 2010, accessed at http://www.tribuneindia.com/2010/20100922/jkplus.htm#1

9

Rapid Action Force (RAF)

Origin

Since its inception in 1939, the Central Reserve Police Force (CRPF) has been deployed extensively in internal security duties, maintaining law and order during communal disturbances and riots, etc. Ever since the early 1990s, the deployment of the force for counter-insurgency duties put an additional strain on the already stretched manpower and resources of the force. Hence, a need was felt to raise a separate and a specially trained force for tackling communal disturbance which had been erupting with alarming frequency in the country at that time.

Consequently, five battalions of the CRPF were specially trained, equipped and converted into the Rapid Action Force (RAF) on 7 October 1992. Five more battalions were converted soon thereafter. "Ideals of secularism were especially inculcated in its members and a Dove, the universal symbol of peace and amity was chosen as its insignia. It was dressed in blue camouflage dungarees, for blue signifies peace, prosperity and plenty. Thus even at first sight the force projects a people friendly image".[1]

Ever since its raising, the Rapid Action Force battalions have remained deployed in extremely sensitive cities and towns of the country and have managed to contain many explosive situations. The force has also provided contingents to United Nations peace-keeping missions in Haiti, Kosovo which is a testimony to its effectiveness and achievements.

Organisation

The RAF is an integral part of the CRPF. The IG, RAF reports to the DG CRPF. The organisational structure of the RAF is different from that of standard CRPF battalions.

DG CRPF
↓
IGP RAF SECTOR
↓
DIGP RAF RANGE
↓

↓	↓
Comdt Accts	Comdt Staff

Organisational Structure at Battalion Level

Commandant
2IC
↓

↓	↓	↓	↓
DC (Adjutant)	DC (Ops & Trg)	DC (QM/MTO)	DC (General)
↓	↓	↓	↓
A COY	B COY	C COY	D COY

PLATOON-I   PLATOON-II
↓
TEAM × 3 (14)
(Riot control element, Firing Element, Tear Smoke Element)

Each RAF battalion is commanded by a Commandant rank officer. A battalion is organised into four companies, each commanded by a Deputy Commandant. A company has two platoons, each commanded by an Assistant Commandant. A platoon is composed of two teams. The teams have three specialised elements, viz, the Riot control element, Firing Element, Tear Smoke Element. A Team is commanded by a Team Commander of the rank of an Inspector. The teams have a strength of 14 personnel each.

The official publication of the Rapid Action Force describes the specialised role of each element within a team.

Tear Smoke Element: It is the first element that comes into action in controlling a mob. It is headed by a Head Constable with two constables working under him.

Riot Control Element: This is the lathi-wielding element that steps into action it and when the situation demands. It is composed of one Head Constable and five constables.

Firing Element: This is the third element that moves forward only as a last resort to disperse the riotous crowd. One Sub-Inspector, one Head Constable and three constables constitute this team.

The 10 RAF battalions are tactically located at communally sensitive areas which have a history of incidents in the past. Stationing of these battalions at these locations makes it possible for them to rapidly deploy at the site of a disturbance. The RAF battalions are deployed at:

- 99 Battalion—Hyderabad
- 100 Battalion—Ahmedabad
- 101 Battalion—Allahabad
- 102 Battalion—Mumbai
- 103 Battalion—Delhi
- 104 Battalion—Aligarh
- 105 Battalion—Coimbatore
- 106 Battalion—Jamshedpur
- 107 Battalion—Bhopal
- 108 Battalion—Meerut

Equipping Profile

The aim of the RAF is to quell rioters with the application of minimum force. Thus, in addition to the standard SLR rifles issued to its personnel, the RAF is equipped with non-lethal weapons to deter the rioters and not main or kill them. Such equipments include shock batons, rubber truncheons, rubber bullets and plastic pellets. The purpose of these weapons is not to injure or kill anyone but to dissuade the rioters from making mischief and disperse.

The force is also supplied with special tear smoke munitions and stun grenades. The stun grenades produce a flash and a deafening sound which helps in dispersing the crowd without causing any injuries. Some of the tear smoke inventions in the RAF inventory are: Single way grenade, Three way grenade, Stun lac grenade, Stinger grenade, Dye Marker, Stun Shell Normal & Electric, Dual Shell Normal & Electric, Two-in-one Shell, Short Range Shell, Long Range Shell, Wood Piercing Shell, Stun Grenade Lac, Stun Grenade Mark-II, Dye Marker Grenade, Multi-Barrel Launcher and Vehice-mounted Tear Smoke Devices. The dye marker is an effective device that stains the cloth of a rioter and makes him easily identifiable. The riot control vehicles, 'Vajra' are mounted with the Multi-barrel launcher which can fire shells in any direction.

RAF units are also equipped with fire tenders and recovery vehicles. Other equipments include protective clothing, water jet blankets, extension ladder, bolt cutter, portable chemical fire extinguishers, etc.

Other modern equipments like safety reflective vests, portable spot light sets, industrial emergency light system and other fire fighting equipment are being procured for riot control and disaster relief tasks. Riot intervention vehicles and water canon jets would make it possible for the men to enter narrow by-lanes in pursuit of the rioters.

Selection and Training

The duties performed by RAF personnel can be strenuous and extremely taxing at times. A high-level of mental alertness and robustness has to be developed by the personnel. Personnel with quick reflexes and a mature outlook are preferred for the job. To maintain a young age profile, the constables in the RAF are between the age group of 20-27, junior leaders are in the age group of 30-35 and the officers are not older than 45 years of age.

The RAF has Mahilla troops to deal with women rioters and constitute 7.5 percent (as of 2003) of the force.

Due to the sensitive task of the force, due care is taken to ensure that the personnel selected are of a secular character. The candidates are put through a series of psychological tests and interviews to determine their secular orientation. The secular character of the force is maintained by giving adequate representation to all communities and sections of society. Due care is taken that the minority communities get adequate representation in the force.

The personnel inducted into the RAF have already received their basic training at the CRPF Regional Training Centres. Further in-service training is imparted on them at the unit level to improve their efficiency and make them suitable for riot control tasks. All aspects of training programmes are so designed to change the CRPF men into disciplined, proficient and responsible members of the RAF, who are able to discharge their duties with full confidence and efficiency in their changed role.

The various specialised training capsules of the RAF are briefly mentioned below.

Conversion Training: This initial training lasts for about three months with the aim of familiarizing the personnel from the CRPF with the role and working of the RAF. The new entrants are taught effective methods of riot control drill, use of tear smoke munitions and other equipments. They are also made proficient in signaling, fire fighting, martial arts, rescue and relief works and providing first aid. The other specialised courses which a RAF personnel has to undergo are:

Tear Smoke Course
Fire Fighting with rescue and relief operations
First Aid Course
Refresher Training
Refresher Course for SOs

In addition, the RAF battalions frequently undertake FAMEX or Familirisation Exercises to gain full knowledge of the people, topography, social structure and communal equations, inter-community and inter-caste relations, occupational and law and order situation of their area of responsibility. A period of a week or more is spent on these exercises to gather local intelligence and a layout of the locality. Such exercise result in a quick deployment and to gain a firm hand on the situation during a contingency.

Past Operations

1992-94

The first deployment of the RAF was to control the communal riots that had broken out in Sitamarhi district of Bihar in October 1992. The RAF deftly handled the tense situation and earned tremendous goodwill of the people by providing medical aid to riot affected people.

Thereafter, the force was deployed handled in communally sensitive pockets during the bye-elections in Bombay in November 1993 and during the general elections in Ayodhya (January 1994). It also handled the communal disturbances in Siwan, Bihar.

On 7 October 1994, the RAF moved in swiftly to prevent clashes in Bangalore after tension was simmering following the decision to broadcast Urdu News on Doordarshan.

1994-96

The year 1994 saw the deployment of the RAF in Hubli, Karnataka where tension was in the air following the decision to unfurl the National Flag on Republic Day in a minority community dominated area.

The RAF effectively quelled communal rioting in Moradabad on 11 February 1995. It's deployment also prevented violence from breaking out during a Maha Shivratri procession in Varanasi during the same month.

Six companies of the RAF were deployed in Kerala after communal violence had broken out between two minority communities in the state.

The presence of 21 companies of the force ensured peaceful conduct of Janma Asthmi celebrations at the Krishna Janambhoomi in Mathura in July 1995.

As part of its welfare activities, 105 Battalion of the RAF carried out Shramdan in July 1995 to construct a road in Village Chatelallor of Mallapuram district as part of the Civic Action Programme. 108 Battalion of the RAF distributed free medicines for common ailments to a large crowd of patients on Ghaziabad, UP.

The RAF played a major role in distributing medicines and other relief material during the Surat plague of September 1995. The RAF men ventured into the worst affected areas which even the doctors were shying away from entering.

1996-98

The RAF set up a lost and found camp to provide guidance to thousands of pilgrims during the Kumbh Mela in 1996. Companies of 101 Battalion rescued trapped persons from the debris of a wall collapse in Ayodhya during the same year.

As part of its civic action programmes, RAF battalions organised medical camps in Karimnagar, Andhra Pradesh and in South Delhi to prevent the outbreak of dengue.

1998-2000

In May, 1998, the RAF acted with true professionalism to keep the peace in Moradabad, UP after the outbreak of communal riots.

RAF men provided great relief and succor to the people of Kandla Port in Gujarat during the cyclone of June 1998.

2001-03

RAF carried out extensive rescue and relief work in Gujarat following the devastating earthquake of 26 January 2001. The RAF was instrumental in saving many lives and provided the victims with immediate medical care and distributed blankets, etc. The RAF saw a major deployment in Gujarat following the Post-Godhra riots of 2002. The deployment of the force in sensitive areas of the state prevented further violence from breaking out following the Godhra train carnage of 27 February 2002.

The RAF was also deployed in the outer cordon of the Akshardham temple to assist the NSG in carrying out its operations to flush out the two holed up terrorists inside Akshardham temple in Gandhinagar in September 2002.

Ten RAF battalions remained deployed for a total number of 5146 days during the year 2002 to prevent the outbreak of riots and communal clashes.

UN Missions

A company of the RAF comprising 120 personnel were deployed with the US Army 504 Military Police Battalion (Dragon Fighters) in UNMIH from 31 March 1994 to 31 March 1995. The RAF contingent carried out tasks such as mobile patrolling, saturation patrolling and manning of police stations and the national prison. It also imparted training to prison personnel and conducted presidential elections in the troubled region.

The RAF contingent was integrated with the US Army battalion to form the first ever US-Indian battalion under UN control.

Two companies of the RAF were inducted to Kosovo as the Indian Special Police Unit (ISPU) since 2000. The duties included providing reinforcement, border duty, guarding vital installations and sensitive localities with mixed population, prisoner's escort, etc. The extensive patrolling and area familiarisation exercises conducted by the RAF contingent earned them the goodwill of the people.

Deductions

The outbreak of frequent communal disturbances in the country saw the need for the formation of a dedicated and specially trained rapid response force to tackle incidents of rioting and communal disturbances. The need was also felt to minimise civilian casualties and prevent high-handed behaviour at the hands of the local police and other stretched central forces which were often rushed to contain communal violence.

The organisational structure, training modules and equipping profile of the RAF fulfils all the parameters of a rapid response force for handling emergency situations. The ten battalions of the RAF in their twenty years of active service have been able to effectively tackle numerous challenges in major cities and towns of the country. The professional conduct and deft handling of communally charged situations has often resulted in the cooling of tempers and return of peace to an area. Due to their secular outlook and mature handling of the situation, the RAF has a high degree of credibility among the local communities. It is due to this reason that it is able to effectively tackle a situation and bring it under control in no time. In fact, in several instances, the sheer presence of RAF personnel in their trademark blue dungarees is enough to prevent violence from breaking out.

The RAF was formed to specifically provide speedy aid to control a deteriorating law and order situation. The RAF battalions are headquartered at 10 major cities of the country which have a sizable population of the minority community and have had a history of communal disturbances and rioting. Over the years, the presence of RAF in these cities has provided them with accurate knowledge and information of the demographic profile, socio-economic patterns and relation between different communities in sensitive pockets of the cities. The regular area familirisation exercises undertaken by the RAF battalions in their respective areas of responsibility have provided them with information of the terrain, routes, landmarks, etc of localities prone to rioting and communal disturbances. This knowledge is useful in carrying out a rapid mobilisation in the event of a contingency. Also, during these exercises, the RAF personnel are able to build an effective rapport with the population, particularly with the community elders. This helps in winning the trust of the local communities and helps understand them better. It also provides an insight into the local dynamics and equations playing out in a particular locality and the likely causes of discontent that may lead to clashes between two communities residing closely together in an area. The famiiarisation exercises also helps in pre-identifying potential trouble makers and ring leaders who may rip up passions and incite the people to create disturbances. The establishment of relations with the local communities and undertaking of social welfare measures by the RAF in these areas also acts as a deterrent value and prevents the people from resorting to violence.

The permanent deployment of RAF battalions has prevented major incidents of violence from breaking out in these communally sensitive cities. In the event of a disturbance, the swift deployment of the force prevents a situation from getting out of hand and take a dangerous turn. The deployment of the RAF often has a salutary and a deterrent effect in containing a situation. The RAF has more credibility than the local police in some cases. The population has much more faith in the RAF during volatile situations because of their secular outlook and impartial behaviour. The RAF due to there area familirisation exercises and community welfare activities have been able to win the trust and confidence of the population in communally sensitive areas.

Despite their excellent track record, the deployment of the RAF battalions in only towns has often been a handicap as far as their deployment in the event of a breakout of riots in far-flung areas of the country is concerned. The critical factor in arresting a deteriorating situation is speed and rapidity. A rapid deployment is of the essence to prevent large scale casualties and destruction of public property due to rioting and arson. Although the RAF battalions are effective within minutes in deploying within their areas of responsibility, their deployment to other towns and cities may take several hours or even a day resulting in crucial loss of time. Therefore, the RAF should have its own dedicated fleet of vehicles to deploy anywhere in quick time. Reliance on chartered transport dents their mobilising capability and hence their effectiveness.

The RAF is effective in riotous situations as it is meant exclusively for that purpose. The use of the force for other routine tasks like 'bandobast' duties or supplementing the strength of the local or state police forces to manage large crowds, provide security during a major event or VIP visit should be avoided. The use of the RAF for every minor incident of rioting or civil disturbance in a small locality over petty issues should also be refrained from as too much visibility of the force would erode its deterrence value. Similarly, the RAF should also avoid frequent interactions with the local communities as part of their area familiarisation exercises. Too much interaction also has the inherent risk of losing their edge when large scale violence breaks out as the population would have become familiar with their operating patterns and tactics.

In the overall analysis, there is no doubt that the RAF has evolved as an effective and highly-skilled professional force in dealing with communal disturbances and rioting. It has proved its mettle by deftly handling large scale disturbance across the country and in UN Missions in Haiti and Kosovo. Despite, this, the strength of the RAF is fairly limited to tackle all incidents of rioting and violence. The force due to its location at 10 major cities of the country is often handicapped in aspects of time and distance to be able to react to incidents of civil agitations in the interiors and far-flung parts of the country. At times when large scale disturbances break out even within their areas of responsibility, the RAF deployment has to be complemented by other Central forces.

The purpose of the creation of a separate and dedicated force for dealing exclusively with communal disturbances and rioting has not taken the pressure off from other central forces for being deployed for such tasks. It must be kept in mind that the RAF was raised as the CRPF and other central forces were unable to provide men for these tasks by the late 1980s and early 1990s. Given the large size and huge population of the country it is beyond the capability of the 10 RAF Battalions to be present everywhere and contain every situation by themselves alone. Yet, the degree of professionalism exhibited by the RAF in dealing with the tasks it is meant for is far better than the state police and other central police forces. Therefore, it would be prudent to raise more RAF battalions for them to be able to effectively cover most parts of the country. Today, a radius of 250 Km forms the area of responsibility of one RAF battalion. Additional raising of battalions would increase the coverage and presence of RAF companies in smaller towns of the country as well.

In the past few years, incidents of communal violence have come down but incidents of large scale civil agitations and civil protests have increased manifold. In the coming years with an uncertain socio-economic outlook and increase in the youth population of the country, this trend is likely to continue. Therefore, the RAF should shift its focus from communal violence to riots and arson emanating due to socio-economic causes and political violence. The area familirisation exercises and surveys should be extended to this bracket of the population which is likely to cause civilian unrest in the future.

In the past five years, there has been a frequent breakout of violence due to socio-economic and caste politics factors. These movements have often stemmed from a small area and then engulfed larger areas within a state and have continued for months. A few examples of such civil agitations or protest movements which ultimately assumed a violent form are the Gujjar Sangarsh Samiti agitations of 2007 and 2008, the Gorkhaland agitation in Darjeeling district of West Bengal, the Telengana Movement in Andhra Pradesh, and farmer protests in Western Uttar Pradesh.

The state of Jammu and Kashmir has since 2008 frequently witnessed large-scale protests and violence breaking out in the summer months due to political and religious reasons. The recent Jan Lokpal Bill movement has so far remained non-violent but the large-scale mobilisation of people always has the potential of sparking a violent incident.

The notable aspects of all these incidents of civil disturbances mentioned above have seen the mobilisation of a large number of people, spread of the movement and the long duration of the agitations. Some of the agitations have displayed the tendency of re-erupting after a brief hiatus. Worryingly, in most of these disturbances, the RAF was either not used at all or had a piecemeal deployment as part of a larger deployment of other central police forces and state armed police. Also, in several instances, the situation warranted the deployment of the Army for a short period to contain the situation. All this points to the need for taking a re-look at the numerical strength and deployment pattern of the RAF. The RAF is quite effective in dealing with incidents of violence on a small scale but in large scale disturbances, the quantum of force deployed is often the only way out to keep people away from the streets. Also, it needs to be analysed whether the RAF should be used instead of regular CRPF battalions in dealing with the frequent outbreak of mob violence in Srinagar city. The RAF is specially equipped and trained to deal with such situations but, presently, the force is not deployed in that city.

Therefore, an increase in the number of RAF battalions is essential for it to deal with incidents of all hues across the country and relieve the burden of the Army and other Central Police forces in dealing with Internal Security duties.

NOTE

1. Quoted from, "In Service of the Nation", official publication of the Rapid Action Force.

10

Sashastra Seema Bal (SSB)

Origin

The Sashastra Seema Bal (SSB) was raised in 1963 to promote a sense of security among the population residing in border areas in the wake of the Chinese aggression of 1962. The aim was to inculcate among the population a sense of nationalism and build a resistance force to tackle aggression by the enemy in the future. The SSB was deployed in the frontier regions of Ladakh, Himachal Pradesh, Uttar Pradesh, North Bengal and Assam. The scheme was later extended to Manipur, Tripura, Jammu (1965), Meghalaya (1975), Sikkim (1976), border areas of Rajasthan and Gujarat (1989), Manipur, Mizoram and some more areas of Rajasthan and Gujarat (1988), South Bengal, Nagaland (1989) and Nubra Valley, Rajouri and Poonch district of Jammu and Kashmir (1991). The endeavour of the force has been to "present a benign face of the government among border populace in the far flung and inaccessible areas subscribing to the ethos of Service, Security and Brotherhood. The local populace always found SSB standing steadfastly with them during difficult times".

Role and Tasks

Following the recommendations of the GoM formed in the aftermath of the Kargil conflict, the SSB was designated as the border guarding force for the Indo-Nepal border. It took over the responsibility for guarding the 1751 kms long Indo-Nepal border along the states of Uttarakhand, (263.7 km., Distts.-03), Uttar Pradesh (599.3 km., Distts.-07), Bihar (800.4 km., Distts.-07), West Bengal (105.6 km., Distt.-01) and Sikkim (99 kms). In 2004, it was also entrusted the responsibility of guarding the 669 kms. stretch of Indo-Bhutan border along the states of Sikkim (32 km.), West Bengal (183 km., Distts.-02), Assam (267 km., Distts.-04) and Arunachal Pradesh (217 km., Distts.-02).

The role of the force is to:

- To promote a sense of security among the people living in the border areas.
- To prevent trans-border crimes and unauthorised entries into or exit from the territory of India.
- To prevent smuggling and other illegal activities.

Organisation

The SSB is a Border Guarding Force (BGF) under the administrative control of the Ministry of Home Affairs. The force is organised into 05 FTRs, 11 Sector Headquarters and 54 battalions. In addition it has two reserve battalions (including one for operations) in Delhi and one battalion in Goa.

The following table lists out the present deficiency in the force strength:-

Strength	*Sanctioned*	*Existing*
Combatised	60807	47079
Non-Combatised	4787	2655
Total	65594	49734

The Deployment of the SSB is as under:

FTR Hqrs	*Sector Hqrs*	*Battalions*
Ranikhet	Pithoragarh	Didihat Pithoragarh Champawat
	Pilibhit	Udham Singh Nagar Pilibhit Palia Dehradun (Reserve Bn)
Lucknow	Lakhimpur Kheri	Lakhimpur Kheri Nanpara Bahraich Bhinga Lucknor (Reserve Bn)
	Gorakhpur	Balrampur Utraula Siddarth Nagar Maharajganj
Patna	Muzaffarpur	Bagaha Narkatiaganj Bettiah Ramgarwa Motihari Sitamarhi-I

FTR Hqrs	*Sector Hqrs*	*Battalions*
		Sitamarhi-II Ranchi (Reserve Bn)
	Purnea	Jaynagar Rajnagar Birpur Bathnaha Araria
		Patna (Reserve)
Kolkata	Ranidanga	Kishanganj Thakurganj Ranidanga Khaprail Bhadrak (Reserve Bn)
	Gangtok	Geyzing Yuksam Rangpo
	New Jalpaiguri	Kalimpong Malbazar Falakata Alipurduar
Guwahati	Bongaigaon	Gossaigaon Kokrajhar Kajalgaon Bijni Howly
	Tezpur	Rangia-I Rangia-II (For ROP/CP Duty) Mangaldoi Udalguri Dirang Tawang
		Guwahati (Reserve Bn)

Training

Training to force personnel is imparted in the following training centres on Counter Subversion, Border Management, Perception Management, and Survival and Other professional courses designed to enhance performance.

1. SSB Academy, Srinagar
2. TC Gwaldam
3. TC Sapri
4. TC Salonibari
5. TC Ranidanga

6. Telecom TC Kasumpti
7. MTC Shimla
8. ITS-I, Ghitorni
9. IT&T, TC Faridabad
10. TC Shamshi
11. TC Sarahan
12. TC Kumarsain
13. ITS-II, Kolkata
14. DTC Palampur
15. 42ND Bn SSB, Didihat at Almora
16. 43RD Bn SSB, Udhamsinghnagar at Girijapuri
17. 44TH Bn Bettiah at Gorakhpur
18. 47TH Bn SSB, Bijini at Debendranagar
19. 48TH Bn SSB, Dehradun at Jamnagar
20. 49TH Bn SSB, Barasat

Challenges of Border Guarding

The GoM recommendation of designating a separate border guarding force for each of the country's large borders with different countries was an appropriate one and is being implemented with a few exceptions. The SSB is responsible for securing the Indo-Nepal and Indo-Bhutan borders encompassing more than 2000 kms across six states. India's boundary with Nepal and Bhutan traverses low hills with thick forests and fast flowing rivers and streams. The expansive land borders especially in the Uttar Pradesh, Bihar and West Bengal has a high density of population straddled along both sides of the border with mutual interdependence and cultural linkages. Historically, India and Nepal have shared a tradition of having open borders with easy movement of people for trade and travel purposes and other day to day activities. The population on either side especially in the Terai region of Nepal has religious and cultural affinities with the population in India further making it difficult to curtail the free movement of people. India had signed a friendship treaty with Nepal in the 1950s reaffirming the need to have open borders.

Taking advantage of this 'open and porous' border coupled with difficult terrain, the Indo-Nepal border has become a hub for anti-national elements to carry out their nefarious activities. The strength of the SSB is too small to effectively man the entire length of the boundary. Also the absence of a spread out deployment, ie, small (section strength) posts and a border fencing makes this task even more challenging. But given India's friendly and mutually beneficial relations with both Nepal and Bhutan it would be incorrect to replicate the stringent border guarding measures in place along the Indo-Pakistan or the Indo-Bangladesh borders. Such a move may be counter-productive and may lead to antagonising the local population on both sides of the border. Also, given the terrain configuration and vastness of the boundary it would require a large investment in firstly raising the manpower and subsequently undertaking construction of border infrastructure and fencing.

Over the decades, the porous Indo-Nepal border region has become a haven for smugglers, poachers, gun and drug-runners and even terrorists. These anti-national elements find a safe haven in Nepal for conducting their activities. Nepal also provides an easy transit point for poachers and smugglers to send their products across to China.

In the recent decades, the Indo-Nepal border has become a major transit point for terrorists and Maoists to create trouble in India. This route is often the most preferred one to ferry explosives and weapons to India. The porosity of the border and affinity with the population on both sides of it makes it easier for anti-national elements to seek refuge and slip to the other side with relative ease. In several major terrorist attacks in India, terrorists or their over ground workers have taken this route to supply explosives or escape after committing their acts.

Over the years, the SSB has apprehended many smugglers, poachers and other anti-national elements and has effected seizures of large quantities of weapons, ammunition and explosives as also timber, drugs and other banned substances. But, the vastness of the border and a stretched deployment of forces with scattered border outposts makes it virtually impossible to detect all illegal activities. The SSB presence on established border crossing points can be easily evaded by using hundreds of beaten tracks and other crossing points on foot.

To overcome this challenge of rampant illegal activities on our borders with Nepal and Bhutan, it is essential that a better sense of discipline and training is inculcated among the SSB personnel. A vast area of responsibility and stretched deployment in far-flung border areas far away from the public gaze has made the SSB men susceptible to corruption. In several areas, the local population has also developed an uneasy relation with the SSB men accusing them of harassment and high-handedness. Recently, there have been incidents of clashes between villagers and SSB personnel in Uttar Pradesh. There is a need to increase internal vigilance and accountability among the personnel. Prolonged deployment in one sector also makes the men more amenable to corrupt practices as they develop local contacts over the years.

It is virtually impossible nor desirable to man every nook and corner of our nearly 2000 km long borders with Nepal and Bhutan. Several other measures can be taken to increase the efficiency of the force and make border guarding more robust. To cover the long gaps in border surveillance, technology in the form of manned UAVs, CCTVs, etc can be installed at known crossing points. Modern communication equipment should be procured to better communication between the border outposts. Increased patrolling, both mobile and on foot should be undertaken to cover the large ground and establish better contact and amicable relations with the villagers. More four and two wheeled motor vehicles and boats should be procured for the force to improve mobility and speed.

A disciplined conduct by the men would instill a better sense of confidence among the local populace. The SSB can also take a leaf out of the Army's Sadhbhavna activities in J&K and the North East to assist the civic authorities to reach out to far-flung border villages and bring rural employment schemes, medical and other community development facilities to the population. A favourable image of the force would go a long way in improving the information flow and curtail illegal activities in the border regions.

Above all, the intelligence wing of the SSB at the battalion level should be strengthened to detect illegal activities. More civilian sources on both sides of the border should be co-opted to gather human intelligence. There is a need to establish closer integration between the police and all intelligence agencies operating in the border belt.

There is a need to take a re-look at the rotation policy of SSB battalions. A battalion deployed in one sector should be pulled back to a training centre for rest and re-fit. But given the limited number of SSB battalions this type of rotation between peace and field areas seems to be a difficult proposition. More recruitment from the border belts would instill a sense of belonging and pride among the personnel. In addition, family welfare measures and more benefits and post-retirement measures of the SSB personnel need to be adopted.

The SSB is performing an onerous and lonely task of guarding the often neglected and remotest border regions of the country. The Border Guarding Force is scattered over a large frontage interspersed with difficult terrain and a floating population. The free movement of terrorists across the Indo-Nepal border poses a tremendous challenge to the SSB. It is very difficult to detect these terrorists as they often move unarmed in small groups and there are a large number of unmanned and even undetected border crossing points. In the past three to four years, many militants apprehended in J&K have confessed to have gained entry from the porous land borders in the states of Uttarakhand, Uttar Pradesh and West Bengal. They then board a train or a bus to Jammu for their onward journey to their respective destinations in J&K. The Maoist cadres of both Nepal and India move across the border to seek refuge on either sides. A major consignment of Maoist arms and funds also flows across the border. The Maoists have refrained from committing any incident in the border belt to keep the focus away from this region and facilitate their easy and safe movement.

In the event of a major military offensive launched against the Maoists in the Indian hinterland there may be increased pressure on the Indo-Nepal border. A large number of armed Maoist cadres may take this route to escape the security forces dragnet into Nepal. In such an eventuality, the scattered and miniscule deployment of the SSB would not prove very effective in cordoning off this vast border and cut their escape route. Therefore, in the event of such an offensive against the Maoists it would be prudent to put an effective outer cordon in the areas of operation or beef up the deployment of CPOs along the Nepal border as well. The former option appears to be more viable given the likely tactics of security forces operation. The density of population along the Indo-Bhutan border is much less and the terrain is more interspersed with forests and fast-flowing small rivulets. In addition to the activities of wood-cutters and poachers, North East insurgent groups like the ULFA and NDFB use the border as a transit point to their bases in Bhutan. Although a large number of insurgent camps were wiped out during Operation All Clear in December 2003, there have been reports of the NDFB re-establishing camps in Bhutan. The SSB has to be strengthened to take on armed militants crossing the borders. This is a difficult task for an organisation which lacks orientation and basic training for counter-insurgency operations. In an ambush on 26 July 2010, NDFB militants killed four SSB personnel in Panguri PS area in Chirang district. In another ambush, three SSB personnel were killed in Kokrajhar district on 04 April 2011. The NDFB had ambushed a BSF vehicle in the same district on 14 March 2011 killing eight BSF personnel and injuring seven others.[1]

NOTE

1. Major incidents of violence in Assam 1990-2012; www.satp.org, accessed at http://www.satp.org/satporgtp/countries/india/states/assam/data_sheets/majorincidents.htm

11

Railway Protection Force (RPF) and Government Railway Police (GRP)

Railway operations began in India with the laying of the Bombay-Thane railway line in 1854. Since then, the Indian Railway network has expanded to include 114,500 kms tracks over a distance of 65,000 km across the length and breadth of the country. Indian Railways has the fourth largest rail network in the world which covers 7,5000 stations. As for rolling stock, IR owns over 240,000 (freight) wagons, 60,000 coaches and 9,000 locomotives It is the world's second largest commercial or utility employer, with more than 1.36 million employees.[1]

Railway Security

It is estimated that nearly 30 million passengers travel every day on Indian Railways. 2.8 million tons worth of freight is also transported by rail in a single day.[2] In 1854, the Railways had its own police force to handle security while the responsibility of protecting its properties and goods were entrusted upon "chowkidars". By 1882, a formal division into 'Government Police' and 'Private (Companies) Police' took place.[3] However, the Chowkidari system was found unviable as a large amount of theft and pilferage of goods took place due to the connivance between chowkidars and local low-level officials. This problem magnified during the two world wars. Post-Independence, a committee under the then Director of the Intelligence Bureau, Mr BN Mullik recommended the raising of a separate Railway Protection Force headed by an Inspector General rank officer. The IG was also to act as an advisor to the Railway Board on matters of security, training, postings, promotions. The force was also to have its own security wing. The Railway Protection Act was finally enacted by the Parliament on 29 August 1957 and the RPF regulations were formulated in 1966. An amendment was made to the RPF act in 1985 for the construction and maintenance of the force as an armed force of the Union.[4]

The RPF functions under the Ministry of Railways and is funded by the Rail Budget. The strength of the RPF is 65,000 which include the Railway Protection Special Force (RPSF) Battalions and fire-service wing.

Role and Tasks

The duties of the force as governed by the RPF Act of 1957 and modified in 1985 includes, to protect and safeguard railway property, to remove any obstruction in the movement of railway property and to do any other act conducive to better protection and security of railway property. The Act empowers the personnel to arrest and search any person or property within railway limits in the absence of an arrest warrant or the presence of a magistrate.[5] In addition, several provisions of the Code of Criminal Procedures, 1973, CrPC and the Railway Act of 1989 are applicable to RPF personnel for specific actions.

Organisation

Security Directorate in the Board Office

↓

- DIG/RPF (Jt Director) Sec I
  ↓
  SO (Dy Director General Security & Crime)
  ↓
  ASO / Asst Director Security (Crime)
- AIG RPF (Dy Director General
- DIG RPSF (Jt Director General)
  ↓
  - Asst Comdt (Central Stores)
  - Asst Inspr of Arms
  - Under Secy (Defence)

Zonal Railways

↓

Chief Security Officer

↓

Security Officer (Division)

↓

Asst Security Officer/Under Security Officers (Crime, Intelligence, Special Intelligence Service, Prosecution)

↓

Company Commander

↓

Inspector

↓

Platoon Cdr (ASI incharge of Outposts)

The responsibility for overall command, recruitment, discipline, internal economy and administration lies with the Chief Security Officer. At the Zonal level, the Chief Security Officer shall keep the Inspector General and the Zonal Manager fully informed on all matters pertaining to protection, security and railway property and premises. His Headquarter is at the same location where the General Manager has his headquarter. The force on each zonal railway consists of the Executive Branch (comprising of protection, investigation and intelligence wings), prosecution and Fire Services Branch.[6]

RPF Battalions

RPF is an armed force of the Union organised into battalions headed by a Commandant with two Assistant Commandants and an Adjutant, who are both Assistant Security Officers. The strength of each battalion is four companies and a headquarters wing. The Company Commander is an Inspector rank officer assisted by sub-inspectors (platoon commanders). Each company has 10 Head Rakshaks, 10 Senior Rakshaks and 96 Rakshaks plus the normal component of followers.[7]

Government Railway Police (GRP)

A part of the police forces of each state is entrusted with the responsibility of prevention and detection of crimes against the person and property of passengers and maintenance of order in railway premises. The GRP falls under the jurisdiction of the state governments and the Railways Ministry has no control over them.[8]

The system of Railway Police first came into being in 1866 when the Government approved the recommendations of the Inspector General of Lower Provinces to depute regular policemen at railway stations. This force under the supervision of the Deputy Superintends of Police was, however, placed under the disposal of the East India Company. The Special Police Force of the East India Company was raised on 1 January 1867. In 1870, two distinct railway police forces came into being, while one performed the duties pertaining to traffic and was paid for by the government and the other carried out watch and ward duties and paid for by the railways.[9] Over the years, several re-organisations took place in the railway security system.

The existing system of separation of powers between the GRP and RPF is based on the recommendation of the Railway Committee of 1921. As the constitution of India provides for law and order to be a state subject, the system was continued as crime committed at a railway station is connected with the overall law and order situation prevailing in that state. It was also thought that a departure from the existing system would greatly weaken the co-operation between the local and railway police force.

The Government Railway Police is a special branch of the State Police force.

Jurisdiction

The Railway Police takes cognizance of all crimes which occur on the railways between two distant signals and also of crimes which are committed on running trains. Crimes occurring on railway lines are beyond the jurisdiction of the district police. In some states, the jurisdiction of the railway police extends to the entire limits of the railway stations and the railway track upto the limit of fencing on both sides. The District Magistrate has complete jurisdiction over all areas even beyond the outer signal within a district. For administration, the area is divided under police circles under a police station. Police stations are located at important railway stations. Outposts with four or five constables are located at smaller stations. A number of police stations are placed under a Sub-Divisional Officer and two to three sub-divisions come under a district under the charge of a Superintendent of Police. The overall control of Railway Police in a state is under a DIG or IG of Railway Police.

Expenditure Sharing

The GRP is divided into crime and order police. The state governments pay for the crime police and the cost of the order police is borne by the Railways. Crime Police constitutes railway policemen carrying out investigation work, surveillance, patrolling and prosecution of crimes. Platform duties, traffic control at booking offices fall under the category of order police. The unrealistic system of expenditure sharing has led to several complications. It is also very difficult to distinguish between police personnel carrying out crime and order duties. The same personnel may be deputed to perform both the tasks at a time.[10] In addition, the Railways also pay 25 percent of the expenditure on supervisory staff of the GRP.

Recommendations

- The jurisdiction of the GRP and RPF should be clearly laid out. Ideally, Railway Police should function under the Central Government. But as law and order is a state subject in India, an element of the Railway Police in the form of GRP may continue to function under the respective state governments due to the direct relation between the local crime scenario and those committed on railways in a state.
- For increased efficiency and better management of railway security, the tasks of both the RPF and GRP should be segregated. The RPF can be made responsible for ensuring security on long-distance trains and tracks beyond the two outer signals of a railway station and other railway infrastructure. The GRP in turn should be responsible for protecting railway stations and managing crowds on platforms, booking offices,

etc. A centralised control room at railway stations would improve the co-ordination between different agencies involved in railway security. The role of the local police and CPOs such as the CRPF for protection of railway infrastructure in some areas should be reduced.

- Due to the vast length and huge number of trains operating in a single day, ensuring security of railway infrastructure is an uphill task. There is a need to increase the professionalism of both the RPF and GRP to gear up for this uphill task. The RPF should be modernised and oriented on the lines of an effective CPO like the CISF. A more all-India composition, with increased discipline, training and regimentation needs to be drilled into the force. There is also a need to filter out corruption and politics prevailing among the ranks at the local level.
- The manpower gap in manning the vast rail network in the country can be overcome by harnessing technology. Better hand-held radio sets, light weapons, cargo scanners, metal detectors, CCTV cameras should be deployed at railway stations.
- The ability of the RPF to conducting rail opening tasks in insurgency affected areas of J&K and the North-East is fairly limited. These tasks are primarily performed by the Army or CRPF in these areas. There is a need to take a re-look at the organisation, orientation, training and equipping profile of the RPF so that the force is able to take over such tasks from the Army/CPOs. This would ensure that the force completely takes over the charge of railway protection thus freeing the other forces to concentrate on their own tasks. Even the safety on Delhi Metro is ensured by the CISF, a force already stretched in providing security to industries, airports and other government infrastructures. The security on the Kashmir rail between Anantnag and Baramulla is provided by the CRPF.
- In the future, the RPF should be modeled as an effective CPO with the latest technology, skills, training and discipline akin to any other CPO. It should operate like a battalion with lesser strength divided between railway stations in a zone. A more effective intelligence wing would better address the vast needs of the safety of the rail infrastructure in the country.

The aspect of railway security is connected with the overall national security. Time and again trains and railway stations across the country have borne the brunt of terrorist attacks. Due to its sheer size and vast network, railways would continue to be a preferred target of terrorist and insurgent groups. Railways are also a prime carrier for movement of military assets and troop both in times of conflict and during peace times. Therefore, the need for railway security assumes greater significance. At present the RPF and GRP are not geared-up to independently ensure railway security in India. This problem is further compounded due to the fact that a substantial chunk of rail lines criss-cross the maoist-affected red corridor of central India. Therefore, railway security has to be complemented by CPOs given the lack of resources and capability on part of the Railway police forces and also due to the widespread railway network and infrastructure passing through troubled regions of the country.

The railway infrastructure in India has always borne the brunt of the public ire in the form of frequent blocking and damaging of tracks and trains during agitations. The Gujjar agitation and the more recent one for the demand of a separate state of Telengana are a few pointers to this. Therefore, given the complex set of challenges posed to railway security and un-hindered movement of trains, the task of railway security cannot alone be performed by the RPF and GRP. The local police authorities may invariably get involved in the event of blockades and local thefts on railway stations and trains, etc. The present nature of the Maoist challenge also makes it beyond the capability of the two railway police forces to ensure free and safe movement of trains through the red corridor. But, a desired capability building and expansion of both the RPF and GRP should at least ensure that the two forces become completely sufficient to be able to ensure security on passenger and goods trains and of all railway stations and tracks in most parts of the country. Other CPOs can complement their role in difficult areas and in emergency situations as and when required.

NOTES

1. Indian Railways Yearbook (2009-10), Ministry of Railways, Government of India.
2. Ibid.
3. Giriraj Shah, Paramilitary Forces of India, p. 251.
4. Ibid, p. 252.
5. Ibid, p. 253.
6. Ibid, p. 257.
7. Ibid, p. 257.
8. Ibid, p. 274.
9. Ibid, p. 261.
10. Ibid, p. 263.

12

Central Industrial Security Force (CISF)

Origin

The CISF came into being in 1968 following the enactment of the CISF Act by the Parliament. Its first deployment was in 1969 at FCI Trombay. The inquiry into a major fire incident at Heavy Engineering Corporation Ranchi in January 1964 underlined the need to have an industrial security force under the control of the central government. This incident coupled with other incidents of communal disturbances in Ranchi, Jamshedpur and Rourkela highlighted the inability of the local watch and ward staff to protect industrial units. Thus, following the recommendation of Justice B Mukherjee, former judge of Allahabad High Court, the CISF was envisioned.[1]

In 1969, three battalions were raised to provide security to PSUs in the country. They functioned under the IG and Zonal Ranges. But, this pattern was given up in 1974 for a need based system where manpower at each industrial unit was provided according to the requirement at that particular unit. Today, the sanctioned strength of the CISF stands at 1,31,000. It has become a multi-skilled security agency responsible for protecting industrial units, airports, some important heritage monuments, nuclear installations and sensitive government buildings. The force provides security coverage to 307 buildings of national importance. The CISF's dedicated fire-service wing also provides fire security to 83 installations across the country.[2] In addition, it also handles responsibilities ranging from VIP security to disaster relief.[3]

Organisational Structure

The CISF is led by a DG rank officer at Force HQ in New Delhi with an IG (HQ), IG (Adm) and IG (APS).

There are six DIGs for:

DIG (Pers)

DIG (Int/Ops)
DIG (Admn & Prov)
DIG (I&P & Trg)
DIG/DM
DIG/Fire
DIG (Pension & Welfare).

In addition, there are 14 AIGs at the Force HQ for providing effective assistance to the DG.[4] The CISF has five Zonal DIGs (including DAE Zone) and six plant DIGs. There is one DIG exclusively for Atomic plants under the DAE and one for Fire organis[5] ations.

The CISF is divided into six sectors:

(i) Airport Sector
(ii) North Sector
(iii) South Sector
(iv) East Sector
(v) West Sector
(vi) North-East Sector

There are seven reserve battalions at Barwaha, Bhilai, Ranchi, Ghaziabad, Arrakonam and Jaipur.

Training Institutes

National Industrial Security Academy (NISA) at Hyderabad is the primary institute for conducting the basic as well as in–service courses for CISF officers and various courses and seminars for the officers of others organisations. The Fire Service Training Institute (FSTI) is co-located inside the NISA campus. NISA was awarded the "Centre of Excellence" in the field of industrial security by the Home Ministry. It has six Recruit Training Centres at Arakkonam, Barwaha, Bhilai, Deoli (two) and Mundali.

Training

Basic training such as PT, Drill, Weapon handling and shooting, mob dispersal, training of women personnel, etc are imparted to the recruits at the six RTCs. In addition, promotion cadres and capsules are provided to direct recruit constables, Head Constables, Assistant Sub Inspectors (ASI), Sub-Inspectors/Executive. These capsules include commando training (STF Commando course), short-term commando course for Sub-Inspectors, Unarmed combat, Quick Reaction Team (QRT), Intelligence, Weapons & Tactics, D&M, IED, etc are also held at these centres. Previously, the CISF had to rely on training facilities of other CPOs for these specialised courses.

FSTI, which is the premier fire service training institute in the country, imparts professional training in fire fighting and fire prevention.[6]

NISA Hyderabad conducts courses for CISF officers and personnel during various stages of their career. Some of these are listed below:

1. Disaster Management Course for District Level officers
2. Vertical Interaction Course for IPS officers of state and CPOS
3. Duties of quarter master/provisioning and procurement action for DC/ ACs
4. Safety awareness course for DC/ACs/ Inspectors.
5. Legal and Establishment course for DC/ACs
6. Course on computer and MIS for DC/ACs/ Inspectors
7. Staff officer course for DCs
8. DDO Course for DC/ACs
9. Yoga and Meditation course for DC/ACs
10. Intelligence course for ACs/ Inspectors
11. Integrated Industrial Security Management course CO/DC of CPOs.
12. TTC on aviation security for GOs and SOs.
13. Senior level industrial Security course for Comdt./Dy.Comdt./ACs of States/Uts/CPOs.
14. Refresher course for AC
15. Departmental Inquiry course for SOs
16. JLIS course for SOs /ASOs of States/CPOs
17. Aviation Security Course for SO's
18. Pre-Promotion course for GOs upto the rank of IG
19. Promotion cadre course for SI/EXE,SI/MIN
20. Promotion cadre course for ASI/CLK
21. Yoga and Medication Course for SOs nand ORs
22. QM course for SOs
23. Legal and Establishment course for DC/AC/Inspr.
24. Indoor Instructor course
25. Tactical and WT course for GOs and SOs
26. Training of trainer course for SOs
27. Computer Course for Sos
28. Human Right Course for Gos
29. Assistant Commandant (DA) Basic Course
30. SI/Exe Basic Course
31. HC/CLK and SI/Steno Basic Course.[7]

NISA conducts the following courses for personnel of other organizations:

1. Disaster Management Course for District Level Officers
2. Vertical Interaction Course for IPS Officer
3. Integrated Industrial Security Management course for DC/AC,CPOS and State Police

4. Senior level Industrial Security Management course for DC/ACS for CPOS
5. Junior level Industrial Security course for Inspectors/SI of state and CPOS
6. Junior level Industrial Security Course for Parliament security officers
7. Junior Level Industrial Security course for DAE Security officers.[8]

Role and Tasks

The CISF is an armed Force of the Union of Indian under the Ministry of Home Affairs and is engaged in performing the following functions:

(a) Ensuring effective security and protection of public sector undertakings (PSUs), including some state government undertakings, on specific demand;
(b) Providing fire-safety cover to the PSUs;
(c) Deploying the force for Internal security and law and order duties in any part of the country as and when ordered by the Union Government;
(d) Modernising the Industrial security and Fire-protection system by introducing scientific gadgets and providing expert security consultancy service to the Industrial undertakings.

The CISF is responsible for protecting Category 'A', 'B' and 'C' industries of the Government of India. Industries falling under these categories are those whose products or services are vital to the country's national economy and defence preparedness and whose products cannot be replaced in case of total or severe damage or which can be replaced to a certain extent. Some examples of Category 'A' industries include power houses, steel plans, ship building yards, aircraft industries and oil refineries, etc.

The scope of CISF cover broadly covers the following sectors:-

(a) Space Centres
(b) Super Thermal Power Plants
(c) Major Ports
(d) Steel Plants
(e) Fertilizer Plants
(f) Coal Fields
(g) Ship Yards
(h) Oil Refineries
(i) Petro-Chemical Complexes
(j) ONGC installations
(k) Hyder-Power Projects, etc.

Today, the CISF is engaged in providing security cover to more than 200 undertakings across the country. Post the terrorist attacks in Mumbai on 26 November 2008, the mandate of the CISF has been extended to cover some sensitive industries in the private sector as well. At present, it is providing security cover at the Infosys campus in Pune and Bangalore. It has also provided consultancy services to 65 units in the private sector. The CISF is the primary agency responsible for protecting airports and metro stations all over the country. In addition, it provides the inner security to the Taj Mahal at Agra which is a world heritage site and the Red Fort in Delhi.

Critique

- *Organisation.* The CISF was conceived as a Central Government organisation to keep its personnel away from local influence. Its functioning on the battalion pattern was not possible as its personnel were deployed in a scattered manner across the nation in different industrial units and installations. Such a deployment pattern also precludes timely rotation of entire battalions. Therefore, the CISF except for having a few reserve battalions is a need based force. To check local influences from seeping in and uphold discipline, the personnel need to be rotated frequently both within and outside the sectors. The personnel should have a mixed-bag of experience of protecting vital installations, industries and airports instead of long tenures in one station only.
- *Recruiting pattern.* The CISF recruits constables, ASIs, SIs and Inspectors directly. It also absorbs retired personnel from the Armed Forces at the Constable/Head Constable levels. Although the latter category of personnel carry a huge reservoir of service experience with them, they are utilised at fairly lower levels in the force. They are also aged and less physically suited for tasks such as static guard duties, frisking, etc. There is a need to better utilise the pool of retired personnel in the force. They should be directly recruited at the ASI level and upwards for supervisory functions after imparting specific training as per their job description. The direct recruit constables should have a better chance of promotion till the Inspector level. Their minimum education qualification should be higher secondary or graduate levels as the job-profile requires frequent public interactions and contact. Direct recruitment of ASIs and above should be done away with. This would not only increase motivation levels at the constable level as they would stand a greater chance of promotion but would also increase efficiency and placement of experienced personnel at the supervisory levels in the force.

  At the officer level, the proportion of direct recruitment should be increased as against deputations from police and other CPOs. A proportion of short-service commission officers from the Army may be absorbed at the Assistant Commandant level and upwards.
- *Training and Human Resource management.* In addition to basic pre-

induction training there is a greater need for imparting specialised training and soft-skills on the personnel. As the deployment of the force includes sensitive installations such as nuclear plants, airports, etc, the personnel need to be oriented towards specific security and technical parameters at these locations. NISA Hyderabad offers various specialised training capsules to the force personnel.

The CISF is endeavoring to impart soft-skills to its personnel deployed at public places such as airports, metro stations, government offices, etc. But long working hours and prolonged periods of deployment at one place are contributing to high stress levels among its personnel. Along with holding yoga classes, there is a need to increase the frequency of postings and overcome manpower deficiencies at sensitive locations. This along with requisite infrastructure development at these locations would improve their interaction with the general public and also improve efficiency. More opportunities of promotion by restricting deputations from other services as mentioned in the preceding paragraphs would also go a long way in improving motivation levels in the force. Welfare measures such as better living conditions, health and education facilities for family, etc need to be improved.

An effective command and control system which is open and flexible to address the grievances and difficulties of its personnel would go a long way in bringing down stress levels among the personnel. This would help in preventing incidents of suicides and fratricides in the force. As the deployment of the CISF is at sensitive and public installations, morale of the personnel is an important element which needs to be watched round the clock as adverse reaction even by one person can create damage to infrastructure or risk to public life. In the past, there have been incidents of fratricides and suicides by CISF men deployed at airports and metro rail stations.

Role and Tasks. The CISF deployment stretches across a wide spectrum and covers several PSUs, government buildings, transportation hubs such as airports and metro stations, vital installations, etc. For better efficiency, the CISF should be withdrawn from providing security cover to some VIPs as it is totally against the mandate of the force. It also has no role in disaster relief and this task should be exclusively handled by the NDRF battalions. The latter should have personnel from deputation from other PMFs/CPOs to start with but gradually recruit from its own pool.

The CISF as per its mandate was created to protect industries. In addition to PSUs and industrial manufacturing units in the defence and other sensitive sectors, its mandate has been expanded to include the private sector as well. Following the hijacking of an Indian Airlines flight from Kathmandu to Kandahar in 1999, the CISF took over the security duties at all domestic and international airports in the country. With a few exceptions, it continues to provide both external and internal perimeter cover at most airports. The newly created Delhi Metro Rail also saw the deployment of the CISF due to its experience in handling airport security and also due to the absence of a well-trained force. Though, it can be argued that the security of metro property should have been provided by the Railway Protection Force or the Government Railway Police. As the metro service expands to other tier I and tier II cities in the country, there will be increased pressure on the CISF's resources to provide security.

Over the years the mandate of the CISF has expanded beyond the PSUs. But keeping in view the fragile internal security situation and continued threat to the nation's economic and public infrastructure from terrorists, the CISF is the best force available to the Central government for providing first-line deployments at these locations. With better training, human resource management and procurement of modern surveillance equipments, the efficacy of the force will be enhanced manifold.

Although the CISF is the primary security agency for guarding several government buildings, airports and vital installations across the country, it is still far away from being able to contain or neutralise a terrorist attack on any of these installations. The services of specialised forces such as the NSG and other agencies would be required in the event of a major contingency. Nevertheless, the role of the CISF can not be belittled in a country facing an existential security threat from a multitude of sources coupled with the enormous public pressure at these installations. Therefore, the CISF is the best suited force for the day to day securing of premises and screening of passengers, workers and office employees at these installations as the first-responders.

Review Weapons being deployed at Airports, Metros

The requirement to deploy pistols, small sub-machine guns rather than lackadacsical and aribatry deployments of light machine guns, automatics and support weapons which can cause greater collateral damage to innocent civilians through disproportionate fire.

NOTES

1. Giriraj Shah, Paramilitary Forces of India, p. 159.
2. CISF Observes 43rd Raising Day, *Sunday Times of India*, 11 March 2012.
3. Ibid.
4. Ibid.
5. Ibid.
6. Official website of the CISF, accessed at http://www.cisf.gov.in/nisa/nisa.htm
7. Ibid (5) above.
8. Ibid (3) above.

PART 3

Paramilitary Forces of China & Pakistan

13

Paramilitary Forces of China

China's National Defence

The Annual White Paper on China's National Defense in 2010 lists the national security priorities of the People's Republic of China. The paper accords primacy to the country's strategic objectives and defence strategy for its regional neighbourhood. It briefly highlights the role played by its internal security of paramilitary forces in safeguarding the country's land and coastal borders and in maintaining 'social stability'. The PRC is graduating to a concept of sharing responsibility between the military and local authorities in safeguarding the territorial and maritime borders of the country. The *White Paper* underlines the main responsibilties of the Border public security force as follows:

> "Border, coastal and maritime public security administration, entry-exit frontier inspection at ports; prevention and crackdown on illegal and criminal acts in border and coastal areas, such as illegal border crossing, drug trafficking and smuggling; and organization of and participation in counter-terrorist and emergency-management operations in border and coastal areas. Organs of maritime surveillance, fisheries administration, marine affairs, inspection and quarantine, and customs are responsible for ensuring legitimate rights, law enforcement, and administration. The State Commission of Border and Coastal Defense, under the dual leadership of the State Council and the Central Military Commission (CMC), coordinates China's border and coastal defenses. All military area commands, as well as border and coastal provinces, cities and counties, have commissions to coordinate border and coastal defenses within their respective jurisdictions."[1]

The paper goes on to emphasize the progress made by the 'border public security force' in the areas of border defence and control, counter-terrorism, and maintenance of stability. In addition, concerted efforts to maintain law and order, port security and curbing drug and arms trafficking have reaped rich dividends. The paper points out that in the year 2009 alone, 37,000 cases were solved and

3,845 illegal guns confiscated. This also goes on to highlight the wide spectrum of activities undertaken by China's

Internal security forces in support of the local police and other civil enforcement departments.

PEOPLE'S ARMED POLICE FORCE (PAPF)

Origin

The People's Armed Police Force (PAPF) is a paramilitary force of the People's Republic of China (PRC) responsible for performing internal security tasks. The origin of the force can be traced to the establishment of the PRC in 1949. The division of the People's Liberation Army (PLA) looking after internal security and policing was separated to form the Public Security Army under the Ministry of Public Security of the People's Republic of China. After several re-organisations, the People's Armed Police came into being on 19 June 1982 as a para-military unit separate from the PLA.

The PAP consists of the Internal Troops, as well as four specialised branches: Forestry Troops, Gold Mining Troops, Transportation Troops, and Hydropower Troops, which are non-combat paramilitary organisations tasked with economic development roles. In addition, the PAP also provides manpower for the three paramilitary police forces: Border Defence Troops, Firefighting Troops, and Guard Troops, which are subordinate to the Ministry of Public Security (MPS).[2]

Organisation

The PAPF consists of internal security forces, gold mine, forest, water conservancy, electricity power, and transportation forces. The frontier police force, fire brigades and security guards are also included into the Armed Police Force. The internal security forces are composed of contingents and mobile divisions.

The PAPF functions under a dual command structure of the Central Military Commission (CMC) and the State Council. The latter exercises control over the PAPF through the Ministry of Public Security. The control of the CMC led to a closer integration of the PAP with the PLA. By the year 1996, demobilisation of 14 PLA divisions further bolstered the strength of the PAP. In 2009, a separate legislation was enacted to give statutory authority to the force to respond to emergencies, riots and acts of terrorism.[3] Previously, the Armed Police was governed by the Military Service Law.

The strength of the PAPF is estimated between 6,60,000 to 8,00,000 personnel.[4] This includes the 14 demobilised PLA divisions transferred to the PAPF in 1996.

The PAPF Headquarters is located in Beijing.

Role and Tasks

The White Paper describes the PAPF as the State's backbone and shock force in responding to emergencies. It highlights its role in assisting other public security forces in maintaining social order and ensuring peace and stability. The paper states:

> "Since 2009, it has handled 24 acts of serious violence and crime, including hostage taking, participated in 201 operations of hunting down criminal suspects, and fulfilled the task of security provision during the celebrations of the 60th anniversary of the founding of the People's Republic of China, the Shanghai World Expo, and the Guangzhou Asian Games.
>
> In November 2010, the CMC approved and promulgated Regulations on Emergency Command in Handling Emergencies by the Armed Forces, which specifies for the armed forces regulations concerning their organization, command, force deployment, integrated support, and civil-military coordination while carrying out missions to maintain social stability and handle emergencies".

The primary role of the PAPF is the maintenance of Internal Security. The border security units of the force guard the country's land and sea frontiers, airports, sea ports, etc. The Armed Police is responsible for guarding government buildings, (including party and state organisations, foreign embassies and consulates), provide personal protection to senior government officials, provide security functions to public corporations and major public events. Some units perform guard duty in civilian prisons and provide executioners for the state. The PAP also maintains tactical counter-terrorism (CT) units in the Immediate Action Unit (IAU), Snow Wolf Commando Unit (SWCU) and various Special Police Units (SPU). The PAPF is also responsible for protecting the country's natural resources such as hydro-electricity plants, forests and mines. The fire-fighting Border Security units operate under the dual control of the Ministry of Defense and Public Security.[5]

The White Paper on China's National Defense in 2002 describes the role of the PAPF as under:

> The Armed Police Force receives unified leadership and management, and its command is delegated to a relevant organ at each level. The Armed Police Force has three echelons of leadership, namely, general headquarters, contingent (division) and detachment (regiment). The General Headquarters of the Armed Police Force, as the chief commanding organ of the Armed Police Force, commands and administers internal security forces, and gold mine, forest, water conservancy, electricity power, and transportation forces. In the nationwide administrative hierarchy, the Armed Police contingents, detachments, and squadrons are instituted at province, prefecture, and county levels respectively. When performing a public security task or relevant work, the Armed Police Force unit is subordinate to the leadership and command of the public security organs at the same level.

In peacetime, the tasks of the Armed Police Force include performing guard duties at fixed points, dealing with contingencies, combating terrorism and supporting national economic development. Guard duties at fixed points chiefly means, among others, security guard, watch and ward, prison and detention guard, escort and patrol. It is specifically responsible for protecting the security of state-designated objects to be guarded, important visiting foreign dignitaries, leading organs of the Party and government at and above the provincial level, embassies and consulates of foreign countries in China, important national and international conferences, and sites of large-scale cultural and sports activities; posting peripheral armed guards at prisons and detention houses; providing armed protection for key departments in charge of confidential work and critical parts of important airports, radio stations, state economic departments, and national defense works, as well as important bridges and tunnels along trunk railway lines, and specially designated large road bridges; and performing armed patrol and other security duties in state-designated large and medium-sized cities or specific zones. Dealing with contingencies chiefly means handling, according to law, sudden illegal incidents endangering state security or social order, such as revolts, riots and disturbances, fights with weapons and other group activities that endanger public security. Combating terrorism chiefly means performing anti-attack, anti-hijacking and anti-explosion tasks. Supporting national economic development chiefly means gold mine prospecting, preventing and fighting forest fire, participation in key state energy and transportation projects, and emergency rescue and disaster relief in cases of serious calamities.

The importance accorded to National Construction, Disaster relief and Emergency Rescue in China can be gauged by the wide range and scale of activities undertaken jointly by the PLA and PAPF in this field. The *White Paper* documents the task undertaken by the PLA and PAPF in the past two years alone.

> "The PLA and PAPF have actively participated in and supported national construction work, of which a key component is the large-scale development of the western region. In the past two years, they have contributed more than 16 million workdays and utilized 1.3 million motor vehicles and machines, and participated in construction of more than 600 major infrastructure projects relating to transportation, hydropower, communications and energy. They have set up more than 3,500 contact points for rural poverty alleviation, and provided assistance to over 8,000 small public initiatives, such as water-saving irrigation projects, drinking water projects for both people and livestock, road construction projects, and hydropower projects. The armed forces stationed in the western region have planted 11 million trees and afforested 3.2 million mu of barren hills and desert land by large-scale forestation and aerial planting. PLA medical and health units have provided assistance to 130 county-level hospitals in poverty-stricken western areas, sent there 351 medical teams and donated 110 sets (items) of instruments and equipment. With donations, the armed forces have financed and built eight schools and one rehabilitation center in earthquake-stricken areas in Sichuan, Shaanxi and Gansu provinces.

> The armed forces of China act as the shock force in emergency rescue and disaster relief. In January 2009, with the armed forces as the mainstay, China formed eight state-level emergency-response professional units, boasting a total of 50,000 personnel, specializing in flood control and emergency rescue, earthquake rescue, nuclear, biological and chemical emergency rescue, urgent air transportation, rapid road repair, maritime emergency search and rescue, emergency mobile communication support, and medical aid and epidemic prevention. In July 2009, China integrated the 31,000-strong PAPF protecting water and electricity supplies and communications into the national emergency rescue system. Provincial level units specializing in emergency rescue have been formed with the joint participation of military area commands and relevant provinces, autonomous regions, or municipalities directly under the central government.
>
> In the past two years, the PLA and PAPF have engaged a total of 1.845 million troop deployments and 790,000 deployments of vehicles or machines of various types, flown over 181 sorties (including the use of helicopters), organized 6.43 million militiamen and reservists, participated in disaster relief operations in cases of floods, earthquakes, droughts, typhoons and forest fires, rescued or evacuated a total of 1.742 million people, rush-transported 303,000 tons of goods, dredged 3,742 km of waterways, dug 4,443 wells, fortified 728 km of dikes and dams, and delivered 504,000 tons of domestic water".

In wartime, PAPF units can be accorded the task of border defence and may also act as Light Infantry troops in support of the PLA.

The two main organs of the PAPF are the Internal Troops and the Mobile Divisions.

Internal Troops

The main body of the PAP Force is the Internal Troops which are composed of provincial general corps and mobile divisions. In China, each provincial-level entity (provinces, autonomous regions, and municipalities) has created a PAP general corps each prefectural-level entity (cities and prefectures) has created a PAP detachment and each county-level entity (county, league, and town) has created a PAP group or PAP squadron.

The Internal Troops are responsible for guarding key targets, such as leading government and party departments, prison and detention centres, foreign embassies and consulates, large airports and seaports, bridges and tunnels on the truck routes of railway and roads, radio and TV stations, and key industrial facilities. Their duties also include escorting convicts and prisoners, reinforcing the public security departments in law enforcement, conducting armed patrol and inspections in metropolitan areas, and assisting in fighting fire and natural disasters. In time of war, the Internal Troops could also be deployed as light infantry for rear security and defence roles.

Each PAP provincial general corps has one or more mobile units, which are not assigned to guard a specific target, but to respond to emergency or crisis such as riots and conflicts. Since the 1980s, there have been several special police units (SPU) created at the headquarters- and local-level within the PAP to deal with terrorism and hostage crisis.

The PAP has also dispatched small teams to station in the Chinese embassies in Baghdad, Iraq and Kabul, Afghanistan to protect Chinese diplomats in these two countries.

Mobile Divisions

The Mobile divisions were composed from the fourteen demobilised infantry divisions transferred from the PLA to the PAP in 1996. They are essentially light infantry troops organised in military order of battle (division-regiment-battalion-company). The Mobile divisions upon their transfer from the Regular Army were stripped of their heavy weaponry such as tanks and artillery gun pieces but retained their standard infantry weapons and support weapons like Mortars, Recoiless guns, etc.

Reserves

China relies on building a strong and effective reserve force for its National Defence. The Reserve force in China comprises of active servicemen and reserve officers and men. It is an armed force, based on the unified organizational structure of the PLA. It functions under the dual leadership of the PLA and the local Party committees and governments. The Reserve force is made up of the reserve force of the PLA, the People's Armed Police Force and the Militia.

The official website of the Chinese Ministry of National Defense describes the reserves as under.

> "After 25 years of buildup and development, the reserve force has become an important component of the national defense reserve. It is made up of the Army Reserve, Navy Reserve, Air Force Reserve and the Second Artillery Force Reserve. The Army Reserve breaks down into infantry, artillery, antiaircraft artillery, antitank artillery, tank, engineering, chemical defense, signals, coastal defense and other specialized forces. The Navy Reserve is mainly composed of reconnaissance, mine-sweeping and mine-laying, radar observation and communications and other specialized forces. The Air Force Reserve mainly comprises ground-to-air missile, radar and other specialized forces. The Second Artillery Force Reserve mainly consists of the specialized missile support force and special equipment maintenance force".[6]

In line with the unified structure and organisation of the PLA, the reserve force has reserve divisions, brigades and regiments, and corresponding leading organs. Reserve units are organised mainly on a regional basis. Divisions are set up in provinces and brigades (regiments) in prefectures (autonomous prefectures or prefecture-level cities). A division (brigade) can be set up in a region covering more than one prefecture (autonomous prefecture or prefecture-level city), and a regiment in a region covering more than one county (county-level city or district).

Over the years, the pool of reservists in China has increased. The focus now is to build close inter-operability between the active forces and reserves to help the latter complement the roles of the former. The thrust is to enable the reserve forces to support the regular forces in their peace time activities.

Militia

The Militia in China functions under the unified leadership of the State Council and the CMC, and the leadership of local Party committees, local governments as well as the local military commands. The General Staff Headquarters supervises militia work all over the country. The military area commands are responsible for militia work in their respective jurisdictions. Provincial military commands, prefectural military commands and people's armed forces departments of counties (county-level cities or districts) are the organs of military leadership and command, and responsible for the militia work in their respective jurisdictions. The grass-roots people's armed forces departments established in towns, urban sub-districts, enterprises and public institutions are responsible for organising and carrying out militia work. Local Party committees and governments at all levels make overall plans and arrangements for militia work.

With force modernisation, the equipment and weaponry of militias has also undergone a transition. The aim is to build a leaner yet effective militia force which is able to support combat and respond to national emergencies. The Militia has been equipped with new types of portable air defence missiles. In recent years, the thrust has been to shift the focus of militias from rural to urban centres and along lines of communication.

Importance has been attached to establishing militia organisations in emerging enterprises and high-tech industries to increase the technology content of the militia force. Equipment for emergency response and stability-maintenance operations has been improved. Some types of weapons have been upgraded. During the Eleventh Five-Year Plan period (2006-2010) the number of militia personnel is scheduled to be reduced from 10 million to eight million.

The website of PRC's Ministry of Defence further describes the training and logistical aspects of the Militia.

"In May 2007 the General Staff Headquarters released a new edition of the Outline for the Training and Evaluation of the Militia. The new outline adds over a hundred training tasks in dozens of categories covering specialties of the Navy, Air Force and Second Artillery Force, marking a shift from traditional single-service to multi-service/arm specialized militia training. Based on the principles of integrating resources, pooling strengths, organizing training level by level and conducting trans-regional training, the military training of the militia has a four-level organizational system: The provincial military commands are the backbone; the prefectural military commands are the main body; the people's armed forces departments are the basis; and the grass-roots people's armed forces departments are the supplement. The militia is improving its technology-based training, and promoting on-base, simulated and web-based training step by step. Prominence is given to such tasks as rapid mobilization of specialized detachments, coordination with active units and operations in complex electromagnetic environments. In addition, efforts are being made to enhance training in emergency response and rescue. The aim is to raise the militia's capabilities in combat operations, emergency rescue, disaster relief, crisis response and social stability maintenance".[7]

NOTES

1. White Paper on China's National Defense in 2010, Information Office of the State Council of the People's Republic of China accessed at: http://www.china.org.cn/government/whitepaper/node_7114675.htm
2. Sino.Defence.com, http://www.sinodefence.com/army/organisation/pap-internal.asp
3. Top legislature passes armed police law. *China Daily*, 27 August 2009.
4. Wines, Michael, China Approves Law Governing Armed Police Force . *The New York Times*. 27 August 2009.
5. White Paper on China's National Defense in 2006.
6. http://eng.mod.gov.cn/ArmedForces/reserved.htm
7. Ibid (6) above.

14

Paramilitary Forces of Pakistan

The Paramilitary Forces of Pakistan along with other police and reserve forces comprise nearly four Lakh personnel. Their primary aim is to maintain internal security and safeguard the country's external borders during peace time.

The strength of Paramilitary and reserve forces in Pakistan are as under:

Service	*Total active duty personnel*
National Guard	185,000
Pakistan Rangers	100,000
Frontier Corps	94,000
Frontier Constabulary	24,000
Airport Security Force	8,930
Pakistan Coast Guard	4,000
Gilgit Scouts	3,697
Maritime Security Agency	2,000
Total	421,627

Organisation

The Ministry of Interior, an organisation of the civilian government in Pakistan exercises command and control over all the 'Civil Armed Forces' in Pakistan which includes the Pakistan Rangers, Frontier Corps, Frontier Constabulary and the Pakistan Coast Guard. The Interior Division of the Ministry is responsible for maintaining law and order in the country. It also regulates the working of various security forces, including Police, to provide protection to the common man and to defend the country. Among the primary responsibilities of the Interior Division of the Ministry of Interior is to:

> Control and administer of Federal Investigation Agency (FIA), Civil Armed Forces i.e. Frontier Corps, Frontier Constabulary, Pakistan Rangers and Coast Guards, Capital Development Authority and Islamabad Capital Territory.[1]

Role and Tasks

The Department of Civil Armed Forces in the Ministry of Interior is responsible for maintaining command and control over the Paramilitary Forces. Civil Armed Forces viz Pakistan Rangers, Frontier Corps and Pakistan Coast Guards are the field organisations of the Ministry of Interior. The roles assigned to these forces are:

- Secure and check illegal border crossing.
- Prevent smuggling.
- Enforce drug control.
- Assist the Provincial Governments in maintaining law and order as and when requested.[2]

The separate tasks accorded to the various Field Organisations of the Ministry of Interior are as under:

1.	Pakistan Rangers, Lahore.	To secure/check border crossing on Indo-Pak border into the Punjab province and to assist the Provincial Government of Punjab in maintaining law & order.
2.	Pakistan Rangers, Karachi.	To secure/check border crossing on Indo-Pak border into Sindh province and to assist Provincial Government of Sindh in maintaining law & order.
3.	Pakistan Coast Guards, Karachi.	To secure sea coast, prevent smuggling, entry of illegal immigrants and enemy agents/saboteurs.
4.	Frontier Corps, North Western Frontier Province (NWFP), Peshawar.	Anti-smuggling measures, maintenance of law & order and drug control along the borders with Afghanistan and in the federally administered tribal areas of NWFP.
5.	Frontier Corps (Balochistan), Quetta.	Anti- smuggling measures, maintenance of law & order and drug control along Balochistan border.

The succeeding paragraphs will briefly describe the inception, organisation, role & tasks and major operations undertaken by the four Civil Armed Forces of Pakistan.

Pakistan Rangers

Inception

In 1942, the British Government had established a special police unit called the Sindh Police Rangers in Karachi. After the formation of Pakistan in 1947, the responsibility of guarding the international borders of the newly formed nation was entrusted to the Armed Police units of the respective provinces. Some of these units were the Sindh Rifles, Bawahalpur State Police and Khairpur State Police, etc. However, this system of border guarding was not found suitable and a re-organisation was effected in the year 1958. The re-organisation amalgamated all the State Border Police forces into one central organisation named the West Pakistan Rangers. After the 1971 War, the Rangers operated under the direct control of the Pakistan Army. In 1974, it was made part of the Ministry of Interior as a Civil Armed Force (CAF). Till 1995, the Pakistan Rangers were two separate forces: the Pakistan Rangers Punjab headquartered in Lahore, Punjab, and the Mehran Force headquartered in Karachi, Sindh. The two forces maintain their different uniforms and chains of command but work under same ordinances, such as the Pakistan Rangers Ordinance, 1959.

Organisation

The Primary responsibility of the Pakistan Rangers is to perform defensive tasks along the country's eastern borders in peace time. In addition, it acts as a reserve force in maintain law and order in the provinces. In the present security situation, the force plays a very active role in maintaining order in the towns and cities of Sindh and Punjab provinces. Due to their role, the Pakistan Rangers is closely patterned on the lines of the Regular units of the Pakistan Army. Most of its officers and men are ex-servicemen. Also, Pakistan Army officers on deputation hold command positions in the force.

Role and Tasks

The role of the Pakistan Rangers is as under:

- Protection of persons and property in the border areas.
- Apprehension of persons unlawfully entering into or going out of Pakistan territory.
- Prevention of smuggling.
- Collection of intelligence in the border areas.
- Reinforce the Police for the maintenance of law and order whenever it is necessary.
- Federal Government may by an order at any time declare a state of emergency on entire border of the Province or a part thereof and thereby place under the operational control of the Army all or any of the units or members of the force for the time being serving within the Province.
- Organization of village defence in border areas.
- Provision of assistance to the police to prevent and detect crime in the border area.
- Reinforce the police for the maintenance of law and order.
- Collection of intelligence and provision of early warning about smugglers movement/concentration.
- Organization of village defence in the border area.[3]

Deployment

The Pakistan Rangers are commanded by a Director General who is a Major

General rank officer from the Army. In Punjab province four border corps are commanded by Colonels and each wing by a Lieutenant Colonel. Presently Pakistan Rangers (Punjab) consist of approximately 16,056 all ranks who are deployed at 414 Border Out Posts along 1283 kilometers of the eastern border with India. Pakistan Rangers (Punjab) Academy is located at Mandi Bahauddin.

In Sindh province Pakistan Rangers (Sindh) consist of approximately 23,000 personnel, of which about 10,000 are deployed in or near Karachi, Pakistan's largest city. They guard 40 consulates and many other important places and installations of strategic importance. Some 13,000 rangers operate in the interior of Sindh, patrolling the border with India and protecting foreign companies' oil installations and gas explorations. Their job is also to maintain a vigil on the railway.

The table below depicts the deployment pattern of the Pakistan Rangers.[4]

Corp Name	*Headquarters*	*Deployment Area*
Chenab Rangers	Sialkot.	Sialkot, Narowal Sector
Sutlej Rangers	Lahore	Wagha, Kanganpur Sector
Desert Rangers	Bahawalpur	Sulemanki, Bahalwalnagar Sector
Cholistan Rangers	Rahim Yar Khan	Khanpur and Sadiqabad Sector

Equipping Profile

The standard issue of the Rangers are the 7.62mm G3A3, 7.62mm G3P4 Rifles, 7.62mm MG3 (Machine Guns), 9mm MP5A2 & MP5P4, 9mm SMG-PK (Sub-Machine Guns), 7.63 mm standard issue pistols. The force personnel are also equipped with AK Series rifles and imported bullet proof vests to battle the insurgents and terrorists.

Training

The selection for rangers lasts 2–3 weeks. Both male and females can join the Rangers and an applicant must be between 18–25 years old. In order to apply for the Rangers, the applicant must passed F.Sc. (an equivalent to U.S. metriculation system) from a government-registered college. An applicant may hold a Pakistani citizenship to join the Force. The Rangers can be deployed at any place either in Pakistan or abroad, according to the Rangers Act of 1959.

In spite of its role as paramilitary, the Rangers have been recognized by Government of Pakistan as one its special forces.

The Rangers Anti-Terrorist Company has been active since early 2004. They were trained by Zarrar Company of Special Services Group (SSG). This company also participated in a recent exercise with U.K. Special Air Service operators and U.S. Army Rangers stationed in Karachi.

Participation in Operations

The Rangers had fought together with the Pakistan Army in several conflicts, namely the 1965 Indo-Pak war and 1971 Indo-Pakistan War.[1]After the 1971 war, the force was federalized underneath the Ministry of Defence as the Pakistan Rangers, and, shortly in 1974, it was made a component of the Civil Armed Forces (CAF) under the Ministry of Interior. Pakistan Rangers guard the borders during peace and war. In 1995, the Mehran Force was merged into the Pakistan Rangers (Sindh). The Pakistan Rangers (Sindh) are credited for providing the Pakistan Army troops for Special Police Units in Kosovo and Haiti Peace mission every year.

These troops are entrusted with the task to provide protection and security to UN officials, provide operational and backup support, respond to threats to public order in coordination with the Kosovo administration, and assist humanitarian agencies.[2] The Rangers also had participated in numerous special military operations along with Pakistan Army Special Forces branch in the past. Since their revitalization and re-building after the 1971 war, the Rangers have been involved in the numerous special military operations in Pakistan. The Rangers have also assisted the Army's Special Service Group in performing special operations. They first participated in 1973, when they, based on the intelligence reports, had successfully accompanied the SSGs to raid the Iraqi Embassy. In 1992, the Rangers were deployed toKarachi, and the Government of Sindh had used Rangers to keep peace in the city. The Rangers had also participated in Operation Blue Fox in 1992 along with the Army

Internal Security Tasks

In the border area and areas with in the country where troops of Pakistan Rangers are called for discharge of Internal Security Duties, all Rangers personnel with the rank of Sub Inspector and above are entrusted with the authority of a Police Officer as regards to arrest and search; under Customs Act and every member of the Force under especially published Government Notification.

Under article 147 of the Pakistani Constitution Rangers can operate within the country when requested by the provincial government. Additional internal security duties include patrolling of National Highways in cases of extreme emergencies. For all large scale search and sweep operations, Pakistan Rangers will provide back-up support to the Police and participate in such joint operations. Areas in the hilly ranges where Police Force is not deployed, Pakistan Rangers will take over and fill in the gaps. This surveillance role would be assigned randomly, and in cases of emergency stationary pickets would also be set up. will remain available as a back-up reserve to be deployed

in sizeable no in case of large scale disorder and rioting. The Rangers will function in support of the Police and prepare to take over certain areas where the situation warrants presence of a well trained strike force. Force will have its own intelligence network and on specific inform, will conduct independent operations. However, in order to cover the procedural and legal formalities they will invariably be accompanied by of Police Officer or a Magistrate. For day to day functioning local commander of Pakistan Ranges will closely coordinate with the concerned District Magistrate and the Senior Superintendent of Police.[5]

Since 2002, the Pakistan Rangers are actively engaged in maintaining order in Punjab and SIndh provinces against acts of terrorism. One wing of Pakistan Rangers (Punjab) are deployed for the protection of the Sui Gas fields in Balochistan Province since January 2003. The troops conduct several Internal security operations such as "Operation Fair Deal", in which troops participated in joint operation with Pakistan Rangers (Sindh) and Frontier Corps Balochistan from 9-16 July 2003 to seal the Provincial border against miscreants fleeing from Provinces of Sindh and Baluchistan, where the flushing operation was launched. Presently 2 x Wings strength are deployed for the Sealing of Tri-junction Border and construction of 2 x Police Stations and 15 x Police Posts in Kashmore and Rojhan area. 20 x all ranks are deployed in Jampur for the protection of PARCCO Staff who are engaged in laying White Oil Pipeline from Umerkot to Mehmood Kot.[6]

Sine 2002, 20 Personnel of Pakistan Rangers (Punjab) were killed and 108 others injured in various internal security operations.[7]

Frontier Corps

Origin

The Frontier Corps is a Federal Paramilitary force of Pakistan. It traces its origins to the Anglo-Afghan wars. Lord Curzon, the then Viceroy of undivided India had raised the Frontier Corps in 1907 by amalgamating seven tribal units operating in the Frontier areas bordering Afghanistan. These were the Khyber Rifles, the Zhob Militia, the Kurram Militia, the Tochi Scouts, the Chagai Militia, the South Waziristan Scouts and the Chitral Scouts.

After 1947, Pakistan expanded the corps further by creating a number of new units, including the Thal Scouts, the Northern Scouts, the Bajaur Scouts, the Karakoram Scouts, the Kalat Scouts, the Dir Scouts and the Kohistan Scouts. British officers continued to serve in the Frontier Corps up to the early 1950s. In 1975, three of the units (the Gilgit Scouts, the Karakoram Scouts and the Northern Scouts) were merged to form a new paramilitary force called the Northern Light Infantry, which is now a full infantry regiment of the Pakistan Army.

Organisation

Today, the Frontier Corps (FC) is subdivided into the FC Khyber Paktunkwa with its Headquarters in Peshawar and the FC Balochistan in Quetta. The FC recruits from the local tribes and its present strength is around 70,000 personnel. The Scouts Training Academy, Mirali in North Waziristan is the primary training institution. The personnel are mainly recruited from the local tribes. Important command positions are held by Pakistan Army officers on deputation. The Inspector General Frontier Corps (IGFC) is a Major-General rank officer seconded from the Pakistan Army.

The various units of the Frontier Corps operating in Khyber Pakthunkhwa and Balochistan are mentioned below. (year of raising/in brackets).

Khyber Pakthukhwa (erstwhile NWFP)

1. Chitral Scouts (1903)
2. Khyber Rifles (1878)
3. Kurram Militia (1892)
4. South Waziristan Scouts (1900)
5. Tochi Scouts (1894)
6. Mahsud Scouts (1944)
7. Mohmand Rifles
8. Shawal Rifles
9. Swat Scouts
10. Orakzai Scouts
11. Khushal Khan Scouts
12. Dir Scouts (1970)
13. Bajur Scouts (1961)
14. Thal Scouts (1948)

Balochistan

1. Zhob Militia (1883)
2. Chagai Militia (1896)
3. Sibi Scouts (1971)
4. Kalat Scouts (1965)
5. Makran Militia
6. Kharan Rifles
7. Pishin Scouts (1946)
8. Dalbandin Rifles (2007-08)
9. Maiwind Rifles
10. Ghazaband Scouts
11. Bambore Rifles
12. Loralai Scouts
13. Bolan Scouts
14. Awaran Militia
15. Panjgur Rifles
16. SOW (Special Operations Wing)

Equipping Profile

The equipment of the Frontier Corps includes G3 rifles, AK-47s, RPG 7, light machine guns, short range artillery and mortars as well as aviation support and APCs and tanks.

Role and Tasks

The primary role of the Frontier Corps includes carrying out patrols in the border regions of Khyber Pakthunkhwa (NWFP), FATA and Balochistan. The force undertakes anti-smuggling and drug control measures in the volatile belts of Pakistan's Frontier agencies.

Since 1970, the FC Balochistan has been engaged in counter insurgency operations in the province. It was not very popular among the local tribes as it used brute force and carried out human rights excesses on the population. Since 2004, the FC has been carrying out humanitarian taks such as construction of hospitals, etc to win the goodwill of the populace.

In the 1990s, the FC was instrumental in the elimination of poppy cultivation in the Dir district of erstwhile NWFP.

Although the FC was primarily used for law enforcement in the volatile Tribal areas, the US led invasion of Afghanistan in 2001 led to an influx of Afghan Taliban fighters into these agencies. The subsequent rise of the Pakistan Taliban led to a radical change in the task undertaken by the Frontier Corps. Today, it is fighting these elements alongside the Army. In fact, its efficiency in controlling the restive tribes and militants has been widely recognised even by the United States which has invested substantially in training and equipping the FC for counter insurgency and counter terrorist operations.

In the year 2007, the FC along with the Pakistan Army was engaged in many bitter clashes with the tribal militants after the breakdown of the peace efforts. In the beginning, the FC took some heavy casualties when it entered the areas controlled by the militants. It was also plagued with a high rate of desertions and mass surrenders.

The situation has improved gradually after the force was imparted training and new weapons for conduction counter insurgency operations. Its efficiency in drug control measures has also increased manifold. it is estimated that in 2007, the Frontier Corps Baluchistan conducted 80 percent of the heroin and morphine-base seizures in Pakistan.

The United States is training and equipping the Frontier Corps to enhance its ability to capitalize on the unique skills, access, and abilities that it has in the border area. The special $75M authority Congress created for the Frontier Corps is an effective tool to aid U.S. efforts, but it too has its limitations - specifically, that it cannot be used for any other non-military force (which excludes, for example, the Frontier Constabulary, etc.).

In October 2008 a small contingent of US military trainers begun a training program aimed at turning Pakistan's Frontier Corps into an effective counter-insurgency force. The Pentagon had spent about $25 million so far to equip the Frontier Corps with new body armor, vehicles, radios and surveillance equipment, and plans to spend $75 million more in the next year.[8]

However, critics argue that training the FC is an exercise in futility. "The 2007 plan to provide U.S. training and assistance to the tribal paramilitary Frontier Corps is misguided, however. Since their inception a century ago, those units have always been poachers-turned-wardens, with well-recognized limits on their reliability; and today they are more deeply infiltrated and compromised by divided loyalties than ever before. The Frontier Corps' problems have little to do with weapons and training, and U.S. troops recruited largely from the inner cities and trained for conventional warfare have little to teach rugged Pashtun hillmen about fighting in their own mountains in any case."[9]

Frontier Constabulary

The Frontier Constabulary is a federally administered Para-Military force of Pakistan drawing its recruits from the Khyber Pakthunkwa. The force operates in all the provinces of Pakistan. The Frontier Constabulary was raised as a Militia Force in 1913 by amalgamating the Border Military Police and the Samana Rifles. Both of the forces were guarding the border between the then settled areas of NWFP and Tribal areas. Frontier Constabulary's main function is to police the border of Khyber Pakhtunkhwa and the Tribal areas against tribal incursions, criminal gangs operating across the border and to check the smuggling of contraband item.

Organisation

The senior officer ranks in the Frontier Constabulary are the Commandant, the equivalent of Inspector General of Police and popularly and are referred to as the CFC who heads the force, Deputy Commandant, the equivalent of Deputy Inspector General of Police, a District Officer, the equivalent of Senior Superintendent of Police and an Assistant District Officer, the equivalent of Assistant Superintendent of Police. The senior hierarchy of FC is drawn from the Police Service of Pakistan.

Frontier Constabulary was created as an independent Civil Armed Force, under the provisions of Frontier Constabulary Act, 1915. under this Act, Frontier Constabulary Rules 1958 were framed. This force is also under the administrative control of the Ministry of Interior. From an operational point of view, the functioning of this force is supervised by the Home departments of the respective provincial governments. The Frontier Constabulary, an armed police force, also operates in a small area bordering FATA and the settled districts. The KPK police does not have jurisdiction over FATA's agencies or the Frontier Regions. Originally, it was aimed at stopping incursions and raids from the tribal areas. Now, its original function has been overshadowed by an increasing involvement in the internal security duties and protection of vital installation as well as embassies.

The force is commanded by a grade 21 officer of the Police Services of Pakistan designated as Commandant FC who is assisted by a Deputy Commandant who is a BPS-20 officer and two Principal Staff Officers of BPS-18/19. The Frontier Constabulary has its own administrative districts and in each district there is one District Officer of BPS-18/19 who is assisted by Assistant District Officers.[10]

Today, the Frontier Constabulary is organised into 17 FC districts across Pakistan and is organised into 547 platoons.[11]

The FC training facilities are located at Shabqadar and Hayatabad near Peshawar. Together, they have the capacity to train 1200 cadets annually.[12]

Role and Tasks

The FC conducted its primary tasks of preventing illegal border crossings and law enforcement in the tribal areas by dividing itself into FC districts where it established a series of pickets to carry out its tasks. However, with the deterioration of the internal security situation in Pakistan, the Frontier Constabulary has been pressed into operations against the militants and has been entrusted with the task of guarding vital installations, embassies, etc.

Over the passage of time, Frontier Constabulary was assigned additional functions such as assisting other federal and provincial law enforcing (LEAs) agencies in conducting operations against criminal elements and supporting them in law & order situations. A large number of FC troops are also manning the security duties in Diplomatic Enclave, Islamabad, and number of multi national companies (MNCs) all over the country.

The primary role of the Frontier Constabulary are:[13]

- To Counter Terrorism.
- To guard the border between tribal and settled area.
- To stop tribal incursions in individual cases or in the form of gangs.
- To check outlaws and their evil designs in the area.
- To stop kidnapping and checking on tribal disputes on the administrative borders.
- To act as a second line of defense in times of grave emergency.
- To assist the local administration in times of need (internal security).
- To control and eliminate poppy cultivation and growth.
- To check trafficking of narcotics, illegal weapons and smuggling.
- To perform any other duties assigned by the government.

Pakistan Coast Guard (PCG)

The Pakistan Coast Guard was raised in the year 1971 and is one of the Civil Armed Forces of Pakistan. It is responsible for maritime law, and maintenance of seamarks, border control, anti-smuggling operations, anti narcotics, search and rescue operations and other services. It has jurisdiction over both sea and land.

Organisation

The Coast Guard operates under the administrative control of the Ministry of Interior during peace time and the Pakistan Army during war. The PCG Headquarters are at Karachi. It is commanded by a Director General of the rank of Brigadier seconded from the Pakistan Army.

Role and Tasks

The primary role of the Pakistan Coast Guards (PCG) is to secure sea coast, prevent smuggling, entry of illegal immigrants and enemy agents/saboteurs. In addition to land based troops, PCG also mainatins a fleet of naval craft to perform its sea-borne duties.

PCG Battalions

PCG Battalions are led by commandants with the rank of lieutenant colonel, seconded from the Army. The Battalions are located as follows:

- 1st Battalion, Uthal
- 2nd Battalion, Korangi
- 3rd Battalion, Gwadar
- 4th Battalion, Pasni

The battalions are each subdivided into 3-4 companies (commanded by majors/ captains seconded from the Army).

Marine Wing (MW)

Pakistan Coast Guards as a whole is spread all over to safeguard coastal belt of 1050 km as well as up to 12 Nautical Miles (NM) Territorial Waters of Pakistan. The Marine Wing of PCG is entrusted with the responsibility of securing the 12 NM of Pakistan's territorial waters. The Marine Wing is based at Karachi and commanded by a lieutenant commander of operation branch, seconded from Pakistan Navy. It is though a small entity, but very much capable of conducting sea worthy operations and activities. MW is equipped with Fast Patrol Crafts, lethal Interceptor Boats and other Utility Boats with latest equipment onboard. The Marine Wing is accomplished with proficient technical staff and adequate facility to maintain its assets.

Mounted Infantry Troop

Animal Transport (AT) Coy is based in Korangi with a Training Wing and is responsible for maintaining horses, camels and cattle for use in the field, as well as a dog section. It is commanded by a seconded captain from the Remount, Veterinary and Farm Corps (RV&FC) of the Army.

Anti-smuggling

To keep a check on smugglers and stop their activities of smuggling (inbound as well as outbound) through the sea routes. PCG Battalions have special check posts all along the coastal belt and also pickets the threatened areas randomly. In addition, *The Intelligence Wing* has a network of agents and informers and establish pickets in consultation with Commandants of the PCG Battalions when a potential smuggling activity is reported to take place. PCG has been equipped with modern communication and surveillance equipment; including radars, to perform this task.

Human Trafficking

The Pakistan Coast Guard has in recent years has undertaken operations against drug and arms and even human trafficking/smuggler networks operating in the coastal waters. The Coast Guard has seen recent successes in combating this issue.

Equipment

In addition to small arms, the PCG is equipped with Fast Patrol Boats (FPB), Interceptor Boats (IB)s and Speed Boats to carry out its tasks.

Counter Insurgency Operations

The Pakistan Army entered the Tirah Valley in July 2002. This was the first time in the country's history that the Army entered the tribal valley for operations against militants. Though, initially, the Pakistan Army suffered some heavy losses, it has in recent years, displayed a stronger resolve to tackle the tribal insurgency. It has significantly bolstered its force presence in Khyber Pakthunkwa (KPK) and FATA. 2,348 security force personnel have been killed and another 6,710 wounded since 2002.

The Pakistan Military has refined its operating skills, tactics and counter insurgency doctrine and this is visible from an improved capability to battle militants on the ground.

The Pakistan Security Forces have also been augmented with state of the art equipment, weapon systems and training from the US Government to fight against the Al-Qaeda and Taliban fighters.

Despite some successes, Pakistan's resolve to completely decimate the militants is weakened due to the country's traditional policy of viewing them as 'strategic assets' against its enemies. As the drawdown of foreign troops from Afghanistan commences, it would move to preserve some of these so-called strategic elements for its own use in Afghanistan and against India. A White House report published in March 2011 opined, "There is no clear path toward defeating the insurgency in Pakistan". Also, the re-deployment of troops from its eastern border against India severely affects its conventional balance against India and is seen as a retarding factor for depleting its conventional resources. Therefore, it needs to be seen as to how far Pakistan can take its fight against the militants.

The Frontier Corps (FC) has fought shoulder to shoulder with the Army in FATA, KPK and in Balochistan since 2002. It has been a force multiplier for the Army due to their knowledge of the terrain, language, traditions and customs of the tribal population. In fact, as the Pakistan Army follows a largely mobile approach towards operations, the FC and other lashkars, militias and levies are utilised for holding the ground.

The strength of the FC in FATA increased from 20,000 in 2002-08 to 34,000 in the year 2010.[14] With a substantial improvement in training and weapons, the FC strength has further increased to 50,000. It has been a major benefactor of the US aid for counter insurgency. Three Low Intensity Conflict Training Centres for security forces have been opened with US assistance in Jharri Kas, Mangla and Pabbi Hills.[15] The historical force in FATA which was till 2002 equipped with World War I vintage rifles has today transformed into an effective counter insurgency force in the Tribal areas.[16] Till 2007, the FC found themselves "outmatched by well-armed insurgents, causing considerable embarrassment to the military, particularly in August 2007, when about 200 soldiers surrendered to militants after falling to take the high ground and getting themselves trapped in a valley against a vastly inferior force."[17] In return, 100 tribal militants had to be freed to secure the release of the FC troops.

The FC suffered 215 fatal casualties in the year 2010. This indicates that the force has been in the forefront in the fight against militants in the tribal areas.[18] In a survey carried out in FATA, nearly 31 percent of the respondents opted for the FC when asked who should take responsibility for security in FATA.[19]

The strength of the Frontier Constabulary, another Civil Armed Force of Pakistan, has also increased to 22,817 FATA and KPK.[20]

The Pakistani state has been battling a restive tribal insurgency in Balochistan ever since its creation in 1947 which intensified in the 1970s. The province comprises 44 percent of the country's territory but only has 5 percent of its population. The province also has rich natural gas reserves. The strain of Baloch nationalism compounded by Pakistan's indifferent treatment of the Baloch people and dominance of Punjabis in the government keeps the embers of insurgency burning. This sentiment is aptly sumarrised by a Tribal chief who said, "I have been a Baloch for several centuries. I have been a Muslim for 1400 years. I have been a Pakistani for just over fifty."[21]

Nevertheless, the region bordering Iran and Afghanistan and with an access to the Arabian Sea is of immense strategic value to Pakistan. Bulk of the supply for NATO forces in Pakistan also transit through Balochistan. In recent years, the People's Republic of China has increased its investments in the province to exploit natural resources and gas reserves. A large number of terrorists and militants operating in Afghanistan, KPK-FATA and Iran often find refuge in the isolated mountains of Balochistan. The region is a major transit corridor for the illegal drug trade and weapons trafficking.

The Pakistan Army and the Frontier Corps have been largely unpopular in Balochistan ever since 1970. The FC has been highly unpopular due to its "heavy-handed tactics, complicity in extra-judicial killings, non-indigenous composition and complicity in criminal activities."[22] The strength of the FC in Balochistan is estimated to be around 35,000-45,000 men.

In the overall picture, the Pakistan security forces have managed to gain a grip on the situation. But, its approach of selected targeting of militant groups, mobile operations and lack of serious will to find a permanent solution to the problem only increase the magnitude of the insurgency instead of containing it. A prolonged presence in the tribal areas will also make them hugely unpopular among the population and further swell the militant ranks. Other factors such as tribal affinities of the security forces with the population and militants further inhibit the fight against insurgents.

Nonetheless, the engagement in the tribal areas since 2002 has been a rich experience for the Pakistan security forces in counter insurgency operations, an area in which it did not enjoy much experience before. It has also combatised the Paramilitary forces like the FC and Frontier Constabulary who are today better equipped, trained and oriented to engage in active combat. The bolstering of their numbers and combatisation would also boost Pakistan's reserves for conventional operations as well.

NOTES

1. Official Website of the Ministry of Interior, Government of Pakistan, http://www.interior.gov.pk
2. Ibid.
3. http://www.pakistanidefence.com/PakParamilitary/PakistanRangers.htm
4. Ibid.
5. Sourced from www.pakistandefence.com
6. http://www.pakistanarmy.gov.pk/AWPReview/TextContent.aspx?pId=139#Internal Security Duties
7. Ibid.
8. http://www.globalsecurity.org/intell/world/pakistan/frontier-corps.htm
9. No Sign until the Burst of Fire—Understanding the Pakistan-Afghanistan Frontier Thomas H. Johnson and M. Chris Mason, *International Security*, Vol. 32, No. 4 (Spring 2008), pp. 41-77
10. Official website of the FC, accessed at http://fc.gov.pk/index.php?page=history.html
11. Ibid (10) above, accessed at http://fc.gov.pk/index.php?page=fcdistrics.html
12. Ibid (10) above, accessed at http://fc.gov.pk/index.php?page=training.html

13. Ibid (10) above, accessed at http://fc.gov.pk/index.php?page=function.html
14. Haider Malik, "The Pakistan Surge", quoted in Vira & Cordesman, Pakistan: Violence & Stability, CSIS, 5 May 2011.
15. Ibid (15) above, p. 70.
16. Vira & Cordesman, Pakistan: Violence & Stability, p. 68.
17. Bill Roggio, "Pakistan frees over 100 South Waziristan "tribesmen"," *Long War Journal*, September 13, 2007.
18. Ibid (15) above, p. 69.
19. Community Appraisal and Motivation Program, "Understanding FATA, Vol. IV".
20. Ibid (15) above.
21. Alexander Atarodi, "Insurgency in Balochistan and Why it is of Strategic Importance", *Swedish Defence Research Agency*, January 2011, available at http://www2.foi.se/rapp/foir3110.pdf
22. Ibid (15) above, p. 92.

PART 4

15

Structural Defects and Organisation Specific Recommendations

A careful analysis of the role, tasks and orientation of the CAPFs have revealed some structural defects which are broadly common to almost all the organisations. It is imperative upon the government to carefully analyse these shortcomings and correct them in order to improve the operational effectiveness of the CAPFs. Some of these structural defects are discussed in the succeeding paragraphs.

Sanctioned Strength of a CAPF Battalion

ORG	*SANCTIONED STR*
ITBP	1450 (HQ + 6 COYs +1 SP COY)
CRPF	1154 (HQ + 7 SERVICE COYs)
BSF	1154 (HQ + 7 SERVICE COYs)

A company has a sanctioned strenghth of 137 personnel although the effective strength varies from 65-80. Each company is futher sub-divided into three platoons.

Nearly 50 percent strength is absorbed in administration and logistics tasks having an unbalanced teeth to tail ratio. The Grid Deployment for CI Ops is stretched and ineffective. In CI Ops, the tasking is done by the Local SP and not the Battalion Commander.

Fighting Fit—Age Profile of Personnel

ORG	*RETIREMENT AGE (Constable)*
ITBP	57
CRPF & BSF	60

Low levels of fitness and morale to carry out difficult tasks. (for eg, a constable receives his first promotion after 18 yrs of service) ; No pension for pers inducted after 2004. A report in Mail Today (13 July 2012) pointed out that nearly 51,000 CAPF Pers quit their jobs in the last five years. Such a high attrition rate is indicative of low morale among the CAPF personnel due to poor service conditions. It is a retarding factor which impedes op effectiveness of a Battalion.

Poor allowances and hardship pay further add to their woes. Ration allowance for one day is Rs 54 for a CRPF constable. Unlike in the Army there is no ration allowance for CAPF officers and they have to pay from their own salaries to procure ration from the open market.

Qualtiy of Officer Leadership

Officers are directly recruited as Assistant Commandants (company commander level in the Army). Therefore, they are recruited a high age of 26-28 years with no ground experience as platoon commanders. Their promotion time-lines are as under:

- Reaches Comdt level after 18 yrs of service & DIG after 28-30 yrs of service
- At Comdt level, an officer will retire at the age of 57 & a DIG will retire at 60

Promotional Avenues for Home (Parent) Cadre Officers

The following chart indicates the ratio of home cadre officers who reach various senior levels. The rest of the percentage of posts at these ranks is filled by IPS cadre officers.

ORG	*DIG*	*IG*	*ADG*
CRPF & BSF	80%	50%	25%
ITBP	60%	50%	–

This aspect is a major bone of contention among officers who are directly inducted into the CAPFs. This factor is further emphasised by taking into account the promotional aspects of directly inducted officers in the CRPF. The CRPF has a pool of 3000 parent cadre officers from which only 131 will become DIGs and 16 IGs. Added to this are the vagaries of officer. A 1992 Cadre CRPF Officer would have spent 17 years in field and only five in peace stations due to the prolonged deployment and frequent movement of CRPF battalions from one operational area to another.

Therefore the junior leadership in CAPFs are weak and inexperienced. They have nit cut their teeth as Platoon commanders; an essential pre-requisite for leading the men in effective operations. The absence of officers directly leading patrols and large parties in an operation is a major lacuna which alarmingly affects troop morale. For instance, there was no officer casualty in the Chintanlar ambush of April 2010 in which 75 CRPF men were killed. It is difficult to imagine such a large body of troops operating without being lead by an officer in the Army. There is lack of regimentation and cohesion to fight as a unit.

Deployment and Training

Training facilities and modules at recruit level largely are largely ineffective as most of the modules at recruit training centres are designed to impart basic training for handling law and order tasks and ordinary policing. This needs to change with the evolving roles being undertaken by the CAPFs. The specialised CIAT schools are a step in the right direction but more hardened training needs to be imparted at the entry level for men.

Some of the other defects in deployment pattern are:

- Battalions remain deployed in different operational areas for prolonged periods.
- ITBP battalions remain deployed for three years in High Altitude Areas whereas even Army units cannot remain deployed for more than two years in such terrain.
- Less time spent in peace stns leaves limited opportunities for collective training, field firing, etc.

Equipping Profile

The CAPF battalions are well equipped with the following Small Arms and Light Weapons:

- 5.56 INSAS—Standard Issue
- 1 × LMG per section
- 1-2 × 84 RL per Bn
- 1-2 UBGL per Bn
- 1 × 51 mm Mor per PL

In addition, BSF and ITBP battalions also hold the following support weapons:-

- 08 × MMGs per Bn
- 06 × 81 mm Mor (1 Section)
- Some BSF BOPs have RCL
- AK-47 RIF issued in Sector Store

However, there is a need to procure only those weapons which are required and the men can handle. Due to lack of practical experience there are at times tendencies to deploy weapons which are not suited for a particular operating environment and can result in uneccessay collateral damage. A few examples would be the CISF deploying LMGs at airports and the ITBP men using Rocket

Launchers to patrol the Arthur Road Prison in a heavily populated area of Mumbai. Then there is also the factor of loss of sophisticated weapons to Maoists. It may be noted here that a large chunk of automatic weapons in the Maoist armoury are looted from police armouries or snatched away from CAPF personnel after an attack.

Uniform

Donning of Combat fatigues by CAPF personnel dilutes the shock value of the Army as it is very difficult for ordinary citizens to distinguish between Army / CAPFs. Therefore, the CAPFs must now blindly ape the Army in weapons, equipment, Uniform and titles.

These defects in the basic organisation of the CAPFs indicate that the CAPFs neither have the status of police nor the benefits of a paramilitary force.

The preceding chapters have illustrated the role played by India's Central Police Forces (CPFs) in upholding national security and maintaining the internal cohesion of the state. The nearly 15 Lakh strong force complements the state's Armed Forces in preserving the territorial integrity of the nation. They also aid the often under-resourced and stretched state police forces in maintaining law and order and social order in society.

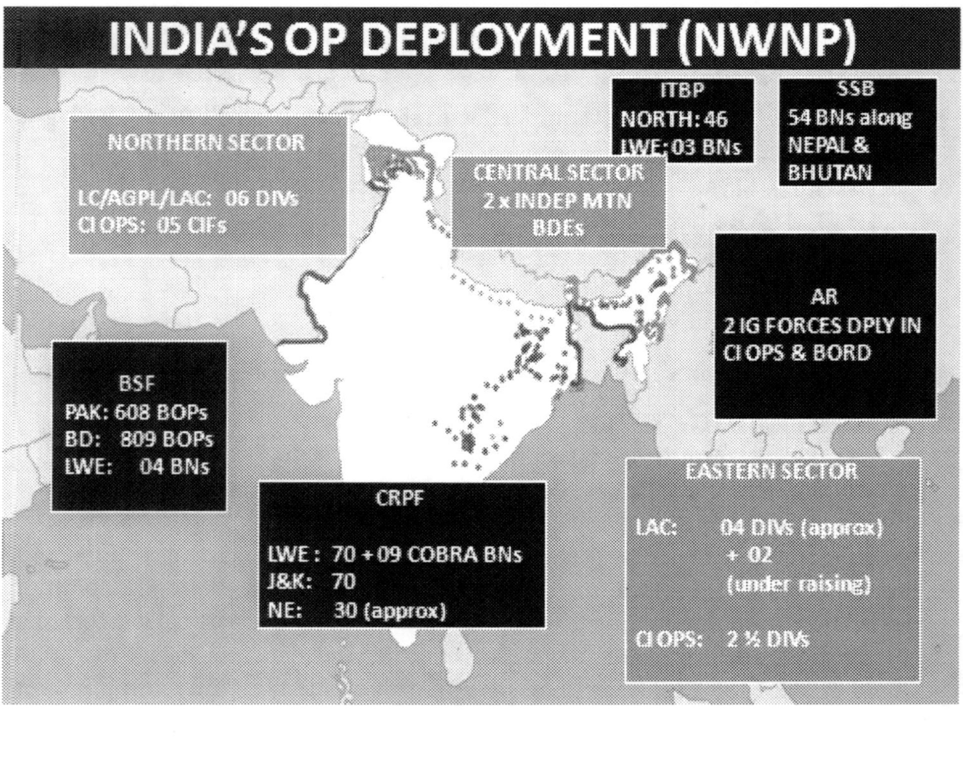

A Role Overview

Type of Force	BORD	HROP	RAS	CT	CTF	SCT	Spec Ops	VAs VPs VIPs	LAW	CB	TXN
AR	v	v	v	v				v		v	
RPF								v	v		v
CRPF			v	v	v			v	v		
ITBP	v	v	v	v				v			
SFF	v			v		v	v				
BSF	v	v		v				v	v	v	
CISF				v				v			v
Coast Guards	v			v							
NSG				v	v	v	v	v			
RR		v	v	v	v						

- BORD – Guarding/ borders Surveillance during peace time.
- HROP - Holding role, deployment in less threatened sectors, delay lines during war.
- RAS - Rear Area Security, def lines of communication/ logistic modes.
- CT - All agencies used in CT some time or the other.
- CTF – Designated CT force.
- SCT – Special/ Surgical/ anti hijacking CT ops.
- Spec – Special ops in Conventional Warfare.
- VA, VP, VIP - Vulnerable Areas / Points, Very Important Person protection.
- LAW - Law & Order.
- CB - Cross border Smuggling during trafficking, crime, refugee management.
- TXN - Transportation Corridor.

The following map and chart highlights the deployment and role of the various CPF organisations as also the different tasks they are capable of conducting or are expected to perform under different circumstances.

Organisation Specific Recommendations

Let us now examine what role each PMF and CAPF would play in the emerging dynamics of India's internal security management and how best to orient them to undertake their tasks in an effective manner.

Assam Rifles (AR)

The oldest Paramilitary force in the country has blooded itself in the Second World War and was a key instrument of both the British and Indian governments in establishing their first presence in the ungoverned tribal belts of the North East frontier. It has also operated in tandem with regular Army units to suppress the turbulent insurgencies of the North East and Jammu & Kashmir. In fact, in practice, the Assam Rifles is similar to any regular Infantry battalion of the Army and operates under its chain of command. It is also officered by the Army. The force is however under the Ministry of Home Affairs and is funded by the Home budget.

The primary task of the AR is that of Border Guarding and surveillance during peace time. It is the designated border guarding force for the Indo-Myanmar border and is deployed for the same in the states of Nagaland, Manipur and Mizoram. In addition, it also carries out Counter Insurgency operations mainly in the state of Manipur and to a certain extent in Tripura.

During War time, the AR would be required to perform additional tasks such as holding role, deployment in less threatened sectors or delay the enemy's lines of communication under the direct command and control of the Army's field formation in the theatre of operations.

Judged by the record of its past operations, proficiency of training, morale and motivation level of troops and equipment profile, the AR is worthy and capable of undertaking any task assigned to it.

In the foreseeable future, the area of operations of the AR may expand to include more sectors in the Counter Insurgency grid of the North Eastern states (primarily Manipur and Assam) in the event that regular Army formations may be pulled out for other tasks elsewhere or in the event that the security situation deteriorates in these areas. There can also be a remote possibility of a few AR battalions being pressed into Anti-Maoist operations in the Indian heartland. The force is more or less equipped and oriented to take on these additional Counter Insurgency roles.

In the worst-case threat scenario, the AR battalions will be required to perform their secondary tasks of holding/defending a less-threatened sector. This scenario is likely to play out along our northern borders. Undertaking this task requires the force to carry out an appraisal of the logistics, transport, equipment profile and other administrative requirements for the move of battalions from their present CI grids to the high altitude areas in the North East sector. Army field formations and the AR should war-game such moves and carry out exercises to gauge the mobilisation and deployment capabilities and address the short-comings that may emerge. The Army field formations should also maintain reserve stocks of specialised high-altitude equipment, clothing and stores for AR battalions in their contingency planning. The AR should undertake similar exercises and planning for deployment in the Maoist-hit areas in the event that such a deployment may be necessitated.

In light of the above and future operational commitments that the force may have to undertake in case the threat scenarios play out, it is recommended that the strength of the Assam Rifles is raised to at least 60 battalions. This would entail raising four new battalions. The force would then be in a position to effectively address an increased commitment for counter insurgency operations as also carry out defensive conventional operations under the Army's chain of command. The Home Ministry can easily release funds for the new raisings or squeeze out money by slashing the number of new CRPF and BSF battalions that have been sanctioned. Also, the earlier pattern of recruitment of men from the North-east region should be reverted. Local population have a larger stake in the security of their region.

Border Security Force (BSF)

The primary role of the Border Security Force is Border Guarding and surveillance during peace time. It is the designated border guarding force for the Indo-Pakistan and the Indo-Bangladesh border. Due to its primary task and permanent deployment posture on the International Borders, the BSF is also responsible for countering cross-border smuggling, drug trafficking, crime and refugee management up to a certain distance form the border. In its secondary role, the BSF has been extensively deployed for counter insurgency operations in several parts of the country. As a key instrument of the central government, it has also assisted the state police forces in the maintenance of law and order, protection of VIPs apart from performing other static duties and deployment during elections, etc.

The dynamics in the Afghanistan-Pakistan region post the withdrawal of International forces from Afghanistan is likely to have a bearing on India's security too. A deteriorating situation in Afghanistan may increase the pressure on our western borders. The BSF should be prepared to counter increased pressure of terrorists and other inimical elements on the International Border in that eventuality. The Government of India is building new BOPs to reduce the inter-BOP distance and improve border management along the Indo-Pakistan border.

The government's proposal to raise 28 new BSF battalions in 2014-18 would help in reducing the AOR of one BSF battalion along the border and provide additional manpower to occupy the new BOPs. In addition, the Ministry of Home Affairs should enhance the surveillance capability of BSF battalions by procuring sensors, night vision devices, battle-field surveillance radars and communication devices to reduce the burden on manpower and increase the ground coverage. BSF battalions do hold some of these equipments but their numbers need to be increased further. Hand-held Micro-UAVs and satellite imageries can become effective force multipliers for border management.

As has been brought out earlier, the state of training and equipment profile are adequate for the BSF to carry out both its primary and secondary tasks. Better and increased avenues of promotion for BSF cadre officers and PBORs will raise the morale of the forces and enable them to carry out their tasks more effectively.

The duration of deployment of BSF battalions along the borders should be reduced to increase their efficiency. The raising of new battalions and relieving the force from tasks such as Law and Order, VIP protection and Counter Insurgency operations are measures that can improve the peace to field rotation of BSF battalions. In peace stations, the BSF battalions can serve as reserves for assisting state governments for the maintenance of law and order in extreme situations or for performing election duties, etc. These battalions can also be expected to deploy for counter insurgency or anti-Maoist operations at a short notice in case a grave situation unfolds. Maintenance of an effective reserve at peace locations would allow adequate time for battalions for training, rest and recuperation.

Central Reserve Police Force (CRPF)

The CRPF is the largest Central Armed Police Force (CAPF) in the country today. It has performed a variety of tasks and remained deployed across the length and breadth of the country throughout its existence. The main role of the force is to act as an effective reserve of the Central Government in maintaining internal security and order. It is the designated counter insurgency/terrorism force of the country. The other tasks of the force include maintenance of law and order, security of rear areas during war time and protection of Vital Areas/Points.

Presently, the CRPF is stretched in its deployment for counter insurgency operations in Jammu & Kashmir, Assam and in select districts of other North-Eastern states. It is at the forefront of the state's fight against Maoist terrorism and a large number of its battalions are deployed in the Maoist-hit areas of the hinterland. In addition, a substantial chunk of the CRPF perform various static tasks such as protection of sensitive installations, VIPs, etc in the states where they are deployed for conducting counter insurgency operations as also in other parts of the country.

Going by its present pattern of deployment and the likely internal security challenges the state is likely to face, the role of the CRPF to address these situations will only increase. This would impose a further strain on the already stretched resources of the force and expand their coverage area of deployment.

The raising of additional 38 battalions of the CRPF will address these issues to a certain extent but there is a need to cut-down the variety of tasks the force presently undertakes and streamline its deployment pattern. The Government has to evaluate the performance of the CRPF and the myriad tasks it carries out and designate it for the task it best performs.

If the CRPF is the designated counter insurgency task of the country then bulk of the force should be deployed for that task only. The other half should be present in peace stations where they can be utilised for other tasks in support of state government such as maintenance of law and order and deployment for the conduct of elections, etc. The prime factor contributing to stress among CRPF personnel is its frequent long-distance movements for various kind of tasks. This should be avoided and CRPF battalions deployed in states for counter-insurgency operations should not be moved outside the state for ad-hoc deployments. Also, the CRPF should be pulled out from static deployments such as protection of government buildings, residences of politicians and government officials, etc and this task should be handed over to the state Armed Police/Reserve Battalions.

Alternatively, there is also a widely held view among security analysts that the CRPF is not the right force for conducting counter insurgency operations and that it has failed to effectively combat the Maoists in the hinterland. The argument is that the CRPF has never conducted hard core counter insurgency operations independently. In Jammu & Kashmir and the North East, the CRPF has operated in a security grid primarily dominated by the Army. Even in the Naxal-hit states, the role of the CRPF is only to assist the state police forces to conduct operations against the Naxals even though they out-strip the local police in terms of number of personnel deployed. The CRPF is deployed in a piecemeal manner and their operations are directed by state police officers and carried out in conjunction with the local police stations. This school of though opines that even after more than a decade of deployment with adequate equipment, the CRPF has failed to effectively combat the armed guerrillas and have incurred heavy casualties. Therefore, they suggest that anti-Maoist operations should be undertaken by the Army as the Maoists pose a grave threat to the security of the nation. In case this happens, a large number of CRPF battalions would be freed for other tasks.

Notwithstanding the contrarian views on employment of the CRPF in counter insurgency operations and the fact that the Army's commitments for conventional operations is only going to increase, it is unlikely that see the CRPF will be withdrawn from anti-Maoist operations in the next few years at least. Also, in the coming years the commitment of the CRPF for the management of internal security will increase if we take the mis-match between the burgeoning youth bulge of our population and the lack of available avenues for employment. Social strife and unrests may become more frequent when sections of the population squabble over limited resources and demand a large share of the pie for themselves. As the coverage area of the CRPF is wide and covers most parts of the country it would be expected to deploy rapidly and prevent internal disturbances from spilling over.

Therefore, the role of the CRPF for both counter insurgency operations and Maintenance of law and order will increase rapidly in the coming decades. For this the CRPF should re-orient itself and address the following issues:

- There is a need to undergo a transformational change in the training, orientation, organisation and tactics involved for undertaking active counter insurgency operations.
- Maintain an effective balance between the number of battalions deployed in the Counter Insurgency grid and those in peace stations.
- Avoid the diversion of battalions deployed in the CI grid for other tasks outside the state of their deployment.
- Improve the level and effectiveness of training of personnel and orient them for taking part in direct combat rather than for performing static duties.
- Address the issue of junior leadership; improve promotional avenues for officers and men.
- Improve transportation and logistics capabilities of the force.
- Ensure adequate time for rest and re-fit for battalions in peace stations and simultaneously maintain their training levels and preparedness for other tasks.
- Accelerate measures for welfare of men and their families and provide housing, medical and educational avenues for their families.

National Security Guard (NSG)

The NSG is the elite force mandated with carrying out surgical counter-terrorist and hostage rescue operations anywhere in the country in quick time. The operations in Mumbai highlighted the need for the force to acquire modern equipment to carry out rapid mobilisation and reduce the time taken to complete its operations. Following the expansion of the force due to the creation of four regional hubs and a regional centre, there is an urgent need for the force to acquire new weaponry and incorporate them into their tactics and training. In the coming decades the NSG should be in a position to:

- Procure new and modern weapons, gadgetry, electronic surveillance and communication equipments, vehicles for speedy mobilisation and other imaging devices for special operations.

- The force should evolve a new doctrine for carrying out special force operations to include counter-terrorism and hostage rescue. The doctrine should factor in the emerging scenario and situations in which operations will have to be carried out. The new procurements should be dovetailed into the doctrine in order to streamline tactics and training. Once in place, the force can put the new doctrine can be war-gamed and put to test by way of carrying out exercises.
- In the coming years, the NSG should prepare it self for carrying out specific and high-value operations in a rural environment. It has experience in operating in the insurgency environment of Punjab and J&K in the past but the terrain of the Maoist hotbeds of the hinterland is a different ball-game altogether. Some of its procurements and positioning of hubs should be guided by this factor too. If the frequency of kidnappings by Maoists to fulfill their demands increases, a situation of carrying out swift hostage rescue operations may arise.
- In the age of terrorism, the NSG must also equip, train and gear-up for countering new threats and challenges like NBC warfare. For instance, It should, in co-ordination with other specialised agencies be in a position to react to a contingency where terrorists might attempt to detonate a 'dirty bomb' in a major city or port.
- The NSG has to ensure that its training standards and operational efficiency are not diluted due to an increase in its strength. The 'eliteness' of the force has to be maintained at all times.

Special Frontier Force (SFF)

In the emerging security scenario, the role of this elite and secretive Special Force of the union may expand rapidly. In addition to the covert and overt tasks it may be required to perform in its traditional area of operations, the force should also be in a ready state to be utilised for a limited period in a rural insurgency scenario in grave circumstances. The government should make up the deficiencies in special equipment on a fast-track basis.

Should such a need arise; it may be used as a force multiplier to bolster the efforts of security forces already deployed to contain insurgency. The SFF already possesses the equipment and training for operating in a low-intensity environment. It can impart training modules tailor-made to the peculiar and specific operating conditions prevailing in that insurgency environment. Transportation assets and logistics support for building up and sustaining a deployment should be worked out in advance with the relevant agencies.

RECOMMENDATIONS

Review of Command and Control structure

The Naresh Chandra Commitee in its report to the Government of India has recommended that all Special Forces in the country including from the Army, Navy, Air Force, NSG and SFF should operate under a Special Operations Command (SOC) to tackle Out of Area contingencies, Non Traditional Threats, Irregular warfare and Assymteric threats more effectively. This is a step in the right direction and the government should adopt this measure on a war footing to better utilise our Special Forces capabilities. The NSG which is a Special Force should be orbated under the SOC for all special operations to be undertaken in the hinterland. Similarly, the SFF which is almost similar to Army Special Forces in orientation and training should also be placed under the SOC. Both these Special Forces which are presently operating under the Ministry of Home Affairs and the Cabinet Secretariat are forces with a high level of training, motivation and orientation and should be better managed for effective operations. For example, it is not justifiable for the NSG, with all its capabilities and prowess to be categorised as a Central Armed Police Force (CAPF).

Similarly, the BSF and the ITBP have all the parameters which place them at the same level with other border guarding forces arcoss the world. They have proved their mettle in continuously guarding the countries' vast frontiers since the 1960s and also in counter-insurgency operations whenever required. Their equipping profile and organisational structure are also similar to that of a Paramilitary force. Therefore, there is a strong case for the BSF and ITBP to be categorised as Paramilitary forces of the nation. The argument that goes against categorising them as Paramilitary is that they are not officered by the Army.

The Assam Rifles (AR) should be amalgamated into the Ministry of Defence and the Army. It is in any case functioning under the operational command of the Army. A dual control of the force makes very little sense especially when it is officered by Army officers on deputation and is organised, trained and equipped on the pattern of Army battalions. The non-Army officer cadre should then be absorbed into the Army. The command and control passing on to the MoD would increase the burden on the Defence budget but the same can be balanced after decreasing the outlay in the Home budget.

One Border One Force

The recommendations of the GoM Report of 2001 should be implemented in spirit as well. We must continue to work on this to ensure for instance, that the Assam Rifles assumes responsibility for the Myanmar border while the BSF does the same for the borders with Bangladesh and Pakistan. Similarly, the SSB should only guard the borders with Nepal and Bhutan and the ITBP should be responsible for the borders along Tibet.

One Task one Force (OTOF)

There is a definite requirement to take a relook at the way the PMF/CPOs are used to carry out all tasks vizz, VIP protection, protecting VA/VPs like airports, nuclear installations, etc. Given the large number of VIPs that the state has to protect in the country, a separate force for VIP protection should be raised. While the SPG should continue protecting VVIPs, this exclusive force can be carved out by drawing strength from the elements of NSG, CAPFs and other state police forces who are presently committed to this task. Presently, all CAPFs are doing all duties which at the operational level is bad for troop morale as a CRPF trooper chasing Maoists in the jungles is more risk prone that his own colleague 'protecting a VIP'.

One force concentrating on one task will also increase the effectiveness and enhance the operational capabilities of the CAPFs considerably. Concentrating on one dedicated task, the force can put into effect a lean structure to better manage its human resources, weaponry, logistics and equipment. Better planning and optimum utilisation of all available resources would lead to enhancement of performance levels of the force.

If Army is the predominant arm in J&K, then all supporting organisations should function under the Army – taking the Unified Command function organisation a step further. Likewise, all organisations must function under the CRPF in anti-naxal operations.

Officers on deputation from all organisations to OTOF should provide synergy, operational guidance to advice, intelligence dissemination, etc. This OTOF must also be available at the state level as advisor to the Chief Minister.

Annual Review of PMF/CAPFs

Do not reinforce strategic and tactics which have been failures in the previous year. To be constituted under the National Security Advisor (NSA) and comprise leads of Army, Navy, Air Force, PMF, CAPFs, NIA, IB, R&AW and the like.

A periodical audit of doctrines, organisational structures, weapons and deployment matrics should be carried out to apportion accountability for actions, results achieved and keep the forces in tune with the emerging security landscape and future battlefield scenarios and technology.

Induction of Officers

The officers in CAPFs must be directly inducted as Platoon Commanders and undergo a short training capsule at the IMA/OTA in addition to their respective training academies. In the short run, Short Service Commission officers from the Army should be laterally inducted into the CAPFs to improve the operational efficiency at the unit level. The home cadre officers of the CAPFs must rise up the chain and be able to achieve the highest rank. The system of inducting officers from the IPS cadre at the DIG and above levels should be done away with. Even then, if IPS officers have to be inducted, they must be first inducted as Company Commanders.

The issue of lateral transfer of SSC officers from the Army has often been met with resistance by the IPS and CAPF officers. Similarly, PBORs from the Army can also be inducted into the CAPFs. Therefore, there is a need to take up this issue at the National level.

Quality of personnel and age profile

There is an urgent need to provide faster promotions to personnel. This would go a long way in enhancing their morale and performance. The system and timelines for promotion and retirement of PBORs in the Army can be replicated for the CAPFs as well. At the same time, a constable who does not receive his promotion after a stipulated period should be asked to reitre instead of continuing in service till the age of 57-60. Such a high age profile for a constable is not only de-molarising but also provides the organisation from having an agile work force.

Improve Service Conditions

Besides providing better quartering facilities and provisions in operational areas, there is a also a need to introduce hardship allowances/dearness allowances and increase the amount of existing ones for both CAPF officers and men. If the government cannot pay pension then it should adequately compensate the men by providing them with alternate employment opportunities especially for those retiring at an age of below 50 years. The Government has recently sanctioned a project for building family quarters for CAPF personnel in peace stations which will help improve their living conditions.

Training

A single training academy with common drills and standards should be raised to provide centralised training to all CAPF officers. The Recruit Training Centres of CAPFs should introduce new and effective training modules matching with the operational requirements of the CAPFs. A system of psychological tests should be introduced for IPS and CAPF officers as is done at the Service Selection Boards.

Procurement

A single organisation for procurement under a DG Acquistions could be created to streamline purchases of all CAPFs.

Fied to peace rotations

At 222 battalions, the CRPF is better endowed then ever before to manage a good peace to field ratio for all its personnel to allow its personnel to rest and refit and give them time for their families. A motivated soldier carries out tasks more efficiently. One more reason for CAPFs to graduate from the fallacy of 'security in numbers' to 'security in quality'.

Force Structure

There is no good justification for a paramilitary battalion to have only 50 percent operational capabilities with the remaning 50 percent be used for administrative back up. This tail to teeth ratio needs to be reworked and administrative requirements like logistics, repair and recovery be outsourced to civilian contractors.

HQs must move up

All successive intermediary HQs must move up to where the action is with the Commandant being right there with the troops and higher HQs located to more contiguous operational deployment areas. CAPF Companies should operate directly under the operational control of the Battalion Commander and not that of the local SP or MHA. They should be deployed in a grid pattern and not in a piecemeal manner spread over several areas.

Border Management

No War No Peace (NWNP)

India's vast borders include vast contested swathes along the Line of Actual Control (LAC) and Line of Control (LOC). Particularly, along the LAC, owing to the terrain and the PLA's capabilities, the likelihood of losing lightly held unheld areas to the adversary is growing. The PLA has the capability to capture a few hundred square kilometers of such areas and cause huge political embarassament to the country. Importrantly, recapturing lost territory will take time and interventions by other countries may well leave these captured areas in emeny hands causing loss in bargaining power. Such a scenario necessitates abinitio holding holding of passes along the LAC, human and electronic surveillance of lightly held, unheld areas round the clock, round the year in all weather conditions. The road ahead, therefore, necessisates:

- *Raising of more ITBP Battalions*: Six each in Himachal Pradesh, Uttarakhand and Arunachal Pradesh. The Government has already sanctioned 13 new battalions and existing ones are being re-patterned on a six company basis.
- *State of art surveillance capabilities*: The 'human eyes and ears' of ITBP battalions need to be beefed up.

- *Mobility*: In addition to mobility by foot, aerial transportation mobility to beef up manpower in lightly held/unheld areas need to be thought of. Procurement of transport helicopters by the Air Force will address the requirements of CAPFs as well.
- *Eyes and Ears across the borders*: Along the LAC, India will have to continuously monitor troop levels and never allow a Kargil type situation to re-emerge. Although the LAC is the domain of the Army, we may consider attaching company/platoon strength of ITBP and Assam Rifles personnel to increase the Army's capanbilities to hold and cover more lightly held and unheld areas along the LAC.

  There are operational plans to co-opt ITBP and Assam Rifles in the defensive battle plans along the LAC. These include using them to fight on the passes, along successive delay lines and to hold less threatened sectors. These plans need to be constantly updated, upgraded to match the growing PLA capabilities. In case such reviews so warrant, these ITBP and Assam Rifles battalions need to abinitio hold passes, delay lines and less threatened sectors, rather than waiting for the balloon to go up and thus effect deployments with enemy using the surprise factor to occupy the passes, unheld areas.
- *International Borders:* Along the International Border (IB), some accretion in BSF strength is taking place and is necessitated to hold Border Out Posts (BOPs) in greater strength. Due to nuclearisation of both India and Pakistan, future conventional battles may well be shallow, moving away from classical deep penetration and manoeuvre battles involving capture of territory in depth. In addition to force accretion, BSF may better prepare to fight battles along the border and totally remove concepts of withdrawing to hold nodal points, strong points and screens once they have given enough battle to make the enemy delay, re-depoly to discern its intentions and direction of attack. Even in NWNP scenario, abinitio deployment of BSF battalions along the borders with Pakistan and Bangladesh is a demanding task due to the challenges of infiltration, smuggling and other anti-national activities. The perinneal aniomosity with Pakistan and the scourge of cross-border terrorism will require constant and a high state of vigilance by the border guarding force. The threat posed by illegal migration and movement of insurgents along the vast and difficult terrains of the Eastern and North-Eastern frontiers pose no less challenges either to the BSF, SSB and Assam Rifles guarding these borders.
- *Counter Insurgency grid in J&K & North East:* As the situation keeps on improving, the CRPF must gradually take over all second tier and third tier interception and counter infiltration lines to relive the Army to concentrate totally on the LOC. To give better 'baptism by fire' and

blooding in use of CRPF personnel, the Army must use CRPF platoons and companys integrated with Infantry/RR rifle companys in the hinterland. This will better prepare the CRPF to assume the role of the prime Counter Insurgency force of the country. Operational capabilities so gained will allow the CRPF to start reducing manpower in step with greater capabilities to effectively tackle insurgencies in J&K on their own, rather than bolstered by Army presence. Due to improvement in the general situation in Assam, the CRPF can similarly assume a more direct role in conducting counter insurgency operations in the state. This will also enable regular Army formations to concentrare more effectively towards their primary tasks in the theatre.

A Bloated Internal Security Structure

More than a century since the North east insurgency and the Maoist insurgency started, India is still at the cross roads. Various other insurgencies picked up momentum and others started anew. But barring a few like Punjab, Mizoram and Tripura, these fires of unrest, in some cases abetted by external powers (J&K and North East) have continued to brew in some form or the other. Commensurate to the spread and growth of insurgences, the PMF/CAPFs also continued to expand. From a couple of thousand to begin with, these numbers have assumed astronomical proportions reaching a mind boggling, almost 14-15 lakhs, more than the strength of the Indian armed forces. Such figures show that "enemies within" are perhaps more than the external enemies. For a country touted to be a future power, such a bloated internal security structure is quite embarrassing, to say the least. Such high internal security force structures may be justified or more to the point, are to be expected from autarkys and countries ruled by autocrats, monarchs and other repressive regimes. India, therefore, has to get its act, together. Here and now, with no time to waste for reasons more than one. India's tryst with long festering and open ended insurgences has reached an inflection point.

Evolve a National Strategy to Tackle Maoist Insurgency on War Footing

There is no national strategy to combat the Maoist insurgency. There is a lack of coordination between the Centre and states, between the states, between the PMF/CAPFs and the state police who all advocate different strategies and tactics as panacea to eradicate this ulcer.

Success Remains Undefined

To date success remains undefined, although the LWE threat is identified as the biggest national threat.

Elements of National Power Not Applied

The anit-naxal strategy's chance of success depends upon getting the correct definition of problems in order to apply all elements of national power - political, economic and military.

Core of Politico-Socio-Economic Strategy

Tribals in India constitute 8 percent (80 millions) of the total Indian population. Out of these 80 million, only 16 million have households as on June 2011; only 1.2 million have been distributed their rights under the Forest Rights Act i.e 7.5 percent of the tribal households PESA (1996) which conferred traditional rights of indigenous communities over their natural resources is yet to be implemented. This inertia and cocoon of inaction must give way to a sense of urgency. So, the core of the politico –economic strategy must be to first address the historical denial of tribal rights for there are other looming problems on the horizons which, if not addressed soon, will be another breeding/recruiting ground for the naxals leading to more proliferating CAPF numbers which will continue to address the symptoms but not the disease:

- 30 percent of world's poorest live in India with per capita income, 10 percent of the United Kingdom, so what if growth is 6-8 percent, it is because of the combined population of 1.3 billions people with half of them growing up half fed and quarter only educated. 50 percent of Indian children show malnutrition.
- Since 1947, India has added two Indias upto 2005 and one more will be added by 2020 (1.4 billion) and will go upto 1.5 billion by 2050 (16.5 percent) of the world population.
- By 2020, the Indian, labour force will increase by a whopping 32 percent. So, 150 million jobs will be required with at least 100 million in the manufacturing sector, 40 million in constructions and 25 million in retail.
- As agriculture productivity increases through modern methods, jobs will become even less in agriculture.

Expand Writ of States to every Knook and Corner

If agriculture goes into doldrums and non farm hands are also difficult to come by because of poor investments, business environment, (all owed to insecurity spread by Maoist stronghold /part influence in over 240 districts of India), then where does the third India to be added by 2020, go ? Some will obviously go over to the Naxals, some will join some other insurgency and some will commit suicide (a quarter million farmers committed suicide in the last fifteen years) with 20 million peopled added to the country's work force every year, lots of jobs are required. There has to be a national policy to transform the industrial landscape of the country. How is that to happen, if 240 districts and counting continue to reel under the fear of Maoist reprisals against developmental activities ? Just how serious is the problem is seen by the decline in job trends. For instance, TISCO employed 85,000 workers in 1991 and manufactured one million tons of steel ; in 2005 it manufactured five million tonnes but with only 44,000 workers; in mid 1990s, Bajaj was producing one million two wheelers with 24,000 workers ; by 2004 it was producing 2.4 million units with 10,500 workers. These displaced millions will work as servants, street hawkers or even criminals. Will some of them join the Maoist? One is told, the Maoist women cadre is fairly substantial. What is to be expected when one to two lakh adolescent girls from Jharkhand work as maids in Delhi!

Debate the Centre – state Divide over Power to PMF/CAPFs

It beggs disbelief that one of the problems posed in tackling the most significant national threat- the Maoists' is not able to gather momentum due to lack of convergence on the strategy to be followed but also the fear by the states of centre encroaching on their domain – since law and order is a state subject, the Naxal insurgency is to be handled by the state police, which means that even as PMF/ CPOs are sought after by the states as force accretion, they are not be to conferred right to arrest, investigate or detain. Which means that the PMF/CAPFs must coordinate their operations with state police. But it is another matter that on ground a significant number of operations by PMF/CPOs are being launched independently, with the state police, according post-facto legitimacy to these operations! Be that as it may, till this issue is legally addressed, lack of rights will continue to be used as an excuse for failure.

Not only the Indian parliament but the State Assembles should discuss this pot boiler of a problem and be answerable to the nation as to why such a grave threat which seriously retards national well being should have to face self imposed defeats by way of centre- state inability to come on a common platform. Aren't we living in a globalized village, advocating redundancies of geographical borders ! And yet creating barriers over our own internal borders such that they prevent full application of operational forces to target the elusive Maoist. Gravest national threat requires fixing the laws and hold seamless operations.

Police is the Answer

There can be no doubt that like in the 'Punjab insurgency', police is what the doctor ordered in states affected by Left Wing Extremism (LWE). Local police and local thanas are best equipped in terms of access to human intelligence which can take out Maoist infrastructure - its eyes and ears, safe havens, logistic hubs in the villages. Importantly, again killing of local police by Maoists exacts retribution and resentment from the local population denuding popular support for Maoists. The local population is not much affected by loss of the Army; likewise the CAPF can carry out personnel since they hail from different parts of the country. If local police and thanas are the answer, then why are states unable to substantially increase their strength? Is recruitment not a state subject?

If police is the answer, then is there no role for the PMF/CPOs. There is, like in Punjab, the local police action was propped up by vigorous country side/forest sweeps by PMF/CPOs, raids and ambushes around population centres. Together, the police and the PMF/CPOs can reclaim so called liberated zones and take out Maoist infrastructure from within the population. It is another matter that the people's socio-economic problems are simultaneously addressed by the government. We must, also, not lose sight of the prohibitive terrain which aids the Maoist insurgency, unlike in Punjab, where militants had few hideouts, other than Sarkhanda (tall) grasses in which to hide-in. So, CAPFs are required but as back up forces.

Avoid More of the Same

If the state cannot increase its police numbers, cannot coordinate combined flushing out operations on their common borders, are reluctant to cede more powers to central forces, then there is no point in doing more of the same – i.e adding more and more CAPFs and mechanically assigning them to states. If the situation continues as it does, in the next few years the CAPFs are poised to become at least one and a half the size of the Indian armed forces. Can the government and the country continue to fund such large behemoths who absent a political will, cannot deliver ? By what logic the government reinforces a strategy which is a failure?

Set out a Vision Paper

After taking a holistic view of the prevalent and emerging situation the Centre must prepare a vision document to tackle the Maoist insurgency and set time frames to achieve politico-socio-economic-military aims.

Clear Eyed Auditing of Time Lines

Once the problems have been identified, the Centre must demand vision documents from the States, spelling out their own politico-socio-economic-military mantra, which again must be time bound. Once you commit the states in writing to their own panacea for the troubles then they will be accountable to their actions, inactions. Such a vision document must attribute responsibilities down the chain to all the stake holders, bureaucrats, politicians, panchayats, institutions. Give the state time to get their act, together. If targets are not achieved in spelt out time frames then they must gradually cede more and more ground to the Centre. Likewise, Centres' action must be audited by a parliamentary panel which should consist of representatives from all streams of public life.

Do not put Money where there is no Governance

If the Centre-state cannot have its presence felt in an area, it is an abject commentary on its capabilities and will. But even worse is the tendency to mindlessly pump in money in a system which is leaking/non-existent and money is siphoned off. This money goes not only to brokers, contractors, corrupt officials and the like but also to the Maoists as also other insurgencies. This money funds their insurrection. This money funds their procurement of weapons, equipment, training and recruitment.

Monitor the Cross over Point as True Indicators

Some insurgencies/militancies are hierarchical. If you kill its leaders, like Prabhakaran in the LTTE, the militancy dies. But the Maoist insurgency is anything but hierarchical. True test of successful politico-socio-economic-military actions are whether the insurgency has reached a cross over point-meaning, the number of recruits to an insurgency are more than those killed. If this be the scenario then present actions in all its domain need a review, rather than resorting to more of the same-more PMF/CPOs, more jungle bashing, etc. Our political leadership must understand that the very substantial additional deployments, creation of more forces will not leave us in any more favourable military position. All that can be said is that more of the same strategy and more of the same and additional forces will enable us to kill more. This will only provide us more security, only if the Maoist does not offset them by more reinforcements by way of recruitment of his own. Mindless para militarization of areas will only be counter productive and a drain on the exchequer.

Core of Military Strategy

The core of military strategy should be to deny naxals, especially its armed wing safe sanctuaries and prevent it from building safe havens/infrastructure (eyes and ears, logistic and intelligence sustenance) for its over ground workers (OGWs) and its military wing such that governance may emerge.

Aggressive and Innovative Leadership

Technology, tactics and training must all support aggressive and innovative leadership. The CAPFs must invest in junior leadership qualities especially leading by personal example and initiative.

Evolve Centralised LWE Command and Control Structure

Irrespective of the states that they operate in, all CAPFs operating in a continguous region must operate in a newly constituted 'Force India CAPFs, temporary organization to coordinate, plan and execute all operations against the LWE. This organization must also integrate all intelligence inputs, both horizontally and laterally vertically with representatives from IB, SIB, SSB, R&AW, State police, State armed police serving on deputation. In a scenario where all terrorists are coordinating there own actions, this kind of seamless intelligence integration is a must, otherwise the present intelligence apparatus which is compartmentalized and poorly disseminated, will continue to lack sophisticated reconnaissance and technical intelligence. Many forces or force elements reporting/working through separate chain of command is ineffective.

Horses for Courses

If the above integrated structure is not feasible, then have horses for courses on the lines of one border one force concept against the LWE, apply only the CRPF to enable force cohesion.

Manpower Quality and Training

Professional career development for officers, career management for junior leaders and high quality training for high intensity engagements in rough terrain must be done. The present senior and middle rank officer leadership is road bound for critical support and lack training for protracted endurance.

Get rid of Garrison Forces/Bunker Mentality

The CAPFs have to shed bunker mentality syndrome with propensity for relatively static operations in pre-determined areas compounded by lack of obstacle/water crossing expedients/expertise.

Night and All Weather Warfare

Must improve capabilities, inclinations, equipment for night and poor weather warfare. It must be remembered that unless you conduct night patrol, night ambushes, the country at night will be controlled by the Maoists/insurgents who will use this time to recruit, replenish, gain intelligence/counter intelligence through his 'Infrastructure' in the population.

Avoid Set Piece Operations

Country side/jungle sweeps must be undertaken only to improve your initial control over a virgin area. Once that is done and insurgents have been displaced, do not undertake set piece operations as it is difficult to maintain secrecy and surprise. These, 'walks in the sun' or 'safari operations', conducted as a routine results only in fatigue, sets bad example, tends to be repeated and is self-delusionary.

Personal Weapon Is Best There Is

Next to Knife, rifle is the most discriminate weapon there is, by making too many weapons other than rifle available, you are encouraging use of indiscriminate firing, stand off ineffective firing and increase chances of killing innocents. Every time an innocent is killed, a counter insurgent loses ground in battle to win people.

Helicopter and Fire Power

Must not be used as a crutch in lieu of sustained patrolling.

Essence of Combat Operations in CI

Long term patrolling of a small area, pervasive use of night operations, emphasis on intelligence on insurgent as well as his infra structure (eyes and ears) is the essence of CI operations.

Match the Insurgent's Foot Mobility

To match the insurgent's foot mobility in an area characterized by lack of roads, the primary lines of communication for carrying the fight to the Maoist must be jungle trails, inland waterways and air transportation (rotary), otherwise the initiative will remain with the insurgents.

Absorb Casualities

Wars, including CI operations are not only about winning or losing but about absorbing casualties. PMF/CPOs, presently, are very sensitive to casualties and losses and almost always pull down shutters on occurrence of casualties. This limits its operational flexibility in taking risks.

Better to send a soldier than bullet

Guard against better to send a bullet than a soldier phenomenon with overwhelming dependencies on fire power, technology like sensors and radars which cannot distinguish between friend and foe.

Kills?

Kills creates tendency for inflation of body counts and encourages wrong practices which militate against the crux of success in CI operations, which is to take out the Two per cent as the famous T.E. Lawrence had said, "rebellions can be made by two per cent active in a striking force and 98 per cent passively sympathetic. The insurgent must only win over the minds, the counter insurgent has to win over both the minds and the hearts."

Time and Deployment Length

Frequent rotation of units and personnel is counter-productive. Time is required for a unit/personnel to demonstrate its/his abilities, obtain confidence and to establish its/his influence within a AOR/units. Both the unit and its personnel need time to prove their abilities. Time spent on ground imbibing terrain, intelligence, language, culture all are force multipliers, absent which all other force multipliers are superfluous. Good performance of a unit or a person, therefore, depends as much on his efficiency as continuity and stability of effort-two years in a given area is a good time to spend. Results do not show up for months.

Incentives

There should be incentives of promotion, special grade pay, allowances to make hazardous service more attractive. This should be a ticket to promotion and the best people must be promoted.

Indicators of Success

Stability of an area, development and prosperity must be indicators of success and not kills.

Make Force Leaner, Smaller and Smarter

Small operations by small teams once the initial 'area sanitisation' has been completed, is the key. Therefore, have smaller, leaner, smaller units. Such huge PMF/CAPF numbers are redundant and generate only a false sense of security.

Facilitate Peace/Operational Deployment

If force becomes leaner and smaller and fix the battalions to their roles for a certain period of time (two years) they will start producing results and personnel can then have a peace/operational deployment rotation enhancing satisfaction levels beside saving revenue which can be better utilized for modernization. For instance, only about 50 percent of a PMF/CPO unit of 1000-1200 personnel are operational. Can they cut the teeth to tail ratio?

At the end of the day, CI operations have to be waged against the Maoists or other terror groups within the unique socio, economic, political and military dimensions comprising their peculiar forces of conflict, peoples and terrain configuration. But then whatever the form, counter-insurgency capability requires the coordination of a nations economic, social and political assets, as well as its military power. As far as the PMF/CPOs are concerned, smaller and lesser is better. Better still for the local police to do it.

CONCLUSION

A review of India's emerging threats and challenges in Chapter 2 indicates that external threats to the country may evolve into short but intense border skirmishes or hybrid warfare. As has been brought out in that chapter, the changing battlefield landscape would require the Indian Armed Forces to infuse more technology and evolve modern ways of war fighting in a network centric environment. The threat from China has to be addressed by asymmetrical means. And, if India has to don the mantle of a responsible world power, it will have to acquire rapid force projection capabilities for out of area contingencies and contribute militarily for world security.

To achieve all this, it has to first put its own house in order, ie, to achieve internal stability. For this, the Paramilitary and Central Armed Police forces have to get their act together and get a grip on the Maoist insurgency and other internal security challenges. But, the best way to achieve this would be to increase the operational effectiveness of these forces with adoption of better training and modern technology than relying on large numbers. Also, increasing the numerical strength of CAPFs in India is hardly justifiable when despite such large numbers; the Army still continues to play a major and pathbreaking role in dousing the fires at home. Therefore, the CAPFs must achieve quick results and demonstrate their effectiveness on the ground. But, if the Army's committments in tackling the insurgencies in J&K and the North East continues to be at the present level, and if in the future, it is also involved in tackling Left-Wing extremism, then; perhaps the government may look at cutting down the number of CAPF battalions in the country.

The expenditure thus saved should be utilised for boosting the defence budget and hastening up the armed forces modernisation programme to tackle the new threats and challenges to India's security in the 21st century. In the long run, it is desirable that a lean and effective Central Armed Police reserve is maintained in the country. Internal security threats must not be allowed to become open ended. No more raisings of CAPFs should be permitted. Even, the existing CAPF numbers in the country are undesirable.

Despite the recommendations of the Kargil Review Committee to peg Defence expenditure at 3 percent of GDP, it was on reverse trend till this year; from 2.5 percent of GDP in 1999-2000 to 1.9 percent or threabouts till 2012. It has gone up to 2.35 percent in 2012.

India's defence budget is 1/4th of China's. In the next nine years, India's defence expenditure at current rates will be 1/8th of China's.

It is therefore imperative that our CAPFs are set time bound targets. Strength so shed may be used to form reserves.The revenue thus saved should be utilised to bolster the defence budget.

All this must be backed up by evolving and implementing an effective National

Security Strategy. Despite 65 years of Independence no national security strategy has been evolved in the country. The National Security Council (NSC) must articulate it and the Parliament must approve it. The National strategy should cater to the external and internal threats facing the country and shoud be approved by a core team of NSC under the National Security Advisor (NSA). The NSA and NSC must be empowered with executive powers to implement strategy.

These measures are a must to circumvent the current deficiency of inconsistency in policy due to change in national government and impulsions of coalition politics.

The role for all the CAPFs in India in the foreseeable future is set to expand. Jammu & Kashmir has enjoyed a season of peace. But peace in J&K has always been fragile. It takes but one incident to set the sparks flying. The cease fire on the LoC is holding. But that it will continue to hold for an indeterminate time is uncertain. What is certain is that the terrorist infrastructures across the LoC remain intact. Afghanistan is on the boil. So, the CRPF in particular and other CAPFs in general have their tasks cut out in J&K. Elsewhere, along the IB, peace and trade with Pakistan are the new buzz words; it will mean a lot of to and fro movement of people across the IB. There will be some amongst these people who will have interest other than trade on their minds. The BSF and SSB in particular, will need to spread its human intelligence tentacles far and wide; for it doesn't need an army of terrorists to set the country on fire. It took only ten to set Mumbai ablaze in 2008.

In the North East, Manipur in particular and Assam to a lesser degree continue to be nettlesome. Assam Rifles, CRPF, SSB and BSF will continue to be relevant. The CRPF will need to watch out for increasing signs of the creeping shadow of LWE in at least ten districts of Assam.

With Myanmar on the throes of opening up politically and economically, the region is poised for a flood of economic prosperity, infrastructural development, foreign investment, free flow of goods and services not only across the India-Myanmar border but if pursued diligently and single-mindedly, it could well mean that the gateway to South east Asia will finally be opened through multifarious transit points in Manipur and Mizoram. The PMF/CAPFs will then find themselves entrusted with larger roles protecting the 'economic flag' of the country. If they are relevant, then the PMF/CAPFs will undergo more expansion.

Tripura and Assam are two other states which will find the BSF and others entrusted with greater responsibilities as India in the short to middle term seeks more trade with Bangladesh and through Chittagong a shorter route to the Bay of Bengal and to Burma.

In his book 'Breakout Nations', Ruchir Sharma has identified North and Central India as the potential economic powerhouses for the country. But whether Central India, in particular, realises its place under the sun, depends largely on how the state institution' in the region including the PMF/CPOs, in particular, keep up with the legitimate requirements of their people. Central India has resources. It has talented people. But it is also a Maoist fortress. Rest of India has important stakes in Central India shrugging off the yoke of Maoists' shadow.

Central and East India will require a concentrated focus on economic and political policies that foster growth, greater participation of the population in governance and meaningful distribution of tribal rights. They will also need greater police expansion and role. The PMF/CAPFs deployed to these regions will require greater freedom to operate. But then there are Centre-State differences on giving rights to Central forces as is currently the case with the BSF Act, 2011 which has not passed muster in the Parliament. But more than right to arrest and investigate, CRPF, the lead counter insurgent arm, needs the will to act and reform its military operating ways to stay relevant. They owe it to the country to get after the Maoists in the planned, time bound manner. Its success will be measured not by kills but by how much the civil arm is able to extend its reach in Maoist affected areas because of the CRPF's better and effective operating philosophy. Otherwise, all the recommendations on increases in their strength will be wasteful. It must be remembered that all recommendations for increases in strength of any of the PMF/CAPFs will be valid and justified only if the Centre and States evolve a commonly agreed politico-economic-military strategy. If there is a common understanding on the nuts and bolts of strategy and tactics which will be the corner stones of success, then temporary increases in strength of PMF/CAPFs till achievement of laid down time lines, is justified. Absent politico-socio economic-military coherence, these increases in strength will only be a drain on the exchequer, generate false and delusionary sense of security in numbers (as panacea to military success) in a country which has such huge CAPF numbers, which even some dictatorial countries do not have. Absent a will by any of the stake holders, all force accretions will mean a condition which can only be described as 'muddling along'.

India, as so often in the past will get its act, together and the PMF/CAPFs will remain relevant to the country by forging clear cut time lines and the means to achieve them. Conflicts among the people, whatever its strength, cannot be left to open-ended drifts. The end state of dismantling terror in the North east and Maoist insurgency must be realised in the next five to ten years. The PMF/CAPFs and local police must make it achievable.